SECRETS AND LIES

SevenOaks

THIS IS A SEVENOAKS BOOK

Text and Design copyright © 2005 Carlton Publishing Group

This edition published in 2005 by Sevenoaks
An imprint of the Carlton Publishing Group
20 Mortimer Street
London
W1T 3JW

A CIP catalogue for this book is available from the British Library

ISBN 1 86200 237 1

Senior Art Editor: Karin Fremer
Design: Tanya Devonshire-Jones
Executive Editor: Amie McKee
Copy Editor: Mike Flynn
Picture Research: Steve Behan
Production: Lisa Moore

Printed in Dubai

SECRETS AND LIES

David Southwell

EXPOSING THE WORLD OF COVER-UPS AND DECEPTION

SEVENOAKS

CONTENTS

INTRODUCTION

INTRODU

"ruth can never be told so as to be understood, and not be believ'd."
lliam Blake, "The Proverbs of Hell"

nowledge is power. That is why people keep
secrets. That is why people lie. When we talk
about things that people are not meant to know,
what we are really talking about is keeping people
gnorance. Knowledge only ever gives you power over those
o are ignorant of it. This is why those with authority are
ndestine and tell untruths; they need others to be unaware
what is going on to maintain their positions.

n business, ignorance of the shortcuts being taken in
stomer safety avoids lawsuits and means bigger profits. In
itics, ignorance of corruption means re-election. This
lespread ignorance of what is happening has allowed secret
vices and military forces to commit vile experiments on
ir own populations. Whether it is the medical, scientific,
demic or legal establishment, if you are ignorant of the
ts, you can never effectively challenge those in positions of
hority who decide what the official view is

This book is about exposing the secrets and lies that ma
of those in authority would much rather everyone remain
ignorant of. It's about challenging the comfortable world
official versions and established thinking by giving you acc
to the knowledge that makes some people – whether it is
government, business, academia, military, the judicia
media or an established church – uncomfortable.

How do you discover secrets and lies? The m
straightforward answer is to be curious and not lazily acc
an answer if it seems wrong. When I was growing up, a h
tower adorned with strange dishes and antennae loon
mysteriously over the local woods. It intrigued me. In an
before cell phones, no adult I asked knew that it was
microwave relay tower and no one knew who was responsi
for it either. I asked my teachers. I went to the local libra
I wrote to the local council and my MP. No one knew, so I k
on asking questions

right Station to station — microwave relay towers were a rare sight in the 1970s, but not all of them were part of Backbone.

Eventually I learnt what it was, and thanks to Duncan Campbell's investigative journalism in his book War Plan, I also discovered that the mysterious tower of my childhood was part of Backbone – a secret microwave communications system for use in wartime, and a part of the Echelon spy network. I had learnt my first state secret. Since then I've been hooked on discovering the things I'm not supposed to know about.

In a book about secrets and lies, the reader should be able to trust the contents. Previously I've written about conspiracies, but in this book there is no conspiracy, no theory, only fact. I've tried to include enough information so that readers can go away and investigate the reality of these secrets and lies for themselves. If reading this book does nothing else beside entertain you, it should alert you to the dangers of blindly trusting what you are told. If you don't ask questions, you will always have secrets kept from you and be fed a diet of lies.

SPOOKS

1

"Someone who knows too much finds it hard not to lie."
Ludwig Wittgenstein

It's the job of government spooks and spies to keep secrets and to lie. They are paid to be masters of deception and disinformation. We all know this, but few question one of the implications of it: how can we ever trust anything they ever tell us?

Intelligence agents specialize in gaining accurate information and planting misleading information. This means they know more secrets than anyone else and are better at keeping them hidden under a barrage of believable falsehoods. Their campaigns of disinformation can lead to such a widespread belief in misinformation that anyone who challenges the official version of events they have engineered appears crazy. How insane does it sound to suggest British

spies helped terrorists murder their own citizens or that one of the most surreal TV shows ever seen was based on a real secret agent prison?

Under the cloak of protecting the national interest, the security services of the UK and USA have lied to their political bosses and the public about a raft of dirty secrets, ranging from drug running, brainwashing, murder of their own citizens to even running undeclared and illegal wars on other countries and organizations. It's the same across the world – from Israel's Mossad to France's DGSE – the field of espionage provides cover for a range of illegal activities. In the end, the greatest lie we are told is that the spooks' lies are justified to protect secrets that are essential to our safety.

THE TV SHOW "THE PRISONER" WAS BASED ON FACT

ometimes you can get away with revealing highly confidential information openly as long as you don't tell people what you are showing them is classified. When it comes to revealing a secret to full public glare, no-one comes close to George Markstein.

Markstein had worked as a military correspondent during the start of the Cold War. Before moving into writing for television he built up an incredible range of sources within the intelligence community. Through his contacts he heard about the "Mad Major" – an ace British secret agent during the Second World War who was too much of an asset to kill but who had become too deranged be allowed to go back to occupied France.

The "Mad Major" was taken to an establishment known as the "Cooler" – a Scottish castle where he and other spies were to be held until the end of the war. Unfortunately, post-1945 some of them were then transferred to another facility for "prolonged secure retirement".

While working with Patrick McGoohan on the TV show "Danger Man", Markstein told the star about the retirement home for spies and together they created the basis for the cult TV show "The Prisoner" – in which a British masterspy resigns and is taken to the mysterious "Village", where he is held against his will. Later, Markstein revealed even more about the "Mad Major" in his best-selling novel entitled "The Cooler".

Over the years research has shown that the original "Cooler" was at Inverlair Lodge in Invernesshire, an establishment heavily guarded by the Cameron Highlanders during the war. In the early 1980s, Markstein would take close associates to his London gun club where a special firearm – a Walther PPK – was displayed. This gun had once belonged to the "Mad Major" himself.

Even 60 years after the end of the war, the full history of the "Cooler" and the "Mad Major" remain classified. Given that some of the files have been categorized "Maximum Burial" – meaning they remain classified for a hundred years – the secrets of the real life "Village" look set to be kept for some time to come.

left Captive audience - odd as it seemed on screen, Patrick McGoohan's TV show "The Prisoner" echoed the real experience of some World War Two spies.

NUMBER STATIONS – BROADCASTING INDECIPHERABLE SECRETS ACROSS THE GLOBE

If you own a short-wave radio, you may have come across one of the strangest sounds to be found on the airwaves. A female, digitized but distinctly English voice reads out a sequence of apparently random numbers: "65776 56757 58605 64985 28352 02082…"

If the transmission started with a few notes of the old English folk song "The Lincolnshire Poacher" then you listened to a transmission by MI6 to its agents. If you come across a female voice calling out three phonetic letters instead of numbers you are listening to a Mossad transmission. An American female voice counting "1234567890" for ten minutes and then a series of five-digit numbers originates from the CIA. Other voices that can be heard reeling off numbers are often mechanical or those of children.

All of these broadcasts and many more of a similar type originating from a raft of countries, including Russia, Cuba, China and the former Yugoslavia, can be heard daily on shortwave radio. Collectively they are known as number stations. Although no broadcaster or government will acknowledge their existence, their purpose has become known to those tracking the spooks.

The stations operate as a simple, foolproof way for intelligence agencies to communicate with their agents in the field. The numbers transmitted are codes linked to a one-time pad system. This is a theoretically unbreakable method of encryption which relies on the receiver having a pad of numbers corresponding to the message they are hearing. In recent years the messages have also begun to contain data bursts.

The transmissions often originate from embassies, as under international law embassies have the right to maintain radio facilities to communicate with their home countries. You can sometimes spot the antenna needed for broadcast on top of diplomatic buildings. Another source are intelligence agencies' own broadcast facilities, though some national broadcasters such as the BBC are also known to be involved in their transmission.

In recent years drug dealers in America have begun to set up their own number stations to avoid the possibility of electronic surveillance carried out by the FBI.

HOW THE CIA LIED TO CONGRESS OVER ITS DRUG AND GUN RUNNING OPERATIONS

You would expect professional politicians to be able to spot a liar on the basis that it takes one to know one. However, no case in recent history shows the inability of politicians to work out the truth and the ability of professional spooks to lie and keep secrets better than that of William Casey's dealings with the US Congress.

In 1981, Ronald Reagan wasted no time in appointing his election campaign manager William Casey as Director of the CIA. Reagan also wasted no time in attacking the left-wing Sandinistas government of Nicaragua. He accused them of working alongside Cuba in supporting revolutionary Marxist forces in other Latin American countries such as El Salvador.

When the US Congress ordered Reagan and the CIA to stop illegal activities against Nicaragua and to stop military support of the right-wing Contra rebels in the country, most people would have shelved any plans that would have meant directly disobeying Congressional edicts. Not a man to be bothered about such small matters as treason, Casey set about carrying out a covert war against the Sandinistas.

Right from the start, Operation Black Eagle, where he offered favours to the governments of Israel, Argentina and Saudi Arabia in exchange for them providing cash and arms to the Contras, was highly illegal. Next he set a deal with Honduras's largest cocaine dealer to involve the CIA in helping smuggle drugs in return for a share of the profits. Casey also arranged the mining of a Nicaraguan harbour – an illegal action for which the US was found guilty by the International Court of Justice.

Even though there was evidence of many of these clandestine operations, Casey continually lied about them to the Congressional Oversight Committee responsible for monitoring the CIA. Whenever he appeared before them he put on a brave performance, managing to get away with whoppers such as: "I don't know anything about a diversion of funds." It was not until the Iran-Contra scandal was exposed that Congress realized Casey had been lying to them for more than five years.

MI6 WAS PART OF A PLOT TO KILL THE UN SECRETARY GENERAL

Unlike the CIA, Britain's MI6 is not usually held responsible for assassinations, military coups or a host of other unsavoury activities. This does not mean that they do not engage in them, it merely implies they are better at covering their tracks.

The coat of arms of the Secret Intelligence Service (SIS) – the real name of MI6 – portrays a grey brain contained within a green "C" and the motto *Semper Occultus*. The brain represents intelligence; the green "C" refers to the title given to the head of the SIS after the original "C", Sir Mansfield Cumming, while the translation of *Semper Occultus* is "Always secret". One event that MI6 has not managed to keep "always secret" is its role in a plot to kill the UN Secretary General Dag Hammarskjöld.

Dag Hammarskjöld was the second Secretary General of the United Nations. He was elected to the post in 1953, receiving 57 votes out of 60, and was re-elected for a further five years in 1957. A skilful peace maker, under Hammarskjöld the UN took on the problems facing countries gaining independence from colonial rule. When, in 1961, the government of the newly liberated Congo was faced with the secession of its Katanga province, they called on the UN and Hammarskjöld for help.

On route to the Congo to try and bring about a peaceful solution, Hammarskjöld died in a mysterious plane crash. Mourned across the globe, he became the only person ever to win the Nobel Peace Prize posthumously. While there were unanswered questions about the crash, it was not until the post-apartheid Truth and Reconciliation Commission was investigating the work of BOSS – the South African security service – that evidence of a plot came to light.

On August 19, 1998, the chairman of the South Africa Truth and Reconciliation Commission, Archbishop Desmond Tutu, announced that they had found documents indicating a plot by BOSS, the CIA and MI6 to kill Hammarskjöld and that MI6 had helped arrange the sabotage of his aircraft. Maybe the motto should be changed to "always secret as long as someone shreds the evidence"?

top UN Secretary General Dag Hammarskjöld – a man of peace.
right Nicknamed James Bond towers, the HQ of MI6 on the River Thames in London is probably the most ostentatious base for secret agents and assassins in the world.

THE SECRETS OF THE MOST POWERFUL AGENT IN CIA HISTORY

In the annals of espionage, James Jesus Angleton will go down as one of the most secretive, paranoid and powerful counterintelligence agents of all time. The CIA's director of counterintelligence from 1954 to 1974, he still casts a long shadow over the Agency and popular imagination. Whenever you read of a fictional spymaster, there's a good chance that some element of the chain-smoking, fly-fishing, orchid-growing and poetry-reading Angleton is making it on to the page. He was also the creator of the phrase "with extreme prejudice" – a term used to refer to CIA murders.

After the defection of KGB agent Anatoli Golitsin in 1961, Angleton became so convinced that the CIA contained a top-level mole his already paranoid nature went into overdrive. He shredded all of his files, removed 25 safes from his office to his home and refused to believe that any further Soviet defectors were genuine. Fellow CIA officer Edward Petty commented: "He was a lone wolf doings all sorts of things on his own that nobody ever told him to do."

After Angleton was forced to leave his post in 1974, the secrets he kept for decades started to come to light. In 1975, Congress investigated CIA wrongdoing through the Church Committee. They quickly focused on Operation Chaos, an illegal domestic surveillance and dirty tricks campaign against anti-war and civil rights groups set up by Angleton.

However, unlawful spying on US citizens was the least of Angleton's secrets. It emerged that the man who had established Mossad had also been the main force behind Operation Gladio. Created in Italy in 1947, Gladio utilized former SS officers and Italian fascists that Angleton had recruited during the Second World War. He also brought in members of the Mafia that he had previously worked with.

Using profits it made from drug dealing, Gladio financed anti-communist and pro-fascist activities, becoming instrumental in the P2 conspiracy. At its height, Gladio could call upon thousands of high-placed operatives to prevent Italy coming under communist control, and it also played a role in plots to assassinate France's President de Gaulle.

ISRAEL SPIED ON ITS MAIN ALLY THE UNITED STATES

Even in the murky worlds of espionage and international politics, where morality is as rare as a living dodo, spying on your closest ally and stealing its nuclear secrets is still considered a no-no. However, that has not stopped Israel from doing just that to America since at least 1965.

While the official position, according to Mark Regev, a spokesman for the Israeli embassy in Washington, is that "Israel does not spy on the United States of America," and has "no need to engage in that activity," the evidence shows an entirely different picture.

In 1985, American Jonathan Pollard, an intelligence analyst for the United States Navy, was arrested and admitted to conspiracy to commit espionage on behalf of Israel. He was found guilty of passing classified military documents and nuclear secrets to Israel and is currently serving a life sentence in North Carolina. Israel not only used this material herself but also exchanged some of it with the Soviet Union in return for higher Jewish emigration quotas from the USSR. Trumping

that though, 20 years previously, Israeli spies had actually managed to obtain enriched uranium illegally from the US Nuclear Materials and Equipment Corporation.

In the aftermath of 9/11, more than 60 Israelis were arrested under the Patriot Act and later expelled from the country. Under investigation it emerged that several of them were active military personnel who went on to fail polygraph tests when questioned about their clandestine activities. Six of the detained worked for an Israeli-based telecommunications company that has contracts with 25 of the largest phone companies in America. The US National Security Agency believes information Amdocs Ltd obtained on phone calls made in America was being passed on to the Israeli intelligence services. A report from the American government's General Accounting Office showed that Israel continues to "conduct the most aggressive espionage operation against the United States of any US ally".

The fact that Israel is spying on the US is both without doubt and worrying, but not perhaps as much as the fact that Mr Regev expected anyone would believe his denial.

THE CIA WAS INVOLVED IN SINKING A SHIP ON THE RIVER THAMES IN 1964

No one would blink an eye at news that the CIA was behind an assassination or military coup if they heard it was taking place in Latin America or the Middle East, but sinking a ship in a river of America's closest European ally would seem like a breach (of international law) too far – even for them.

However, that is exactly what happened in 1964 when a Miami-based dirty tricks squad from the CIA were involved in sinking the MV Magdeburg in the Thames estuary.

It is well known that the US government (and the CIA in particular) did not like Fidel "Comandante" Castro and his regime in Cuba. After the disastrous Bay of Pigs invasion by a force of 1,400 Cuban exiles, financed and trained by the CIA, and several failed assassination plots against Castro, the CIA set up the JM/WAVE station in Miami to engage in a global effort to strangle Cuban trade.

In 1964, Britain's Prime Minister Harold Wilson refused to bow to US pressure to block a $12.2 million Cuban order for 400 British Leyland Olympic buses. This led Luther Hodges, US Commerce Secretary to declare: "I don't like it one bit. It hurts us." It also led to the CIA taking action.

In 1974, it emerged from testimony of former agents, that JM/WAVE had used the Japanese freighter Yamashiro Maru to hit the MV Magdeburg while it was travelling down the Thames loaded with its cargo of 42 politically sensitive buses. The collision tore a hole in the MV Magdeburg and left it lying on her side on a sandbank, with her cargo of Leyland buses fallen into the River Thames.

The CIA's deputy director of intelligence Ray Cline later admitted: "We were sending agents to Europe to discourage shippers from going to Cuba. There were some actions to sabotage cargoes."

Despite the loose-lipped agents, details of the event remain classified. This is hardly surprising as sinking a ship in the river of a friendly nation would have caused a major diplomatic incident and exposed CIA clandestine operations to worldwide public scrutiny.

above Beloved son – Cuban hero Che looks down on a street short of buses thanks to CIA sabotage.

MI5 HELPED PARAMILITARIES MURDER TERRORIST SUSPECTS AS PART OF THEIR "DIRTY WAR" IN NORTHERN IRELAND

The fight against terror groups such as the IRA by the British intelligence services is as old as the conflict in Northern Ireland itself. While conventional British troops were patrolling the streets, Special Branch, military intelligence, MI5 and MI6 were fighting a secret "dirty war".

When stories about the collusion between British intelligence and loyalist paramilitaries in the deaths of republican politicians, terrorists and civilians began to surface, the British government flatly denied them. They even suggested that such stories were "black propaganda" created by republican terrorists and those sympathetic to their cause and tactics. The truth, however, was that the security services had secretly been heavily involved in using loyalist terrorists to commit political murders.

Captain Fred Holyroyd, who had worked as a military intelligence officer in Northern Ireland, provided the first solid evidence when he exposed the collusion of British army intelligence officers in the death of the IRA's John Francis Green. The Special Investigation Branch of the Royal Military Police carried out its own investigation of his allegations and found them to be true. Shortly afterwards, MI5 and other agencies operating in Northern Ireland began a smear campaign against Holyroyd and he left the army.

In recent years, members of loyalist terror groups, including the Ulster Defence Association (UDA) and the Ulster Freedom Fighters, have admitted that they received so much information from their connections in British intelligence in the late 1980s they could not act on even a quarter of it.

There is no escaping the fact that British intelligence agents were running the UDA's assassins against the IRA – it was effectively a joint military intelligence-UDA assassination programme. The most famous victim of this was Belfast solicitor Pat Finucane, who was murdered by the UDA in 1989. Pat Finucane was not a member of the IRA.

Despite all of the evidence of clear British security service collusion in the murder of several people, many secrets are still being kept and the British public is still largely unaware of the extent of the "dirty war" in Northern Ireland.

THE CIA SECRETLY PERFORMED LSD EXPERIMENTS ON UNSUSPECTING, INNOCENT CITIZENS

For many, learning that the CIA undertook pioneering research into LSD and is responsible for its widespread use today is a revelation. If you are one of those people, the following sentences may be so shocking you'll need to sit down to read them.

In the 1950s, as part of its MK-ULTRA programme researching mind control, the CIA began research to find new drugs to be used as truth serums. After experimenting with a range of pharmaceuticals, including marijuana, morphine, cocaine and near-lethal doses of caffeine, they realised that LSD had the most potential as a chemical tool in espionage.

Upon this discovery, agents began the process of testing LSD in the field. After giving up on surreptitiously dosing fellow agents and having their plans to serve LSD-laced punch at the CIA Christmas party spiked by their superiors, they turned their attention elsewhere.

In 1953, Frank Olson, a civilian biological warfare expert, was given a glass of Cointreau spiked with a massive dose of LSD. Nine days later he met an untimely death falling from the upper story of a New York hotel. However, the testing on unsuspecting civilians continued apace.

The CIA bought a property in San Francisco – 225 Chestnut Street – where they ran a brothel. Entitled "Operation Midnight Climax", prostitutes were paid $100 a night to lure customers. The men would be plied with LSD-laced drinks while CIA agents observed the effects of the drugs and any bedroom action from behind two-way mirrors. They also worked with doctors at the National Narcotics Hospital where they gave unknowing black patients steadily increasing doses over a 75-day period. Plans were also drawn up to try and dose a whole platform of people on the New York subway. Agents even set Timothy Leary on the path to become a global advocate for the drug.

The CIA appears to have stopped testing LSD in 1966, causing one of those involved – George Hunter White, a narcotics officer seconded to the project – to comment: "I was a minor missionary, but I toiled wholeheartedly because it was fun, fun, fun."

USA'S TASK FORCE 121 – THE SECRET UNIT THAT INCLUDES GREY FOX HUNTER-KILLER SOLDIERS – IS ENGAGED IN WORKING WITH TERRORISTS TO PLAN ATTACKS

Task Force 121 is so sensitive its existence is barely acknowledged by the Pentagon. They refuse to provide any details of its make-up or activities beyond that it is made up of intelligence agents and soldiers. This unusual arrangement is explained by Pentagon spokesmen as: "A tightening of the sensor-to-shooter loop. You have your own intelligence right with the guys who do the shooting and grabbing. All the information under one roof."

One of the key elements of Task Force 121 is Grey Fox – a unit made up of CIA officers and members of Delta Force – the American equivalent of the SAS. Originally formed to combat drug smuggling, it specialized in the use of deep penetration agents. It was reformatted after 9/11 to become an anti-terrorist man-hunting group of soldier-spies. Its focus is delicate and dangerous intelligence operations combined with fast-reacting military support.

Grey Fox was engaged in secret searches for Osama bin Laden in Afghanistan and Pakistan. In Iraq, they spearheaded the hunt for Saddam Hussein and other key members of his family and regime. On both occasions members of both the British and Australian SAS were seconded to Grey Fox.

It has also become clear that Grey Fox is heavily involved in a variety of Black Ops. In the summer of 2002, the Pentagon's Defense Science Board called for the creation of the Proactive, Pre-emptive Operations Group (P2OG), to bring together CIA and military covert action. P2OG would launch secret operations aimed at "stimulating reactions" among terrorists and states possessing weapons of mass destruction. They would aim to provoke terrorist cells into action, thus in theory exposing them to "quick-response" attacks by US forces. This worried some intelligence experts who could foresee US forces causing terrorist attacks that they might not be able to stop.

The frightening ideas behind P2OG have been put into practice, but the group is not known by that name. This book can reveal the forces involved in making P2OG and its high-risk plans a reality are in fact those of Task Force 121 and the Grey Fox soldier-spies.

`below`
Search and destroy – after US forces failed to win the world's deadliest game of hide and seek with Osama bin Laden in Afghanistan the Grey Fox unit took over the job.

SCIENCE

2

"A new scientific truth does not triumph by convincing its opponents and making them see the light, but rather because its opponents eventually die out, and a new generation grows up that is familiar with it."
Max Planck

For a field based on evidence, fact and the search for truth it comes as a surprise that science and scientists have been so involved in keeping secrets and telling lies.

Many of science's secrets stem from the fact that no one likes to be proved wrong. No one who is meant to be an authority on a subject likes to be caught out as not knowing as much as they pretend to. The extreme embarrassment factor only increases if something fundamental to your knowledge system is exposed as being wrong. However, some truths are more than discomforting, they can do real damage. Not only do school textbooks get re-written, careers are ended and the authoritarian grip certain established academic elites have held on subjects from beyond living memory is loosened.

It also seems that the scientific establishment tries hard to ensure that information about successful scientists who contradict the public perception of their ranks as a collection of sober rationalists is repressed. It is as if they think that a public who knew that great scientific minds took drugs and believed in the occult would no longer have a belief in amazing discoveries of those scientists.

The biggest lie that many scientists peddle is that their theories are not only absolute, but they arise from totally dispassionate analysis of the facts. The truth is that for many of them their belief in certain theories is almost religious and can only be maintained by ignoring the facts that prove them incomplete.

right Deceptive lizard –
alleged Brontosaurus bones
might not be what they seem.

THE BRONTOSAURUS NEVER EXISTED

Like many other five-year-old boys, I had an incredible passion for, and peculiarly advanced and specialized knowledge of, dinosaurs. Of all of the dinosaurs, the Brontosaurus was my favourite. I knew its name meant "thunder lizard", I knew it was a vegetarian, could reach 90 feet in length and lived 150 million years ago. However, the Brontosaurus never existed. I had been lied to by all of the books, museums and TV science shows.

Since the 1970s the palaeontological community has had to admit that the Brontosaurus never existed and what they and everybody else called a Brontosaurus for a 100 years is in fact an Apatosaurus – a name which, ironically, means "deceptive lizard". However, palaeontologists tend to remain somewhat tight-lipped about the fraud that led to a century of confusion.

In Wyoming in 1874, Othniel Charles Marsh unearthed the most complete dinosaur skeleton ever found. It was an Apatosaurus, but it was missing its head. Not one to let that get in the way of a perfect discovery, he took the head of another type of dinosaur called the Camarasaurus which he had found connected to a body four miles away. Lying in a scientific paper, he claimed that whole skeleton represented a new dinosaur – the Brontosaurus. His colleagues took him at his word and thanks to the magnificent skeleton the Brontosaurus went on to become one the instantly recognisable dinosaurs in the public's eyes.

Despite the fact that knowledge of the fraud had been circulating in the scientific community for dozens of years, the name was not formally removed from the palaeontology books until 1974. It took several further years for many museums displaying skeletons to change their labels and even longer for some actually to replace the heads of the skeletons with the correct and entirely different looking Apatosaurus skulls.

Today the skeleton that started all of this is displayed at the prestigious Peabody Museum of Natural History, Yale University. While it has the right skull, it appears to have the feet of a Camarasaurus. It is definitely a deceptive lizard.

ONE OF THE MAIN AIDS TESTS IS SCIENTIFICALLY INVALID, MISLEADING MILLIONS INTO BELIEVING THEY ARE HIV POSITIVE

The nature, origins and cause of AIDS remain one of the most controversial areas of medical science. Ever since the phrase AIDS – standing for "acquired immune deficiency syndrome" – was used in public for the first time in 1982, scientists have been clashing over the disease.

It has often been a brutal academic conflict. Scientists such as Professor Peter Duesberg, a world-renowned molecular biologist, who proposes that the HIV virus is not the cause of AIDS, have been labelled "scientific dissidents" and ridiculed by researchers. However, one area dissidents and leading conventional experts, including Dr Max Essex of Harvard University, agree on is that one of the main AIDS tests can be highly misleading.

Research by Eleni Eleopulous, a biophysicist at the Royal Perth Hospital in Australia, showed that many people who appear to be infected with HIV could actually be suffering from other conditions such as malaria since they produced a positive result when the standard Elisa AIDS test was used. The research also showed that even flu jabs could impact on test results. Screening in Russia using the Elisa test in 1991 produced 30,000 positive tests, of which only 66 were later confirmed using the more precise Western Blot test. Despite the massive implications, it was initially treated with some scepticism as some scientists saw Eleopulous and her colleagues as "dissidents".

However, Dr Essex later provided collaborating evidence when he stumbled across the apparent flaws in the tests during an investigation into whether leprosy patients were at increased risk of being infected with HIV. One test gave a positive reaction in 85 per cent of the patients who were later shown to be negative when using the other tests. This led Essex's research team to the conclusion that both the Elisa and Western Blot tests "may not be sufficient for HIV diagnosis in AIDS-endemic areas".

Given the mental stress that a diagnosis of AIDS can cause – often triggering suicide – knowing that the standard Elisa test can give a false result due to something as simple as a flu jab is highly worrying.

ONE OF THE SCIENTISTS WHO DISCOVERED DNA WORKED OUT ITS DOUBLE-HELIX STRUCTURE WHILE ON LSD

There is much hype about scientific discoveries. Hyperbole such as "revolutionary" and "paradigm-shifting" are used in the same way advertising people use "major new advance in whiteness" to sell soap power.

In 1953, Francis Crick went into his local pub in Cambridge on a February evening and told the whole pub that: "We have found the secret of life." For once, someone was not exaggerating. Crick and his colleague Dr James Watson had worked out the double-helix structure of deoxyribonucleic acid (DNA) and that it could unzip to make copies of itself.

This discovery revolutionized biology, medicine and how we see the world. It let to the creation of the biotechnology industry and provides hope that through genetics we may conquer some of the worst diseases to afflict the human race. Much has been written about the discovery, but the role LSD played is almost always ignored.

Crick told biochemist Richard Kemp that he often used small doses of LSD to boost his powers of thought and that he had first perceived the double-helix shape while on LSD, using the vision as a basis for his research. This staggering revelation, as well as Crick's idea that life on Earth began when a spaceship from a higher civilization dropped micro-organisms, is rarely mentioned in any scientific literature.

Francis Crick was not alone in the world of science when it comes to the creative use of LSD. Dr Kary Mullis, the 1993 Nobel Prize Winner for Chemistry and inventor of PCR – without which genetic engineering would be impossible – claimed in an interview that: "I doubt I would have invented PCR if I hadn't taken LSD. It allowed me to sit on a DNA molecule and watch the polymers go by."

While there is blue plaque in The Eagle pub in Cambridge city centre to mark where Crick made his dramatic statement, there is no corresponding commemoration of the place where he took the LSD that led to his revelation about the double helix. Were it not for scientific hypocrisy and small mindedness, there would be.

right Acid dreams – Francis Crick's LSD vision provided the staggering revelation that helped him and Watson unlock the secret of DNA.

NOBEL PRIZE WINNING SCIENTIST AND AUSTRALIAN NATIONAL HERO SIR FRANK MACFARLANE BURNET WANTED TO DEPOPULATE SOUTH EAST ASIA WITH BIOLOGICAL AND CHEMICAL WEAPONS

Probably Australia's greatest scientist, Sir Frank Macfarlane Burnet won the 1960 Nobel Prize for Medicine for his groundbreaking work on the discovery of acquired immunological tolerance. His centenary was celebrated as part of Australia's Tall Poppy national pride campaign and he has lent his name to the prestigious Macfarlane Burnet Centre for Medical Research. The image portrayed of the Nobel Laureate is that of a brilliant scientist fighting to eradicate disease, whose work on virology and immunology was so outstanding he was twice nominated for the Nobel Prize.

Professor Frank Fenner, Australia's current leading scientist, described Burnet as "the most original and productive scientist Australia has produced," and the scientific journal *Nature* nominated Burnet as one of the 10 greatest scientists of the twentieth century.

Surely a humanitarian genius such as Macfarlane Burnet is a rightful source of pride for any country – and for science itself? While no one disputes his contribution to modern medicine, top secret files found in Australia's National Archives show their hero in a very different light.

In 1947 Burnet compiled a report for his government urging them to develop biological weapons to use against what he saw as the overpopulated countries of South East Asia. In the report he stated: "Specifically to the Australian situation, the most effective counter-offensive to threatened invasion by overpopulated Asiatic countries would be directed towards the destruction by biological or chemical means of tropical food crops and the dissemination of infectious disease capable of spreading in tropical but not under Australian conditions."

Invited to join a subcommittee of the New Weapons and Equipment Development Committee he wrote a further report in which he argued: "The main strategic use of biological warfare may well be to administer the *coup de grace* and compel surrender in the same way that the atomic bomb served in 1945. Its use has the tremendous advantage of not destroying the enemy's industrial potential which can then be taken over intact."

It's not known whether those reports helped him secure his knighthood, but they might make some Australians reconsider his revered position.

SCIENTISTS HAVE ALREADY TRANSPLANTED THE HEADS OF MONKEYS

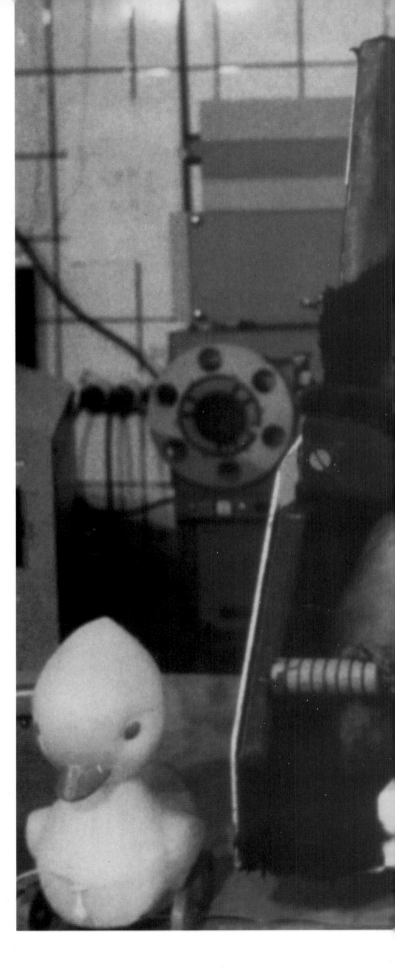

When anyone tells you there is no such thing as mad scientists, that the image of crazed surgeons from literature such as Dr Frankenstein and Dr Moreau are myths with no factual basis in the modern world, turn to them and say "Dr Robert J White".

In 1970, Dr White was the first neurosurgeon to sever the head from one rhesus monkey and transplant it successfully to the still-living but headless body of another rhesus monkey. Working in secret to avoid public outrage and animal rights protests, the operation required two surgical teams. When the monkey with a new body (or a new head depending on your perspective) woke up and tried to bite off the finger of a doctor, everyone in the medical team cheered.

While Dr White's first head-switched monkey lived for only one week, he believes that with the significant improvements in surgical techniques and postoperative care made since the 1970s the operation is ready to be adapted for use on humans. White calls the process of transplanting heads "a full body transplant", as he believes a person's identity can be transferred by the procedure and wanted former *Superman* star Christopher Reeve to be among the first humans to undergo the operation. Some find it ironic that while he is gung-ho for swapping brains in bodies, he does not believe in any form of genetic experimentation using embryonic stem cells.

The idea of monkey head transplants is not the only disturbing idea that White put into practice during his career. As a precursor to his work on swapping heads, he once produced a dog with two brains. In the 1960s, White and his team of surgeons attached another brain to the blood vessels in a dog's neck to see if they could get the second brain working while the original brain was intact. They could.

Professor Stephen Rose of the UK's Open University summed up the feelings of many when he described Dr White's experiments as "medical technology run completely mad" and "a grotesque breach of any ethical consideration".

`right` Two heads are better than one when it comes to Dr. White's head-swapping surgical experiments on monkeys.

THE STARS THAT PROVIDE EVIDENCE THAT EINSTEIN MAY HAVE GOT THE GENERAL THEORY OF RELATIVITY WRONG

Einstein was the first global superstar of science. Even in a later age of mass communication, not even Carl Sagan or Dr Stephen Hawking have managed to achieve his level of popularity and recognition.

While few people could successfully explain his general theory of relativity, almost everyone has heard of it. Given the position Einstein enjoys in the annals of science and the role the general theory of relativity has enjoyed in theoretical physics for 80 years, any suggestion he could have got it wrong is treated as heresy by the scientific establishment.

It was observations made during a total eclipse of the sun in 1919 that seemed to prove Einstein's theory. It successfully predicted that light from a star passing near the Sun is bent by one and a half arc seconds. The theory also explained a discrepancy in the predicted and observed orbit of Mercury. These proofs of his theory brought Einstein instant fame and convinced astronomers his ideas about gravity were correct.

In 1959, astronomer Mogens Rudkjobong suggested that *DI Herculis*, two young blue stars in an eclipsing binary system, would provide another test of general relativity.

However, when US astronomer Edward Guinan made observations of the pair in 1977 they failed to provide the expected confirmation.

As the stars swing around one another, the axis of their orbit rotates or precesses too slowly. General relativity predicts a precession of 4.27 degrees per century. With *DI Herculis* the rate is only 1.05 degrees per century. Guinan found another binary star – *AC Camelopardalis* – that goes against general relativity in the same way.

In normal scientific practice, when observations conflict with theory the theory must be changed or scrapped. It seems scientists have too much riding on the general theory of relativity to do this. More than a dozen possible causes for the anomalies – from the presence of a third unseen body to powerful stellar winds – have been put forward. Upon investigation, none has been convincing.

While the whole of the general theory of relativity may not be wrong, it seems that where strong gravitational fields occur around binary stars the theory certainly fails the test and needs serious rewriting.

EVIDENCE SUGGESTS THAT THE BIG BANG THEORY MAY BE WRONG

Ask almost anyone how the universe started and the answer usually comes back "with a Big Bang". Ask a scientist and you may get the answer that a tiny bubble of space-time, a trillionth of a centimetre across, spontaneously popped into existence out of nothing due to random quantum fluctuation that led to the Big Bang.

Since it replaced the Steady State theory – the previous hypothesis on the origins of the universe – in 1965, the Big Bang theory has become the cornerstone of scientific orthodoxy. It is the ultimate paradigm, even used as a phrase by those who have no idea of the details of the alleged single most significant event in creation.

Given all of this, surely there is no reason to believe that there is good evidence for believing the theory may be wrong? Surely all of those famous scientists we have seen expanding on the Big Bang on television for the last 40 years cannot be wrong?

The case against the theory does not rest on just one single piece of evidence, but a whole phalanx of observations that contradict it. These range from the universe having a much too large-scale structure to have formed in the time allotted, to the fact that the age of some globular clusters seem to be older than the universe itself should be.

In 2004, 33 leading scientists sent an open letter to the scientific community via *New Scientist* magazine. The letter started: "Big Bang relies on a number of hypothetical entities, things we have never observed. Without them, there would be a fatal contradiction between the observations made by astronomers and the predictions of the theory. In no other field of physics would this be accepted as a way of bridging the gap between theory and observation."

The letter called for funding to investigate alternative theorems and an end to the dogmatic holding to the Big Bang theory by scientists, claiming: "Never has such a mighty edifice been built on such insubstantial foundations." Despite this, orthodox scientists continue to promote the Big Bang theory and obstruct research into other views.

US SCIENTISTS HAVE EXPERIMENTED ON ORPHANS AND REFUGEES

Government scientists secretly inject refugees with mysterious substances. Medical companies pay local authorities for permission to experiment on orphans. It sounds like something that would only happen in a horror movie. Surely if this happened it would be on the nightly news?

The truth is awful and the truth is scary, but the facts are that involuntary experiments on people have been conducted in the United States in recent years.

One of the main areas where involuntary human experimentation has gone unchecked in America is the testing of drugs on orphans. Pioneering work by the Alliance for Human Research Protection and investigative reporters such as Jamie Doran and Liam Scheff revealed a system whereby orphanages in New York provided orphans in their care to take part in drug trials.

In 2002 it was shown that some foster homes housing HIV-positive children in the New York City area allowed those in their care to be used in experiments. Many were only a few months old and often no consent of guardians or relatives was sought. Some children have claimed that if they refused to take the drugs they had a hole surgically drilled in their abdomens so that medication could be placed directly into their bodies. All of this appeared to go on with the knowledge of elements of the authorities responsible for the children.

The drug trials were testing the toxicity of HIV medication and went under names such as "The Safety and Effectiveness of Treating Advance AIDS Patients Between the Ages of 4 and 22 with Seven Drugs, Some At Higher Than Usual Doses". Even where there is no illegality in the tests, there is a potential violation of the medical code of ethics regarding informed consent.

The same is true of the experiments conducted on female HIV-positive Haitian women refugees interned at Guantánamo Bay in 1993. They were forcibly injected with an experimental drug with potentially dangerous side effects that had not been approved for use in the US. Perhaps the Statue of Liberty should read: "Bring me your poor huddled masses so that we can experiment upon them."

`right` Yearning to breathe free – some Haitian boat people were used in drug experiments.

THE SCIENTIFIC COMMUNITY SUPPRESSED MANY OF ISAAC NEWTON'S MANUSCRIPTS TO HIDE THE FACT HE BELIEVED IN ALCHEMY AND RELIGIOUS HERESY

When it comes to the names that have shaped the way mankind thinks about the world, the name of Sir Isaac Newton stands among giants such as Socrates, Plato and Galileo. Between 1664 and 1666, Newton developed the groundbreaking theories on mechanics, motion and gravity. By the time of his death in 1727, he was President of the Royal Society, an associate of the French Académie des Sciences and revered as Europe's greatest scientific innovator.

Despite his unequalled scientific reputation, Newton spent the majority of his time working on his real interests: the chronology of fabled kingdoms, working out biblical prophecy, and alchemy. For the last 50 years of his life, he spent more time pursuing the creation of the philosopher's stone in his alchemical laboratory and predicting the world would end in 2060 than he did on conventional science.

When he died, the Royal Society decided that the more than a million words he had written about alchemy and 500,000-plus words he had written about his belief in the Arian heresy and other theological concerns were "not fit to be printed". They were afraid this work would taint his scientific reputation. This set a pattern for more than 200 years in which the scientific establishment tried to hush up Newton's belief in alchemy and various elements of Christian heresy. When Bishop Samuel Horsley edited a supposedly *Complete Works* of Newton that remained the standard Newtonian resource for a century, he removed all reference to Newton's alchemical passion and suppressed letters showing his heretical views.

The majority of Newton's manuscripts were passed down to his niece and after her death were kept in the family. In 1872, the Earl of Portsmouth, the latest inheritor of the papers, gave them to Newton's old college at Cambridge University. All of the papers concerning alchemy, theology and chronology were returned to him as being of no interest.

The economist John Maynard Keynes eventually bought them at Sotheby's auction in 1936. After reading them he said: "Newton was not the first of the age of reason. He was the last of the magicians."

ONE OF THE MAIN FORCES BEHIND THE EARLY US SPACE PROGRAMME WAS ALSO A LEADING OCCULTIST AND FOLLOWER OF ALEISTER CROWLEY

The image of scientists fixed in the public consciousness is of men of logic who have no truck with magic and the supernatural. Jack Whiteside Parsons was a brilliant chemist whose work on the composition of liquid rocket fuel revolutionized space science. At 25, alongside two colleagues, he set up America's first government-backed rocket research group, helped establish the Jet Propulsion Laboratory (JPL) at Pasadena and co-founded the Aerojet General Corporation, which now manufactures the solid fuel boosters used by the space shuttle.

According to journalist Richard Metzger, even Werner von Braun – the Nazi rocket scientist who led the US race into space – described Parsons as the true father of the American space programme. While most men would settle for trying to break the bonds of gravity, Parsons would settle for nothing less than being able to transcend all time and space. Not only a scientist, he was also an occultist. It is for this reason that he has been purposefully excluded from many scientific history books, including those written about the Jet Propulsion Laboratory he helped create.

As a member of the California Agape Lodge of the Ordo Templi Orientis, Parsons was a magical adept and favoured pupil of the infamous British occultist Aleister Crowley who had created the OTO. A fellow member of the Lodge was the founder of Scientology, L Ron Hubbard, who worked with Parsons on a magical ritual known as the Babalon Working before running off with Parsons' mistress and $50,000 of his money. Parsons was also an accomplished philosophical writer, penning *Freedom Is A Two-Edged Sword*, one of the classics of Libertarian thought.

Parson's was investigated by the FBI and hounded out of the country; then, after his mysterious death at the age of 38, his fellow scientists began to erase Parsons' part in the history of rocketry.

However, despite the scientific establishment's campaign to hide all knowledge of the notorious sex-magician in their ranks, Jack Parsons' name lives on. Some scientists working at JPL now affectionately call it the "Jack Parsons Lab", while French astronomers have named a crater on the Moon after him.

left Rocket man – Jack Parsons (left) was the true father of the US space program according to Werner von Braun.

WAR

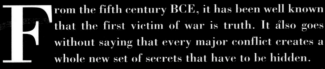

"In war, truth is the first casualty."
Aeschylus

From the fifth century BCE, it has been well known that the first victim of war is truth. It also goes without saying that every major conflict creates a whole new set of secrets that have to be hidden.

It often seems, in the modern age, that the principal secrets kept are the real reasons why countries are taken into war and the largest lies are the false reasons given to justify military action. Whether it's the deliberate falsehoods used to bring America into direct war with communist Vietnamese forces or the lies told to justify an invasion of Kosovo or Iraq, our prime ministers and presidents have repeatedly lied to the public.

Why? Possibly because there would be little chance of re-election for a politician who told the naked truth that soldiers' lives were being risked and billions of taxpayers' dollars are being spent to secure higher profits for oil companies or to ensure NATO could turn part of the former Yugoslavia into a virtual colony.

While a war rages, casualties – especially civilian ones – are kept hidden and propaganda used to hide the harsh horrors of war from the public in case morale and support for the hostilities is undermined. Even when victory is won, the secrets and lies continue to pile up. History is rewritten not just to present the winners in the best light, but also to shield us from the knowledge that war has a tendency to make monsters and murderers of all who fight in it.

THE US MILITARY PREPARED PLANS TO INVADE CANADA

When Oscar-winning documentary maker Michael Moore made a satirical comedy in 1995 called *Canadian Bacon*, some critics labelled its plot – which saw a US president declaring war on its friendly neighbour in the north – as "totally unbelievable". Trey Parker and Matt Stone, creators of "South Park", used the same plot device in the movie version of their hit show. Again, critics assumed an American invasion of Canada was an absurd notion with no possible basis in reality.

As usual, Michael, Trey and Matt were a lot closer to the truth than their critics.

In the 1930s, the US military drew up a "Joint Army and Navy Basic War Plan – Red". To be put into effect in the event of a war with the United Kingdom, the plan provided details of the strategy that would be implemented in a US invasion of Canada. Key elements of War Plan Red included seizing the port of Halifax to prevent British resupply, cutting communications between eastern and western Canada by capturing Winnipeg and creating bridgeheads at Buffalo and Detroit.

As the invasion progressed, the Americans would occupy Montreal and Quebec City. Taking control of Ontario and the Great Lakes area to gain control of most of Canada's industry was the next priority.

On the basis of War Plan Red, in 1935 the US War Department obtained $57 million to build air bases on the American-Canadian border for use in pre-emptive surprise attacks on Canadian airfields. In the Great Lakes area, the base's real intention was to be disguised by its use as a civilian airport that in wartime would, according to a Congressional report, "be capable of dominating the industrial heart of Canada, the Ontario Peninsula". (Testimony relating to this was meant to be secret but was released by mistake).

Any Canadian sighing with relief that the plan comes from before the Second World War should remember that more recent war plans containing operational details that would be put into place today remain classified. Later versions of War Plan Red are still listed as secret.

below You can't make anything up – the South Park storyline of a US invasion of Canada bizarrely echoes actual military plans.

COLIN POWELL WAS INVOLVED IN THE COVER UP OF THE MY LAI MASSACRE BY US FORCES IN VIETNAM

Colin Powell is a hero to many black Americans. Born to poor Jamaican immigrant parents in Harlem, he made it to the top of the military as the first African-American Chairman of the Joint Chiefs of Staff. He was even seen as a potential presidential candidate and a popular choice when appointed US Secretary of State in 2001.

Until his role in the presentation of inaccurate intelligence in the run up to the invasion of Iraq, he was also a hero to many American liberals. The phrase used about him was "whatever you think about his politics, you have to admire the man".

Yet his heroic image and integrity are called into question by revelations of his conduct in Vietnam and his role in the attempts to cover up the My Lai massacre. War has a unique way of bringing out the worst in humanity and the actions of Charlie Company of the 11th Brigade American Division on March 16, 1968, qualifies as an expression of all that can be considered dark in the soul of man.

Despite the fact that there were no Viet Cong targets in the village of My Lai, over three hours the GIs murdered more than 500 unarmed civilians. Old men were bayoneted, praying women and children shot in the back of the head, at least one girl was raped and babies were placed in a ditch and then killed in a scream of machine gun fire.

A young soldier, Tom Glen, learned of the massacre and wrote to General Creighton Abrams, commander of all US forces in Vietnam. In December 1968 Glen's letter was given to Powell to check out. Making no effort at serious investigation, he reported that Glen's claims were false except for "isolated instances" and that "In direct refutation of this portrayal is the fact that relations between American soldiers and the Vietnamese people are excellent".

Despite this attempt by Powell to dismiss the massacre, the truth about it surfaced in 1969, linking forever the name of My Lai to the horror of war.

below The brutally murdered victims of the My Lai massacre.

above Everyone loves a man in uniform – before entering politics, Colin Powell was already regarded as an American military hero.

above Addicted to speed - amphetamine use is rampant amongst fighter pilots.

FIGHTER PILOTS ARE REGULARLY GIVEN AMPHETAMINES TO ALLOW THEM TO FLY MISSIONS

Allowing a pilot pumped full of amphetamines and depressants to handle an aircraft capable of flying at 1,500 mph (2,414 km) and armed to the teeth with multibarrel cannons, air-to-air and air-to-surface missiles sounds insane. However, as leaked secret files show, it not only regularly happens, in the United States Air Force it's official policy.

The practice of the USAF encouraging pilots to use stimulants had long been suspected, but an investigation into two F-16 pilots in Afghanistan who mistakenly bombed a group of Canadian soldiers helped expose the truth about the USAF's use of amphetamines. When pilots Harry Schmidt and William Umbach were put on trial for "reckless behaviour and violating the rules of engagement", it emerged that both men had been given "go pills" by their base's flight-surgeon.

Pilots occasionally used amphetamines during the Second World War, but the USAF expanded their use during the 1991 Desert Storm campaign. Half of the pilots in the conflict took amphetamines They were prescribed for the nocturnal bombing runs. Depressants, or sedatives – "no-go pills" – were given to help them sleep through the heat and noise of the day. John Pike, a senior defence analyst, describes the policy as: "Better bombing through chemistry."

While the drugs are legal when given by a doctor and pilots can refuse to take them, by the time of the US war in Afghanistan almost no pilots were drug free out of fear of what would happen to their careers if they said no. The "go pill" most commonly used by the USAF is Dexedrine. Made by the UK's GlaxoSmithKline, it is used in medicine for treating narcolepsy. The company warns it has a "high potential for abuse" and "may impair the ability to engage in potentially hazardous activities such as operating machinery or vehicles".

Even the flight surgeon's Guide to *Performance Maintenance During Continuous Flight Operations* mentions that likely side effects are "euphoria, depression and addiction". It also mentions "idiosyncratic reactions" such as increased paranoia and aggression, which probably sound quite attractive to the military.

CONGRESS WAS LIED TO ABOUT THE GULF OF TONKIN ATTACKS ON US SHIPS THAT LED AMERICA INTO THE VIETNAM WAR

George W Bush is not the only US president who has lied to the American public to justify a foreign war. In 1964, the conflict between North and South Vietnamese forces was a remote struggle in a faraway land. The US Congress and public did not support American intervention in South East Asia. Restricted to intelligence gathering and technical support for the South Vietnamese, President Lyndon B Johnson allowed the US Special Operations Group of commandos (SOG) to begin secretly harassing North Vietnamese forces.

On August 2, SOG teams undertook raids designed to provoke retaliation. The raids occurred just as the *USS Maddox* – a destroyer and intelligence-gathering vessel – entered the Gulf of Tonkin. The destroyer clashed with North Vietnamese torpedo boats that were scouring the area in the wake of the raids.

When the *Maddox* retreated, President Johnson himself ordered it to return to the Gulf accompanied by a second destroyer, the *USS C Turner Joy*. On August 4, another series of SOG raids occurred after which the two American destroyers filled the night with their blazing guns as they thought they were under attack by the North Vietnamese. It quickly became clear that there was no attack; the nervous US ships were blasting at misidentified radar blips and banks of fog.

Even though the White House knew this, President Johnson ordered the first US air strikes against North Vietnamese bases. The alleged attacks on the *Maddox* and *C Turner Joy* were sensationalized, creating a climate that allowed Johnson to get the Gulf of Tonkin Resolution through Congress.

The Resolution gave the president the power to take the country to war without the need to seek Congress's explicit permission. The lie of the non-existent attack was the trigger for America's disastrous involvement in Vietnam. Initial military incompetence was manipulated into a conflict costing 47,378 American and two million North Vietnamese lives.

General Maxwell Taylor, a key White House advisor in the early stages of American involvement in Vietnam, has said in interviews regarding that period in time: "The president's men think they had a license to lie that never expires."

`below` Blast them out - an American naval ship blasts suspected enemy positions during the Vietnam War, ironically started by a non-existent attack on a US ship.

THE BRITISH WERE GUILTY OF COMMITTING WAR CRIMES DURING THE SECOND WORLD WAR

None of us are so innocent as to have escaped the fact that it is the victors who write the history of any conflict. None of us should be naïve enough to believe it is also the victors of any war who decide on the justice for its many victims.

In October 1945, the United States, Great Britain, France and Russia set up the International Military Tribunal at Nuremberg to try Nazi war crimes ranging from systematic genocide to murder of captured troops. This was despite Winston Churchill's wish that any surviving Nazi leaders should be "hunted down and shot". The Nuremberg trials were seen to bring justice to many of the millions of victims of Nazi atrocities, but they made no attempt to tackle the war crimes committed by the British and other Allied forces during the conflict.

A typical example of the suppressed British war crimes was the action of Royal Navy Commander Anthony Cecil Capel Miers (known to his men as "Crap"). After his submarine sank two German ships in the Aegean Sea, he ordered the survivors shot with Lewis machine guns. His first lieutenant, Paul Chapman, reported: "Everything and everybody was destroyed by one sort of gunfire or another." This was not an isolated incident. Miers later went on to order the shooting of seven disarmed German survivors who had been captured because in his view "submarines do not take prisoners". Miers was a charming chap who often threatened to shoot the men under his command if they seemed reluctant to follow orders.

If Miers had been a Nazi U-boat commander instead of a Royal Navy submarine commander, he would have been tried at Nuremberg and executed. Instead, he received the Victoria Cross – Britain's highest military honour – and went on to achieve the rank of Rear-Admiral.

British atrocities did not stop after the war. Guards murdered many German prisoners without any action being taken against them and the British forces occupying northwest Germany from Bonn to Hamburg after the war ran internment camps where inmates were regularly tortured. No prosecutions were made.

HOW THE US MILITARY HAS SECRETLY TESTED CHEMICAL AND GERM WARFARE ON ITS OWN CITIZENS ON A REGULAR BASIS

In war, everyone understands there are often good reasons why the first casualty in any conflict is the truth. Most of us would see no peacetime reason for an army to lie and keep secrets from the people of its own nation. Unless, of course, it was performing secret chemical and germ warfare on the very people it was sworn to protect.

Between 1956 and 1958, the US army conducted a series of experiments involving mosquitoes as means of transmitting disease. The surprising fact here is not that they were undertaking research into using the insects in biological warfare, but that the experiments involved releasing mosquitoes into residential areas in Savannah, Georgia and Avon Park, Florida. Unknowing citizens founds themselves swarmed, with some subsequently falling ill. A number died. After the releases, members of the US army research team impersonated public health officials to allow them to test and photograph those who had become unwell. Full details of the experiments remain secret to this day.

It would be comforting to think that this was an isolated example. However, as far back as 1950 the US Navy sprayed clouds of bacteria over San Francisco to monitor how germs used in warfare would spread through an urban population. Despite naval claims that the bacteria were "harmless", many residents developed the symptoms of pneumonia directly after the spraying.

"Harmless" gas was released over five US cities in 1953, while a "harmless bacillus" was released into the New York subway system in 1966. The army report on the releases of gas showed higher than usual occurrences of respiratory problems for those living in the cities. Like the report into the army's release of whooping cough in Tampa, Florida, in 1955, after which 12 people died, the full report remains classified.

The army were not doing anything illegal. Until it was modified in 1997, US Public Law 95-79, Title 50, Chapter 32, Section 1520 stated: "The use of human subjects will be allowed for the testing of chemical and biological agents by the US Department Of Defense."

THE IRA COLLABORATED WITH THE NAZIS DURING THE SECOND WORLD WAR AND CARRIED OUT SABOTAGE AND BOMBING MISSIONS AGAINST THE BRITISH

Admitting you supported the losing side is never easy to do, even if it is just over backing Chelsea instead of Arsenal in the 2002 FA Cup. When you have to admit that not only did you back the wrong side in a war (the Nazis), you were also working with them against the eventual victors, even the most brass necked could find the confession sticks in the throat. This explains why the Irish Republican Army (IRA) do not promote their role in the Second World War when soliciting for their struggle to overthrow British control of Northern Ireland.

In 2003, the statue of the IRA's former leader Sean Russell in Fairview Park in Dublin was attacked. When responsibility was claimed by an anti-fascist group, it lifted the lid on Russell's – and the IRA's – collaboration with the Nazi regime during the Second World War.

Russell died in 1940 on a German U-boat off the coast of Galway as he and fellow IRA man Frank Ryan secretly travelled back from Germany on a mission codenamed Operation Taube (Dove). Russell, a public and vocal supporter of Hitler, had been in Berlin receiving training and planning how a joint Nazi-IRA campaign could deliver the maximum damage to the British war effort against Germany.

If he had lived, Operation Taube would have seen Russell leading the IRA on attacks against British military installations in Northern Ireland and trying to overthrow Ireland's government, led by Éamon de Valera, which remained neutral during the conflict.

The British authorities suppressed reports of bombings and acts of sabotage undertaken by the IRA during the war for propaganda reasons. They also concealed successful acts of sabotage undertaken by Welsh nationalist terrorists. Full details of the extent of nationalist attacks against the British war effort were placed under a 100-year embargo in 1945 and remain classified to this day.

Every year, Irish Republicans continue to gather in Fairview Park to commemorate the life of Russell claiming: "We don't know what was in the depth of his thinking, but we are sure he was never far from the position of a patriot, preferring death to slavery."

below True colours – Irish Republican hero Sean Russell died on a Nazi U-boat taking him back to Ireland to start a joint IRA-Nazi campaign of terror.

NON-EXISTENT ATROCITIES WERE USED TO JUSTIFY THE WAR IN KOSOVO

Only the mentally disturbed could be happy to hear that their country had gone to war, but if your country is fighting to prevent genocide and widespread systematic mass-rape, you could be forgiven for having a touch of pride in your nation's leaders for doing the right thing.

When Bill Clinton and Tony Blair led the way into taking NATO forces to war with Yugoslavia over Kosovo in 1999, they did so proclaiming that the intervention was both necessary and moral due to the atrocities that Serb soldiers were committing against the civilian ethnic population of Kosovo. Blair even claimed that NATO attacks were needed because Yugoslavia was: "Set on a Hitler-style genocide equivalent to the extermination of the Jews during World War Two."

Whilst the propaganda was more sophisticated than that used by the US and UK during World War One, there was no more truth to claims of mass murder than there was to the earlier lie that German soldiers ate Belgian babies. Ahead of the NATO attacks, its officials made claims of mass graves and massive systematic campaigns of rape.

Two months before the war was launched – pictures were broadcast of 23 dead Albanians. German Defence Minister Rudolf Scharping claimed this was evidence of a Serbian massacre, even though the picture was a hoax. This was typical of the media manipulation that helped create a climate of belief for US Defence Secretary William Cohen's claims of: "The murder of up to 100,000 Kosovars by the Serbians." The UK's Minister of State at the Foreign Office Geoffrey Hoon placed the figure at "at least 10,000."

Many atrocities did happen. Whilst one rape or one murder is one too many and a crime against all humanity, the justification for war was the mass murder, rape and other atrocities by the Serbs. After the war, no hard evidence to back the claim of 10,000–100,000 murders emerged. The European Union forensic team sent to Kosovo after NATO had taken control of it found only 187 civilian corpses and reported that less than 2,500 had died during the Serbian-KLA conflict between 1997–1999.

THE US ARMY PLANNED TO KILL ITS OWN CITIZENS TO PROVOKE AN INVASION OF CUBA

How corrupt, crazed and totally lacking in morality would the military of a nation have to be to suggest murdering its own civilians as an excuse to go to war? The answer is as shady, demented and unprincipled as the American military was in 1962.

Still smarting from the fiasco of the CIA-sponsored Bay of Pigs Invasion of Cuba and with no sign that Fidel Castro was going to give them a legitimate pretext for war, Chairman of the Joint Chiefs of Staff General Lyman Lemnitzer began to plot ways to convince the world that America had the right to mount a full-scale military invasion of the island.

In March 1962, the Joint Chief of Staff presented US Secretary of Defense Robert McNamara with their proposals for a project codenamed Operation Northwoods in a document entitled "Justification for US Military Intervention in Cuba".

Among the ideas put forward was that of committing random acts of terror on American citizens "in the Miami area and even in Washington". This would be achieved by "exploding a few plastic bombs in carefully chosen spots, the arrest of Cuban agents and the release of prepared documents substantiating Cuban involvement". If this was not shocking enough, the report also suggested "sinking a boatload of Cuban refugees *en route* to Florida".

If that was not enough to stir up US public and international opinion, the Joint Chiefs of Staff recommended "hijacking attempts against civil craft" and "creating an incident which will demonstrate convincingly that a Cuban aircraft has attacked and shot down a chartered civil airliner *en route* from the United States to Jamaica".

Another part of the plan was to stage a fake attack on the US military base in Guantanamo Bay and even "blow up a US ship and blame Cuba". Becoming more elaborate, they also proposed the "use of MIG type aircraft by US pilots to attack surface shipping and destroy US military drone aircraft".

The people of both Cuba and the United States should be relieved that President John F Kennedy personally rejected implementing the proposal.

THE LIES TOLD TO JUSTIFY THE INVASION OF IRAQ

Despite George W Bush proclaiming himself the "War President", electorates in democracies have always shown a strong aversion to conflict. It's only in dictatorships that leaders get away with declaring "shock and awe" on whomever they want to without having to explain the reasons. This might be behind Bush's statement: "A dictatorship would be a heck of a lot easier."

To persuade the people in the countries constituting the "coalition of the willing" that the 2003 invasion of Iraq was justified, the leaders of America, Britain and Australia told a series of lies. In fact, more than 30 direct lies or gross instances of spin (in politics, spin is often just a posh word for lying) were perpetuated to validate the loss of life and multi-billion dollar cost of Operation Iraqi Freedom.

The central lie was that the aim of the war, as voiced by Tony Blair speaking for the coalition, was to "Disarm Iraq of its weapons of mass destruction". Given that prior to the invasion chief UN weapons inspector Hans Blix backed Saddam Hussein's claim that he had got rid of all of his chemical, biological and nuclear capability, a series of deliberate misrepresentations was made to convince the public he still had weapons of mass destruction (WMD). Not one of the assertions Colin Powell made in giving "evidence" to the UN concerning Iraq and WMD was right.

Another key lie put forward as a pretext for the invasion was that Saddam supported al-Qaeda. George Bush claimed that: "Iraq has trained al-Qaeda members in bomb-making and poisons and deadly gases." Pentagon advisers claimed al-Qaeda's Mohammed Atta "...met Saddam Hussein in Baghdad prior to September 11. We have proof of that." There was never any proof of the meeting or of Saddam being linked to al-Qaeda.

Even though subsequent events in Iraq have made the falsehoods self-evident, it has been worth mentioning some of them again in print, just so you don't feel you have been hallucinating – yes, President Bush and Prime Minister Blair really did get away with telling such whoppers.

left Babylon is burning – on TV it seemed like a firework show, on the ground the tactic of Shock and Awe seemed like the end of the world for many Iraqis.

BIG BUSINESS 4

"Nothing is illegal if a hundred businessmen decide to do it."
Andrew Young

Money is allegedly the root of all evil and it certainly seems to be at the core of some of the most closely guarded secrets and lies perpetrated by big businesses.

There are legitimate reasons for large companies to keep secrets. Details about their products and future plans are market sensitive and need to be protected from their rivals and share-dealing speculators. However, it is also obvious why certain companies make so much effort to repress historical information about their business activities: greed.

The reason why IBM does not want its customers reminded of its role in the Holocaust and why Bacardi does not want its drinkers to know how an ex-boss funded the CIA, gangsters and terrorists intent on bringing down Fidel Castro is money. Activities from the past such as this could have a huge impact on their corporate reputations and therefore their profits. This probably also accounts for why Coca-Cola doesn't tell the full story of the creation of Fanta or Coke on their website.

From Microsoft paying leading journalists to write seemingly objective reviews of its products to the Ford Motor Company covering up its safety record, our culture not only permits big businesses to get away with lying to us, we almost expect them to do it. We know deep down that the majority of ads we see on TV contain untruths and that the major corporations wrote the book on media manipulation and spin, yet we rarely challenge it.

THE IMPACT OF THE PROMOTION OF NESTLÉ INFANT FORMULA

Given the vast profits that Nestlé make across the globe, it's surprising to know that there's a consumer boycott of their products in force. It's a campaign against the company that has attracted support from a number of famous names ranging from Pulp's Jarvis Cocker to Hollywood stars such as Emma Thompson and Julie Christie.

The root of their anger and the anger of thousands of customers was summed up by Christie in 2001 when she said: "I've been supporting the Nestlé Boycott for years due to the company's irresponsible marketing of baby food. This has brought about children being deprived of the early natural immunization that breast milk provides. The use of contaminated water is another issue in rural areas."

Whilst Nestlé disputes the view of Christie and others who support the boycott, there is no getting away from the fact that in the 1960s and 1970s, it engaged in promotional practices that could have persuaded some mothers in developing countries to use baby-formula rather than breastfeed their children. These ranged from giving free samples of infant formula to mothers, placing posters promoting Nestlé infant formula in health facilities and giving gifts to health workers involved in infant care.

Powdered baby milk is not as effective as the mother's own milk at providing nutrition to infants. Mother's milk will contain antibodies that ward off infection and disease. The United Nations Children's Fund – UNICEF – are on record as saying: "Marketing practices that undermine breastfeeding are potentially hazardous wherever they are pursued: in the developing world. The World Health Organisation estimates that some 1.5 million children die each year because they are not adequately breastfed. These facts are not in dispute."

However, Nestlé has been quick to point out it is often the victim of lies by some pro-breastfeeding campaigners who have selectively quoted international bodies and neglected to mention those bodies balancing arguments for the appropriate use of infant formula and bottle-feeding. The company claims that: "It now does no public promotion of infant formula in the developing world." Campaigners continue to dispute the record of Nestlé regarding the promotion of infant formula and in 1999, the UK Advertising Standards Authority warned Nestlé over claims it made in an advert including: "Even before the World Health Organisation International Code of Marketing of Breastmilk Substitutes was introduced in 1981, Nestlé marketed infant formula ethically and responsibly, and has done so ever since and stopped such practices 20 years ago."

FANTA WAS CREATED BY THE GERMAN DIVISION OF COCA-COLA IN NAZI GERMANY

On its corporate website, the Coca-Cola Company fact sheet for Fanta proclaims it: "A favourite in Europe since the 1940s." Strangely, there is no mention of the drink's origins or why it was so popular in Europe, thereby neatly glossing over all of the more interesting history of the product.

Before the Second World War, Coca-Cola's strongest foreign success was in Germany, where their operation had gone from 243,000 cases sold in 1934 to shifting almost four-and-a-half million cases by 1939.

Having achieved a position of popularity in Germany, the man running Coca-Cola (GmbH), Max Keith, found himself with a problem when the war interrupted supplies of the necessary ingredients to make the famous Coca-Cola syrup. Having let Coke HQ in Atlanta know that he would do his best to keep the business running in Germany and the Nazi-occupied territories in the rest of Europe, Keith set his employees the task of creating a new drink, which was eventually named Fanta.

Despite containing everything from cheese to apple fibre in its earliest formula, Fanta was popular enough to sell more than three million cases throughout the Third Reich. In 1960, Coke formally acquired Fanta.

right Heil – the German division of Coca-Cola was one of the sponsors of the Berlin Olympic Games

HOW BANKS TRIED TO GET TWA TO TAKE OUT A LOAN IT DID NOT WANT

If you are one the world's richest men running a successful company in which you hold 78 per cent of the stock, you do not expect the banks to kick you around. Yet this is exactly what happened to Howard Hughes and his airline TWA.

The hit film *The Aviator* has helped remind us that there was more to Howard Hughes than the paranoia and eccentricity of his later years. It also demonstrated that whatever passions he may have had for actresses such as Katherine Hepburn and Jean Harlow, the one true love of his life was flying.

This affair with aircraft saw him not only design planes and set new aviation records, it also led him to buy the struggling airline Transcontinental and Western Air in 1939. Renaming it Trans World Airlines (TWA), under his leadership the company expanded rapidly, becoming a major international player by innovating over routes, customer comfort (TWA was the first airline to show movies) and the aircraft it used. Hughes took a hands-on interest in the company, even piloting some of TWA's commercial flights.

In 1961, needing additional finance after investing heavily in a new fleet of aircraft, Hughes declined a loan from financial institutions due to the high interest rate and the fact that it would allow the banks two votes on the board compared to his one. In an effort to get Hughes to change his mind about the loan, a top Wall Street lawyer started a legal action against him. The plan was to wrest control of TWA from Hughes on the basis that by refusing the loan he had cost his company $45,870,435.

Hughes could not believe that the company he owned was suing him for control for not taking a loan he did not want. The bitter 12-year-long case rumbled on until 1973 when Hughes was eventually vindicated in the US Supreme Court. It was a hollow victory, however, as Hughes had sold his stock for $547 million five years into the case.

right Get off of my cloud — Howard Hughes fought the banks who tried to seize control of the airline he had spent years building up.

above Never again - given the IBM role in Nazi Germany, their slogan 'Solutions for a small planet' has a painful irony for survivors of the Holocaust.

IBM TECHNOLOGY WAS USED BY THE NAZIS

For more than 70 years, IBM has stood at the forefront of technological innovation and business efficiency. It is proud to call itself a "solutions" company. Today it is associated with the latest in microchips and computer software solutions, but back in the 1930s the zenith of IBM's technology was its five-digit Hollerith numbers and punch cards.

In his seminal 2001 book, *IBM and the Holocaust*, investigative journalist Edwin Black exposed how the Nazi regime had been able, systematically and efficiently, to compile a list of Jews and Jewish assets and arrange for the monumental movement of Jews, gypsies and others to concentration camps. With the help of IBM Germany, the Nazi regime was able to use Hollerith numbers, punch cards and the latest technology to automate much of its campaign of genocide and terror.

After IBM provided more than 2,000 punch card machines, card sorting operations were established in concentration camps. The first horrific tattoos given to inmates at Auschwitz were Hollerith numbers so that they could be tracked as they moved through the forced-labour system. Hollerith-based numbers were only scrapped when the sheer number of victims and the high death rates made them obsolete.

With the knowledge of its New York HQ, IBM Germany did much more than sell machines to the Nazi regime. They custom designed systems, trained Nazi officers and produced up to 1.5 billion punch cards a year for Nazi use. They also serviced the machines on site once a month.

The vast majority of technology is morally neutral. You cannot blame the car manufacturer for the actions of a drunk driver. The fact the Nazis used IBM's technology at Auschwitz may not directly be the fault of IBM. However, the company's provision of technological support that assisted Nazi efforts to efficiently identify, process and move its prisoners is a secret from their past that cannot be allowed to remain hidden in documents for which IBM has yet to provide public access.

Obviously, there is a big difference between devices to assist in prisoner tracking and devices that are used in genocide. While IBM may have been involved in creating computer systems to monitor prisoners while interned in camps, they were, in no way, involved in the subsequent extermination of Jewish prisoners. There is no evidence that IBM was aware, at the time, that Jewish prisoners were being mistreated or exterminated while in the camps.

SONY RAN A PSYCHIC RESEARCH DIVISION

A vast but secretive Japanese corporation sets up a laboratory to investigate telepathy, telekinesis, controlled synchronicity and other strange powers rumoured to reside in the human but derided by nearly all scientists. They employ one of the world's top researchers into artificial intelligence who ends up making a shattering discovery.

It sounds like the set-up for a Playstation computer game. All it lacks is an indestructible cyborg villain. However, the only link to the Playstation is that the Japanese corporation at the centre of this amazing true-life story is Sony.

Sony had legitimate reasons for keeping the work of AI guru Yoishiro Sako and the Extrasensory Perception and Excitation Research laboratory, (ESPER) out of the public eye. When knowledge first became public in 1991, Yoshihiro Otsuki, a professor at Waseda University said: "By funding psychic research, Sony might as well be saying its products cannot be trusted." Allied to this was heightened Japanese fear of all things paranormal after the 1995 Sarin nerve gas attack on the Tokyo subway undertaken by the spooky Aum Shinri Kyo cult.

Sony founder Masaharu Ibuka believed that: "Some people have the ability to perceive beyond the five senses. The research is intended to investigate how this happens and why and to consider the possibility of machines that would enable us to communicate telepathically." The head of the ESPER division, Yoishiro Sako, was quoted as saying: "If we can understand the mechanism of telepathy, it would totally transform communication methods."

In the summer of 1998, after seven years of research by ESPER, Sony spokesman Masanobu Sakaguchi made an incredibly low-key announcement. He revealed two things. The first was that ESP exists. Secondly, that Sony had decided to wind down its paranormal research. Sakaguchi said: "We found out experimentally that ESP exists, but that any practical application of this knowledge is not likely in the foreseeable future."

It may be fascinating to learn that, according to Sony, ESP exists, but the closure of ESPER was no surprise. After all, Sony is a business. If it cannot find a practical application for ESP, it cannot make money from it.

left Game on - Sony's headquarters in Berlin represents the company' futuristic outlook.

THE OFFICIAL HISTORY OF COCA-COLA DOES NOT MENTION IT ONCE USED TO CONTAIN TRACES OF COCAINE

C oca-Cola is the most successful brand in history. It can also safely claim to be the most popular and best-selling soft drink on the face of the planet. In 2004, it helped generate six billion dollars in cash for the Coca-Cola Company. It is almost impossible to find a corner of the world where you cannot buy a cool bottle of Coke.

Given its unassailable commercial position and the great love its customers have for the product, you would think that the Coca-Cola Company would be proud of the early history of one of the world's top products. Indeed, logging onto the "Heritage" section at cocacola.com you can find reams of material on how it was originally sold for five cents a glass at soda fountains and how Frank M. Robinson penned the world-recognized logo.

However, there is absolutely no mention of how Coca-Cola originally contained cocaine. Contacting one of the company's spokespeople at its Atlanta HQ may even elicit a response that flatly denies that a product once sold with the slogan: "Coca-Cola revives and sustains" achieved this effect with the help of a powerful and addictive stimulant other than caffeine.

As much as the folks in Atlanta may want us all to believe that Coca-Cola's cocaine origins are nothing more than a modern urban myth, the truth is too well established for contradiction. When ex-Confederate army officer and pharmacist John Pemberton developed Coke in 1886, it was originally intended as a patent medicine. Its medicinal ingredients after which it was named were extract of coca leaves and kola nuts. One of the alkaloids present in the coca leaf is cocaine.

Coca-Cola advertising from the 1890s proudly proclaimed: "In a triumph over nature, Coca-Cola Co. of Atlanta have achieved success in robbing both coca leaves and the kola nut of the exceedingly nauseous and disagreeable taste whilst retaining their wonderful medicinal properties and the power of restoring vitality and raising the spirits of the weary and debilitated."

Due to a public backlash against cocaine in the early 1900s, even the trivial traces of cocaine were phased out of Coca-Cola, making its later advertising slogan: "That extra something" somewhat ironic.

HOW CIGARETTE COMPANIES HAVE TRIED TO MAKE THEIR PRODUCTS MORE ADDICTIVE

After the success of the 1999 movie *The Insider*, starring Russell Crowe as whistleblower Jeff Wigand, there can be few who do not know that the tobacco industry was not only aware that cigarettes are addictive and harmful, but deliberately worked on increasing that addictiveness.

It seems unnecessary to point out the depths of immorality associated with tobacco companies. Their products kill more than 2,500 people per day. Yet a major tobacco company recently planned on boosting sales of their cigarettes by targeting a new consumer market – the homeless. They called their plan Project Sub-Culture Urban Marketing. By comparison, even international arms dealers and some minor despots seem virtuous.

Since 1998, the US Surgeon General and the UK's Royal College of Physicians have all concluded that nicotine is an addictive substance and withdrawal from it displays similarities to drugs such as cocaine and heroin. They also report that in as little as a fortnight, nicotine changes the brain's chemistry and addiction can begin.

There is, however, one dirty little secret that should be told. Not content with adding ammonia to the tobacco to jack up the addictive impact of nicotine (a common practice in most brands of cigarettes), a very popular cigarette maker produced genetically modified tobacco to create a higher nicotine content.

Known by the farmers that grew it in Brazil as *fumo loco* (crazy tobacco), the genetically altered plant was developed in American laboratories before the seeds were shipped to South America in violation of US export law. The US Food and Drug Administration (FDA) discovered that Brown & Williamson code-named the high nicotine plant Y-1, and that it had been used as an ingredient in cigarette brands sold in the USA. (This was at a time when the FDA was investigating claims that the tobacco companies had lied about manipulating nicotine levels in their cigarettes.)

The issue remains not the use of GM tobacco (in fact GM tobacco has been developed that is low in nicotine) but the adding of ingredients to the product to make it even more addictive than cocaine.

`below` Field of death – GM technology can be used to make tobacco more or less addictive.

THE LIES TOLD AGAINST BIG BUSINESS BY ENVIRONMENTAL CAMPAIGN GROUPS

Sometimes it is not the nature of the lie told to us that hurts; it is the betrayal of trust by the person or organization that tells it. While we might expect governments and big business to use spin and other tactics to pull the wool over our eyes, many of us naïvely expect better from Greenpeace – the world's largest environmental activist organization. However, in their desire to portray big business as inherently bad, they have not only sensationalized issues, they have told lies.

In 1995, Shell Oil planned to sink the Brent Spar oilrig safely in the North Atlantic. Greenpeace attacked them for using the sea as a "dustbin" and claimed that there were hundreds of tons of toxic waste on board the rig, including some that was radioactive. They organized a boycott of Shell while other environmental activists firebombed Shell outlets in Germany.

The company stopped its planned deep ocean disposal even though it was more environmentally friendly than mainland disposal. Independent investigation showed that there never was any toxic or radioactive waste on the rig. As founding member of Greenpeace Patrick Moore pointed out, when the *Rainbow Warrior* vessel was damaged in New Zealand, Greenpeace had no problem with dumping it in the sea.

In my role as the spin doctor for the British Retail Consortium I experienced first hand the type of stretching of the facts Greenpeace is infamous for among the business community. Its members were picketing supermarkets, claiming in the press that retailers were selling genetically modified milk. Retailers weren't and never did. They were selling milk from cows that may have been fed on GM feed. Just as grass does not make milk green, GM feed does not make it GM milk – especially when there was never any GM protein in the product.

There are huge ecological issues for mankind to face if we are to enjoy any type of future at all, but misrepresentation of the nature of environmental problems by either side of the divide on green issues has now become a massive danger in itself.

HOW DRUG DUMPING BY LARGE COMPANIES HAS CAUSED PROBLEMS IN WAR ZONES AND AREAS HIT BY NATURAL DISASTERS

Big businesses are rarely shy or secretive about donating thousands of tons of their goods to the developing world. Given the poor publicity many of the major drug companies have received over the prices they charge some of the poorest countries on the planet for the drugs to fight AIDS, one would expect them to be heralding their donation of pharmaceutical products.

In fact, when major American pharmaceutical companies send tons of drugs to places such as Rwanda, Sudan and Banda Aceh – one of the areas that suffered the worst devastation from the Asian Tsunami in 2004 – the only people they might rush to tell about their generosity are the US tax authorities. Due to tax breaks offered for "gifts in kind", the companies can receive significant commercial benefit from their donations – sometimes twice the cost of the drug against their tax bill.

The truth behind what on the surface seem like acts of pure altruism is that the pharmaceutical companies often donate drugs that are past their sell-by date and which would otherwise have to be incinerated at considerable cost. The process has become known as "drug dumping". During the conflict in Bosnia, companies donated more than 17,000 tons of useless products such as antismoking devices, hair removal cream, lip balm and slimming agents. Skipping over the insensitivity of sending diet pills to people who may be starving, it cost the Bosnian government $34 million to dispose of the unwanted and out of date drugs safely.

Previously the drug companies were much more gung-ho about trying to obtain publicity for their donations. This position began to change when respected organizations such as War On Want, Medicines Sans Frontieres and Pharmaciens Sans Frontieres began to expose how such apparent acts of altruism were in fact callous, dangerous and exploitative.

Drug dumping in hard hit areas of the world continues apace with thousands of tons of unwanted drugs being shipped to areas devastated by the Asian Tsunami.

HOW THE BOSS OF BACARDI WORKED WITH THE CIA AND PAID THE MAFIA TO TRY AND OVERTHROW FIDEL CASTRO

Millions of drinkers around the world enjoy Bacardi. The world's largest rum company, it has annual sales of more than 245 million bottles in more than 170 countries. For many its famous brand of white rum conjures up images of idyllic Caribbean beaches, hedonistic nights in the Latin Quarter and wild celebrations to voodoo gods.

Mention of Bacardi to its drinkers does not usually spark in them an association with plans to bomb oil refineries, the assassination of a world leader, links to the Mafia and the secret and illegal US war against the Sandinistas in Nicaragua. However, given the secret history of the former head of Bacardi, Jose Pepin Bosch, those are exactly the images that should come to mind.

Bacardi dates back to 1862 when Spanish-born wine merchant Don Facundo Bacardi Masso set up a distillery in Cuba. During the early stages of the Cuban revolution, Bacardi supported Fidel Castro, but the founding family fled when the Cuban government seized control of the company in 1960. From its new base in the Bahamas, the family-controlled company set about re-establishing itself and is now the fourth largest spirits company in the world with sales in excess of $2.7 billion.

However, some elements of the family did not forget Cuba or forgive Castro. According to CIA documents declassified in 1998, former boss of Bacardi Bosch contributed $100,000 of the $150,000 requested by the Mafia to attempt a CIA plan to assassinate Castro, his brother Raul and Che Guevara. Bosch also hired an aircraft to bomb Cuba's oil refineries in an attempt to create a blackout that would lead to looting and other acts of subversion. His plan was cancelled when a picture of the aircraft emerged in a newspaper.

Pioneering investigative journalist Hernando Calvo Ospina also discovered that Bosch paid Luís Posada Carriles to commit acts of terrorism against Cuba. Carriles was eventually sentenced for his role in bombing an aircraft carrying the Cuban fencing team. There were no survivors of the attack. Obviously, these were the actions of Boshch alone, and were not the actions or beliefs of Bacardi as a company.

below Vive la revolución – Cuban forces defend themselves against the Bay of Pigs invasion

POLITICS

5

"The best weapon of a dictatorship is secrecy, but the best weapon of a democracy should be the weapon of openness."
Niels Bohr

From the hidden facts about fraudulent election results and illicit campaign donations to lies over secret drug use and weapons of mass destruction, when you study it, the history of politics is a history of lies.

Politicians are the least trusted group of people according to research, and with good reason. Just look at the lies they tell and secrets they cover up in their climb to, and exercise of, power – and which are revealed in this section – to remind yourself what an untrustworthy lot they are.

Most politicians are professional liars. If they told the truth, it is doubtful most of them would get elected. Once in power, the secrets and lies seem to multiply the higher they climb up the ladder of authority. To them, truth is rare, though it's a word they often use when trying to convince us that they have the answer to our problems.

Politicians lie to keep their jobs and to further their own personal as well as political agendas. None of this should surprise us, but we seem apathetic when it comes to challenging this sorry state of affairs. Even when we learn some of their shocking secrets or the worst of their lies are exposed, the most we seem to do in response is change where we put our "X"s at the next election. Unless the public become better at demanding higher standards of truth, our politicians will continue to treat us with contempt through secretive policies designed to keep us purposefully ignorant.

GEORGE W BUSH'S SECRET DRUG TAPE

Being betrayed by a friend is a terrible experience. You feel as if you have been punched so hard you could double up, not from pain, but from the hollow feeling in your stomach. The closer and more trusted the friend, the worse it is.

When George W Bush woke up on the morning of February 20, 2005, you can easily imagine that feeling going through his body. Once awake, advisors showed him a copy of the *New York Times*. In the paper, Doug Wead, a friend of his and an aide to the first president Bush, had revealed secretly recorded tapes of George W talking about his drug use.

Wead had surreptitiously taped private conversations he had had with Bush in 1998 while Bush was Governor of Texas and considering running for the White House. He released the tapes to the media after pressure from his publisher to help promote his book about presidential parents.

In the tape, Bush can be heard saying: "I wouldn't answer the marijuana questions. You know why? I don't want some little kid doing what I tried. Do you want your little kid to say: 'Hey daddy, President Bush tried marijuana, I think I will?' That's the message we would be sending out. I wouldn't answer the marijuana question."

He also goes on to explain. "It doesn't matter if it's LSD, cocaine, pot, any of those things, because if I answer one, then there will be another one. And I just am not going to answer those questions. And it may cost me the election."

White House press secretary Scott McClellan admitted the recordings were genuine but refused to comment on their contents, saying only that Bush was: "Having casual conversations with someone he believed was his friend."

Bush had previously been accused of heavy cocaine use in the book, *Fortunate Son* by James Hatfield. In July 2001, Hatfield was found dead in a hotel room. During the 2000 race, Bush's team kept the lid on any allegations by stating that Bush had not used illegal drugs in the past 25 years.

THE CORPORATIONS THAT DONATED MORE THAN $500,000 TO EACH OF THE CANDIDATES IN THE US PRESIDENTIAL ELECTIONS

Satirists describe the US presidential elections as a competition between two millionaires funded by billionaires. The line is only funny because it's based on the truth.

In most countries it is rare to find any major financial supporter of one party or candidate also funding its rival. The dominant practice across the globe is to back a person who believes in what you do or who will show you some thanks if elected. This might seem like an obvious approach to most financial backers of politicians, but the big corporations in America have developed an arguably better logic – back both candidates so whoever wins, you do too.

In the 2000 presidential race between Al Gore and George W Bush, more than 60 US corporations gave both candidates donations of at least $500,000 each. Campaigning for president costs $100,000 per day, so all the donations were gratefully received (even though some would think that pride might get in the way of letting you take money from someone who was also funding your rival).

Among the leading companies who have given donations to both candidates during some elections have been household names such as Microsoft, Federal Express, Ernst & Young, Boeing, Disney and Bacardi Martini USA. When challenged as to the size of their donations and the practice of donating to both parties, many of the companies explained their generosity as a way of supporting democracy; some even cited a Supreme Court ruling that found that political campaign expenditures are a form of free speech.

The list of companies also contained some that were less recognizable to the public at the time, such as Enron. The now-bust company was the largest corporate donator to Bush. After the election Enron officials helped to write the Bush administration energy policy bill.

Many of the donations were allowed under the "soft-money loophole" that was closed in 2003. Corporations have no need to despair though; they can donate unfettered toward the inauguration of the winning candidate. More than 100 corporations donated in excess of $100,000 dollars to George W Bush's inauguration fund in 2005.

ALASTAIR CAMPBELL – TONY BLAIR'S DARK PRINCE OF SPIN

When Alastair Campbell was Tony Blair's Director of Communications, many informed observers nicknamed him "the Co-Prime Minister", but no one was joking when they called him: "the second most powerful man in the British government."

Campbell was a writer of pornographic stories under the pseudonym The Riviera Gigolo before becoming the political correspondent of the *Daily Mirror*. With a self-confessed drink problem and suffering from a nervous breakdown, Campbell managed to get his life back on track with the help of former Labour Party leader Neil Kinnock. Campbell went on to become Blair's closest advisor and instrumental in his rise to power.

The role of Campbell in manipulating the presentation of intelligence in dossiers that formed the basis for the UK's role in the invasion of Iraq is well known and much discussed. However, another alleged example of misrepresentation of information involving Campbell dates from the US and UK war in Afghanistan. The London Coalition Information Centre he was involved with were behind reports that British soldiers found evidence in a cave that al-Qaeda terrorists had built a "biological and chemical weapon laboratory". The reports were later contradicted by senior military officers as were claims made by a Blair spokesman "that the Baghdad regime was supplying Osama bin Laden's terrorists with chemical and biological weapons".

Even after leaving his job, Campbell remains a close advisor to Prime Minister Blair and retains his reputation as the ultimate dark prince of spin – a word that detractors have suggested has become a euphemism for outright lying. Whilst most spin doctors see their role as advocates of the individuals, organizations and ideas they are representing, some would say an internal ethical code prevents many of them from bullying journalists or presenting the truth in ways Campbell has specialized in. Others just say he's the best at doing what a spin doctor needs to do.

When Campbell was having his routine MI5 security vetting interview he was asked the standard question: "Have you ever knowingly divulged, or can you imagine any circumstances in which you would do so, sensitive or classified information to unauthorized sources?" Journalist Sion Simon was able to report that: "with a look of disgust on his face, Campbell replied, with the impatient brevity that is his trademark: 'That's my fucking job.'"

`below` Standing in the shadows – no one in Westminster underestimates the power Alastair Campbell has to shape the policies and action of Prime Minister Blair.

Close call – JFK beat Nixon with the help of his father who ensured that even dead men would cast votes for his son.

JFK WOULD NEVER HAVE BEEN ELECTED PRESIDENT IF NOT FOR MASSIVE VOTE FRAUD

The US presidential election of 2000 went down in infamy when George W Bush became president despite receiving fewer votes than his Democratic opponent Al Gore. Bush's victory rested on winning the highly contested state of Florida (the governor of which just happened to be his brother Jeb). When the Supreme Court made Bush president, many commentators and American voters thought the election has been stolen from Gore.

Allegations of large-scale fraud in Florida only intensified the sense of outrage felt by some Gore supporters. It was not the first time that a modern US presidential election had been mired in such allegations and the sense that the wrong person was in the White House due to criminal activity was not new.

In 1960, the bitterly fought election between Richard Nixon and John F Kennedy resulted in Nixon losing by an incredibly slim margin. In the end, the result rested on two states – Texas and Illinois. However, it was clear to all observers that there had been widespread fraud across Texas and especially in Cook County, Illinois.

In Texas there were multiple examples such as counties where there were 4,895 registered voters, but 6,138 votes cast (75 per cent of which went to Kennedy). In Chicago, voters who were actually dead and occupying plots in cemeteries cast votes for Kennedy. One reporter went to visit an address where 56 Kennedy voters were registered to vote only to find it demolished. In total, 677 people in Cook County were indicted for election-related fraud before being acquitted.

Following Kennedy's inauguration, the US Department of Justice performed an investigation into the evidence of voter fraud. The head of the DOJ was none other than the US Attorney General, Bobby Kennedy.

Nixon's campaign manager Len Hall, Republican National Chairman Thruston Morton and others all pleaded Nixon him to challenge the result. He refused, saying: "It would tear the country to pieces. You can't do that". Over the coming years Nixon nursed a grudge and would occasionally tell close colleagues that "That son of bitch Kennedy stole it."

THE US CONSTITUTION HAS BEEN INVALID SINCE 1933

"We the people of the United States, in order to form a more perfect union, establish justice, insure domestic tranquillity, provide for the common defence, promote the general welfare, and secure the blessings of liberty to ourselves and our posterity, do ordain and establish this Constitution for the United States of America."

Thus begins the US Constitution, in many ways the most complete expression of all that is most noble about the United States itself. Seen by most Americans as their greatest protection against government tyranny and their guarantee of everything from freedom of speech to the right to bear arms, the truth is that the Constitution was nullified on March 9, 1933, when President Franklin D Roosevelt declared a national emergency.

A few days earlier, FDR had asked Congress for: "Broad executive power to wage a war against the emergency as great as the power that would be given to me if we were in fact invaded by a foreign foe." The emergency he was referring to was effectively a shortage of gold and Congress agreed to his wish by allowing him to declare a national emergency and effectively suspending the Constitution.

Under the emergency power rules, the president has an almost free hand to control the country including the unconstitutional abilities to seize property, deploy military forces without congressional approval, bring in martial law, restrict travel and censor all communications. Until the president declares the national emergency over, the rules remain in force and the Constitution remains suspended. FDR never declared the emergency over. Neither did any of his successors, realizing that by living in a state of emergency their office had greater ability to govern.

In 1973, Senate Report 92549 stated: "Since 1933 the United States has been in a state of declared national emergency. A majority of the people of the United States have lived all of their lives under emergency rule." Since FDR's declaration, Presidents Truman, Nixon and George W Bush have all added further declarations that need to be annulled by a US president for the Constitution to have full effect again.

UK PRIME MINISTER HAROLD WILSON WANTED THE UK TO BECOME THE 51ST STATE OF THE USA

When Harold Wilson was returned to power as Labour Prime Minister in 1974, he could not have predicted that two years later he would resign from office embittered and paranoid as result of a plot by MI5 officers against him. MI5 and the then leader of the opposition Margaret Thatcher believed that Wilson was secretly aligned with Russia.

If they had had access to secret papers that were declassified under the 30-year rule, they would have realized just how insane their suspicions were. Far from wanting an alliance with the Soviets, Wilson is the only UK prime minister to have seriously considered the prospect of taking Great Britain into union with the USA.

In 1966 when he was re-elected as Prime Minister, the United Kingdom's faltering economy was haemorrhaging, with its trade deficits plunging to their worst levels in history. When asked by colleagues in the cabinet why he did not take a stronger line against America's involvement in Vietnam he gave the frank response: "Because we can't kick our creditors in the balls." Britain was being forced to retreat rapidly from what was left of its empire while French President Charles de Gaulle continued to block the UK from joining the ECC and having a larger role in Europe.

The cabinet was divided on Britain's way forward and it was during this period that documents show that Wilson seriously considered the option of the UK forming an alliance with America that would eventually see it becoming the 51st state.

Wilson believed the option would have solved Britain's growing economic problems, also delivering a new sense of identity and purpose that had been lost in the declining years of empire. He also believed that with LBJ running into increasing problems in Vietnam, America might just consider the idea. Constitutional considerations such as the position of the monarchy were examined (it was reasoned that if Hawaii still had a king, there would be no objection to there still being a queen of England) but the idea was shelved as undesirable to both his political party and the British public. Shame.

left New statesman – Wilson thought the UK had a future as the 51st state of the USA.

HOW THE US PRESIDENTIAL DEBATES ARE FIXED

US presidential debates have been described as a televised interview for the job of the most powerful person on the planet. The impact of the debates on the candidates' chances in the presidential elections cannot be underestimated nor can the image of the debates being beamed across the globe as a symbol of American democracy.

In Great Britain, there are campaigns to have debates introduced on the grounds they play an essential role in informed voter choice. Campaigners argue that although there may be problems counting the votes cast in US elections, the debates are a beacon of free speech, open political discussion and public accessibility to the candidates.

However, the truth is that the debates are not open, accessible arenas of free speech. They are secretly regulated by the Republican and Democratic parties through a private bipartisan corporation called the Commission on Presidential Debates (CPD). In 1992, the CPD – jointly run by former heads of both parties and funded by big US corporations – took control of the debates that had previously been run by the non-partisan League of Women Voters. Every four years they negotiate a secret document called the Memoranda of Understanding which dictate precisely how the debates will be structured and televised.

The CPD control of the debates allows them to exclude third party candidates – even those like Ross Perot who took 19 per cent of the popular vote when he stood in 1992. The latest Memoranda of Understanding ran to 34 pages and contained clauses such as "No follow-up questions by the moderator will be permitted," and "No cross-questions by the candidates or cross-conversation between the candidate will be allowed". No wonder they have become as dull as ditchwater.

Alan Keyes, a former Republican presidential candidate, said: "If you are going to present a partisan brawl, in which you have excluded anybody but your chosen few, I would say just do it. You have the right to do it. It's a free country. Don't pretend, however, to do it under a rubric of non-partisanship... few, I would say just do it. Just don't pretend it's non-partisan or not controlled. That's cheating. That's corruption. That's lying. That's an effort to manipulate the perception of the voters in order to favour your power."

below Democracy in action - no wonder John Kerry and George W. Bush seem so friendly given that both men know the presidential debate is under strict control.

US PRESIDENT LYNDON B JOHNSON WAS MENTALLY UNSTABLE AND LIKED TO FLASH HIS PENIS AT JOURNALISTS AND FOREIGN POLITICIANS

Former US President Bill Clinton was nearly impeached for what he did with his reproductive organs and if George W Bush were to expose his penis it is likely that within 24 hours he too would be an ex-President. However, back in the 1960s, flashing the presidential penis to the press would not have raised an eyebrow among Washington hacks. After all, many of them had seen President Lyndon B Johnson's "pecker" before.

Ascending to the presidency after the convenient death of JFK, LBJ used his power to secure a breathtaking programme of civil rights and social reform. He was also a manic-depressive whose mental instability not only incapacitated him for days while president, but also drove him to incredible extremes in his personal action.

The maxim that power corrupts and absolute power corrupts absolutely did not apply to Johnson. He was already open about his corruption, bragging how he stole his 1948 election to the Senate. However, being President of the USA allowed him to get away with increasingly bizarre behaviour.

During a presidential briefing with reporters in the White House, he became frustrated with questions over why America was fighting in Vietnam. Losing his patience, Johnson stood up, unzipped his trousers and pulled out his penis, waved it at them and said: "This is why." LBJ was very proud of the size of his sex organ and gave it the pet name "Jumbo". When the East German Ambassador came to the Oval Office to present his credentials, Johnson placed "Jumbo" on his desk and told the ambassador: "See that? Good Texan meat. Don't screw with it."

Some have claimed that action was an attempt by Johnson to convince the Soviets that he was mad enough to push the nuclear button if he had to. However, it is unlikely that the Soviets needed convincing. They, like anyone else with an ear to the ground in Washington, knew LBJ regularly flashed and would also force secretaries, officials and cabinet to hold meetings with him while he urinated and defecated. And some dare call George W Bush crazy.

left Mad, bad and dangerous to know? President Johnson had more mental health problems than even his biggest opponents could imagine

THE SECRETS BEHIND THE BUSH FAMILY MILLIONS – FROM DEALINGS WITH THE NAZIS TO DEALINGS WITH IRAN

There are many things that politicians keep secret from the electorate as they attempt to attain public office. Vote rigging elections, drug use and adulterous dalliances with 16-year-olds have been successfully kept away from the public by more than one US president and UK prime minister.

However, keeping your relatives' secrets hidden seems to be a much harder operation. It has proven that way for President George W Bush. He must have thought with one Bush having already occupied the White House, there was little about his family's past that could embarrass him. He was wrong. Daddy must have been much better at keeping people in the dark.

Files uncovered in US National Archives unequivocally show George W Bush's grandfather – the late US senator Prescott Bush – was a director and shareholder of companies that made big profits working for the financial backers of Nazi Germany. Prescott was the director of the Union Banking Corporation (UBC) that represented Nazi industrialist Fritz Thyssen. He was also on the board of at least one of the companies that formed part of a multinational network of front companies to allow Thyssen to move assets around the world.

In the summer of 1942, when America was at war with Germany, it was revealed that the UBC had been buying gold as part of $3 million secret nest egg for "Hitler's angel" and other leading Nazis. The US government seized the assets of the UBC under the Trading with Enemy Act and Prescott Bush was lucky to escape prosecution for giving aid and comfort to the enemy. However, the money made from these dealings helped create the Bush family fortune and set up its political dynasty.

Just when it seemed that the skeletons in the family closet were through making life difficult for the team of denial experts working for Bush, it was discovered that his uncle, Bucky Bush, was involved in a company dealing with Iran – one the countries President Bush had claimed made up an "Axis of Evil". It seems the more things change, the more they are the same.

right Fighting for the wrong side – whilst the Nazi war machine trampled over Europe, Prescott Bush profited from his association with key Nazi financial backers.

TONY BLAIR LIED ABOUT MASS GRAVES IN IRAQ

Cats have nine lives with which they manage to scrape out of tricky situations, but Tony Blair has nine lies with which he is able to get away with any problems over his involvement in Iraq.

Most politicians would have become more cautious about proclaiming dodgy intelligence as proven evidence after Blair's outrageous misrepresentations that led Britain to war. Not our Tony. In November 2003 he told another whopper when he claimed: "We've already discovered, just so far, the remains of 400,000 people in mass graves."

The claim was taken at face value across the world and seized upon by the US administration as a perfect example of why their invasion had been justified even though the earlier pretext of weapons of mass destruction had proved false. The US Agency For International Development reported in its publication *Iraq's Legacy of Terror: Mass Graves:* "If these numbers prove accurate, they represent a crime against humanity surpassed only by the Rwandan genocide of 1994, Pol Pot's Cambodian killing fields in the 1970s, and the Nazi Holocaust of World War II."

Coverage of Blair's claims in the UK and US was accompanied by some TV stations showing shots of an Iraqi building in which rows of skeletons and boxes of bones were displayed. It was suggested that the building housed the remains of Saddam's victims. It later emerged that the building was in fact a store of recently recovered remains of Iraqi soldiers who had died in the Iran-Iraq war and which were awaiting forensic identification.

Tony Blair repeated the claim in December on the Labour party website, where he said: "The remains of 400,000 human beings [have] already [been] found in mass graves."

In the summer of 2004, after an investigation by *The Observer* newspaper, Downing Street was forced to admit that repeated claims by Blair that 400,000 bodies had been found in Iraqi mass graves was untrue and only about 5,000 corpses had been uncovered. In 2005, The US Agency For International Development still displayed Blair's comments on their website without any mention of them being false.

above Senator Prescott Bush confers with President Eisenhower - a former general who had fought the Nazi war machine whilst Bush made millions from his German clients.

MEDIA

"A lie told often enough becomes the truth".
Lenin

When it comes to lies and covering up the truth it seems there are liars, damn liars and the media giants who control and censor what gets reported as fact. That may sound extreme, but it comes from someone who has spent the majority of his working life as a journalist and editor.

It is said whoever controls what you read and see controls what you think. Most journalists don't consciously lie, but the media usually takes its views from official statements that are rarely challenged. By doing this, the media reinforces the official version of events, unwittingly spreading the lies they have been fed until the orthodox but wholly wrong version of events is the only one that we have easy access to.

The Internet was heralded as transforming our access to information and therefore the truth, but the information superhighway is grid-locked by so many lies that it's hard to know what to believe. We spend so much time just trying to get by in our lives and be happy that it's hard to find the time to question the information we are constantly bombarded with.

The harsh reality is that even with the Internet, most of us are as dependent on getting our "facts" from the traditional media as we ever were. It is sometimes hard to sense biases and lies, especially when they come from those you have a great deal of implicit trust in, meaning media manipulation is as widespread today as it ever was.

Behind you! Why aren't the lenses of the world's press used to capture meetings of the world's most powerful people when they attend Bilderberg Group meetings?

WHY JOURNALISTS DON'T COVER MEETINGS OF THE WORLD'S MOST POWERFUL PEOPLE

If you ignore the wild conspiracy theories that go hand in hand with most mentions of the Bilderberg Group and concentrate on the facts, the true picture is of a collection of the richest and most powerful people on the planet who meet up once a year.

Given the type of coverage a gathering like the annual World Economic Forum meetings at Davos in Switzerland generates, you would expect that a gathering of world leaders, fast-rising politicians, key military thinkers, press barons, and the richest and most influential business figures on the planet would attract a few journalists. When the 2004 Bilderberg meeting in Italy drew Prime Minister Tony Blair, President George W Bush, and Melinda Gates, wife of Bill Gates, you would think there would be a press stampede.

In fact there was almost a media blackout of the event. The few papers that mentioned it was due to happen did not send reporting teams to cover it. No major national or international news network attempted to film it. When people who usually draw journalists to them like moths to a flame

can avoid publicity like that, it's fair to say that the Bilderberg Group is as secret as such an impressive collection of the world's high and mighty can ever get.

Why is such an important meeting underreported? In the 1990s, William Glasgow at *Business Week* suggested the reason was simply cost-cutting: "After all, we can't afford to cover everything." But a journalist at *The Economist* - one of the UK's most important magazines – gave an alternative explanation: "The Bilderbergers have been removed from our assignment list years ago by executive order." Whilst policies may have changed, business magazines are still lacking the in-depth coverage that most readers would expect a Bilderberg gathering worthy of generating.

Of course, there's another reason why journalists don't try to cover the Bilderberg Group meetings. In 1998, one plucky and independent-minded Scottish reporter tried to cover the Bilderberg Group meeting at the Turnberry Hotel in Ayrshire. For the crime of doing nothing more than asking questions, he was handcuffed by the Strathclyde police like a violent criminal and thrown into jail.

THE CIA FUNDED AND CHANGED THE ENDING OF THE ANIMATED FILM OF *ANIMAL FARM*

If you were asked to name companies that make animated films, you'd probably respond with Pixar or Disney. Anyone who answered the question by saying "the CIA" would be plain crazy, right?

Wrong. During the Cold War, the CIA waged its secret war in many areas, including opening up a cultural front using film as a propaganda tool against the perceived Soviet threat. Even given this, the fact that the CIA used some of its funding to obtain the film rights to the last two novels published by renowned British socialist George Orwell is somewhat surprising. However, author Frances Stonor Saunders managed to track down the evidence to show that is exactly what occurred.

Buying the film rights to *1984* and *Animal Farm* was the idea of CIA agent E Howard Hunt — one of the Watergate burglars and a man who has lost court actions against claims that he was one of the three tramps seen at the assassination of JFK. He sent two of his men from the CIA Psychological Warfare Workshop to negotiate their purchase with Orwell's widow Sonia. Having got the screen rights, Hunt then chose Louis De Rochemont to be the producer of *Animal Farm* – the story Hunt had judged as the most effective piece of anti-communist propaganda out of the two.

The film was made in Britain by John Halas and Joy Batchelor – earning a place in history as the first animated feature film made in the UK. It took three years to make and was released in 1954. Anyone expecting a faithful retelling of the book would have been surprised by the ending as it had been re-written to show that the communist pigs had become totally despotic, deceitful and degenerate, leading to a counter-revolution by the other animals. Orwell's anti-capitalist observations had also been removed from the film version.

The finished film was something of a victory for the CIA as it was a commercial and critical success. Something no one could say about the live action version of *1984*, which was also made with CIA backing.

WHY JOURNALISTS CONTINUE TO MAKE MISLEADING CLAIMS ON AIDS

Hands up if you believe that the origins of AIDS lies with the African green monkey. Hands up if you know that AIDS spread to the western world through Patient Zero – a Canadian flight attendant who was said to have had sex with over a thousand men? Hands up if you think that the first person to die from AIDS was French?

If you consider any of the above statements to be true, don't be too disheartened to learn that all of them have been discredited. It does not mean that you are not keeping up to date with the latest news; it probably just means that the media you use has continued to repeat the above information long after it has been replaced by more recent and accurate information.

AIDS remains a medical problem with global implications, yet reporting on the topic by the mainstream media often contains misleading claims and out-of-date information. Why? The truth is simple and a little frightening. Most of the misleading information continues to be repeated in the media for one simple reason: the laziness of some journalists.

If a non-specialist journalist is asked to tackle a subject as complex as AIDS and finds himself up against a tight deadline, his capacity for research will be limited. If a story has been strongly covered previously and there is nothing in the cuttings file to contradict it, the likelihood of a pressurized hack doing additional research is low.

This explains why old theories can still be found in today's media. A strong example of this is the number of articles that claim Gaëtan Dugas was the "Patient Zero" who introduced AIDS into North America. The popularity of this story is in part due to the movie based on Randy Shilts' book *And The Band Played On*, which deals with the life of Dugas. No official claimed Dugas had introduced HIV into North America or that he was the first to have the infection identified, but even to this day those claims are made about him in some sections of the media.

THE CIA HAS AGENTS IN EVERY MAJOR BROADCASTER – FROM THE BBC TO CNN

When it comes to having a cover for your information gathering role as an intelligence agent, there are few better than that of "journalist". After all, they stick their noses in other people's business and ferret out secrets. The role of journalist also gives you direct access to the media, making the spreading of misinformation a lot easier. It also allows you to influence the news agenda and know first hand who other reporters' sources of information are.

This is why, since the 1950s, the Central Intelligence Agency has worked tirelessly to place deep cover agents in major national and international broadcasters and key newspapers. They have also developed a network of reporters who feed information into them in return for material for their stories.

A leaked internal CIA memo to a former CIA director is highly revealing. It describes how: "We have agents and contacts with every major news wire service, newspaper, news weekly and television network in the nation." It also reveals how they have successfully had stories scrapped and changed the way intelligence issues had been covered. The CIA currently has agents working both in American news networks and key foreign broadcasters such as the BBC and Al-Jazeera.

While the war in Kosovo was raging, the Dutch newspaper *Trouw* uncovered how five members of the US Army Intelligence – all specialists in psychological warfare, or "psy-ops" – were working at CNN in news production. With their cover blown, they returned to their regular duties at the Fourth Psychological Operations Group stationed at Fort Bragg. CNN later stated that they had in no way been "journalistically compromised".

The practice of using journalists as agents is nothing new. After he left Naval Intelligence in 1945, Ian Fleming (the creator of James Bond) became foreign manager for Kemsley Newspapers which owned titles including the *Sunday Times*.

Fleming set up a separate news agency to supply the papers with foreign news. Many of his hand-picked journalists were also working for MI6, gathering intelligence and reflecting the service's views in their reporting.

right The BBC's motto is "Nation shall speak peace unto Nation" which must seem ironic for any CIA agents working at Broadcasting House.

right Was "ER" on the secret White House programmes to watch list?

HOW TV COMPANIES SECRETLY PROMOTED WHITE HOUSE DRUG MESSAGES

The idea that the White House would have any interest in the content of hit TV shows such as "Sabrina: The Teenage Witch", "Beverley Hills 90210" and "ER" seems ridiculous. It seems even more unlikely that the White House would want to influence the content of the programmes.

As with many things linked to the highest levels of American government, the unlikely and ridiculous often turn out to be the way things really are. An investigation by Salon exposed how the White House Office of National Drug Control Policy (ONDCP) had secretly worked with television networks to broadcast anti-drug propaganda as part of the storylines of some of their most popular shows.

When in the White House, President Bill Clinton had persuaded Congress to pass a plan that approved more than $1 billion to be spent on anti-drug commercials and advertising. The plan also legally compelled the television networks to sell the ad time to the government at half-price. As this meant the TV companies losing up to $500 million, they suggested to the ONDCP that they could drop some of their half-cost ads by incorporating anti-drug messages into their shows.

While some networks have acknowledged they sent final scripts or tapes of shows to an agency representing the ONDCP, some networks actually sent in draft scripts for approval and made changes to them in order to gain ad credits. The credits meant that they were not losing out by having to give the White House cut-price advertising rates on airtime they could have sold commercially.

The ONDCP has also run a similar programme covering magazines where publishers could receive ad credits if the content of the magazine was sufficiently anti-drug. At least six major magazines submitted articles in an attempt to demonstrate that they were "on-message" and suitable to gain credits.

Whatever way you look at it, if programmes or articles have been changed to carry a government message and you do not know that fact while you are watching or reading, you've become the passive victim of secret state propaganda.

HOLLYWOOD IS HELPING TRAIN THE US MILITARY TO DEAL WITH TERRORISM

It is hard to keep a secret in Hollywood. There are too many journalists around. You could be forgiven for dismissing this idea given the amount of positive PR guff published from Tinsel Town, but in Hollywood most secrets are known to the press – even if they don't report them.

The reasons why only a small portion of what entertainment journalists know ever makes it to the printed page vary, but plenty of juicy stuff gets spiked. Sometimes a story doesn't make it because the journalist likes the person involved and is happy to keep the their abortion secret to protect them from the Pro-Life backlash. Sometimes journalists self-censor out of fear that they won't get any further information if they reveal which movie mogul cast the male star of the latest blockbuster in the bedroom.

Often a reporter has done a deal with an agent or a studio to bury one story about a high-profile star in exchange for all of the information needed for a career-ruining story about another less lucrative celebrity.

However, there is one secret in Hollywood that journalists have not been able to crack: just what help and advice did Hollywood film-makers give American intelligence specialists about terrorist attacks in October 2001 in the wake of 9/11.

While neither American intelligence nor the film-makers deny that the meetings took place, or that they may even be continuing, they refuse to discuss any details. All that is known is executives from various companies, *Die Hard* screenwriter Steven E De Souza, and Joseph Zito – director of *Missing in Action* – gave advice on handling attacks. If the scenario was reversed, it would be easy to understand film-makers asking the army about real world disasters, but the need for the army to consult Hollywood is puzzling.

The US Army also funds the Institute for Creative Technologies at the University of Southern California, but the ICT's creative director, James Korris, only confirms that the meetings between the film-makers and the military happened and not what specific recommendations had been made to the government.

SECRET ORDERS ON REPORTING CIVILIAN DEATHS IN THE AFGHANISTAN CONFLICT

The US military learnt some important lessons in Vietnam (though George W Bush seems to have forgotten the one about not being popular with the citizens of a country you're occupying against their wishes). One of the biggest is that in the mass media age, reports of innocent civilian casualties are unpopular with the folks back home.

Rather than changing the way they wage war, military commanders set about minimizing reports of military actions that have caused widespread civilian casualties. A number of techniques was developed, such as labelling civilian casualties "collateral damage" and embedding TV crews with military units to keep them under more control. In recent military campaigns, army press teams have been trained that reports of civilian deaths can be countered with lines such as: "They deliberately placed civilians at known military targets"; and "Collateral damage is inevitable in these situations."

When it came to the US war in Afghanistan reorters had a large degree of help in their work on minimizing the impact of civilian deaths from the US media. CNN ordered its reporters to: "Frame reports of civilian deaths with reminders that 'the Pentagon has repeatedly stressed that it is trying to minimize' such casualties, and to remind viewers that 'the Taliban regime continues to harbour terrorists who are connected to the September 11 attacks that claimed thousands of innocent lives in the US'."

"Fox News" anchor Brit Hume even said about reporting civilian casualties: "War is hell; people die. The fact that some people are dying, is that really big news?" Fox pundit Michael Barone also commented: "Civilian casualties are not news. The fact is that they accompany wars." All in all, an interesting take on Fox's slogan: "We report, you decide."

Many newspapers followed suit, with one paper reminding reporters: "DO NOT USE photos on Page 1 showing civilian casualties from the US war on Afghanistan. DO NOT USE wire stories that lead with civilian casualties from the US war on Afghanistan."

Truth is indeed the first casualty of war – just before the civilians.

below Not on the nightly news - US TV news reports were much less likely to show the innocent victims of the war in Afghanistan than their international rivals.

THE DAILY MAIL SUPPORTED THE NAZI REGIME

The *Daily Mail* is a British institution. Love or loathe its middle-brow approach and right-of-centre editorial stance, no one in the UK can deny its commercial success and the place it has in the lives of its millions of readers.

Current readers, who have grown accustomed to its attacks on ever-closer European integration and bitter tirades about the growth of French and German political strength within the European Union, may be surprised to know that the *Daily Mail* used to take a very different stance on Germanic power.

Up until 1939, the paper was a strong supporter of Hitler, the Nazi regime and the German desire to be the dominant voice in Europe. For many, this revelation is like learning that your great-grandfather, who is forever going on about how Britain is the best country in the world and that the Germans ought to remember who won two world wars and one World Cup, was actually a member of the SS.

Lord Rothermere, the *Mail*'s proprietor, was so keen to support Hitler and the Nazi regime that he hired a glamorous German spy to introduce him to leading Nazi figures. Rothermere paid Princess Stephanie Hohenlohe-Waldenburg-Schillingfurst to help strengthen his contacts with Hitler, Goering and Goebbels. Rothermere and the *Mail* campaigned for Germany's colonies seized under the Versailles Treaty to be returned, and they supported Neville Chamberlain's policy of appeasement. They were against Winston Churchill and anyone else who claimed Hitler did not want peace. Rothermere even wrote "Hurrah For The Blackshirts" in support of Oswald Mosley and his British Union of Fascists.

Previously secret MI5 files declassified at the National Archives also show that Rothermere wrote to Adolf Hitler, congratulating Germany on its annexation of Czechoslovakia and urging the Fuehrer to march into Romania.

It has been alleged that the *Daily Mail* has considered agreements with a leading rival not to run stories on its support for Hitler. It is not surprising they don't want their current readers to be reminded that one of its writers once commented: "The way stateless Jews from Germany are pouring in from every port of this country is becoming an outrage."

left The Daily Mail and its Nazi-sympathizing owner Lord Rothermere supported the disastrous policy of appeasing fascism in Europe undertaken by PM Chamberlain.

right US military power even extended to getting changes made in films such as Black Hawk Down.

THE HOLLYWOOD MOVIES THAT MADE CHANGES ASKED FOR BY THE US MILITARY

During the Second World War, Hollywood swung its full creative talent into acting as a propaganda machine for the US military, but by the time of the Vietnam war there was less of a gung-ho spirit in Tinsel Town.

Movies such as John Wayne's *The Green Berets*, an offensively overblown, pro-Vietnam film, were becoming rarer. Hollywood's overt support for the US military had ended. However, the covert promotion of the US military by the American film industry was just starting to get into swing.

Over the last 30 years, Hollywood's top film-makers have often changed plots, altered scripts and added scenes to their movies at the request of the Pentagon. In exchange they have been provided with access to military vehicles and property during filming. Most of the changes were designed to show the US military in a more heroic light.

Pentagon approval and help was sought for *Armageddon*, *Air Force One*, *Pearl Harbor* and *Top Gun*. The remake of *Day of the Jackal* only got assistance after the marines were given a better role. In *Black Hawk Down*, Ewan McGregor's character was renamed at the request of the army, since the real-life soldier he was based on is currently in prison for the rape of a child under 12.

One film that failed to secure Pentagon approval was *Independence Day*, despite extreme arse kissing by its writer and producer Dean Devlin, who told them: "If this doesn't make every boy in the country want to fly a fighter jet, I'll eat this script." Devlin also agreed to turn the Secretary of Defense character responsible for allowing military installations to be destroyed by the aliens into the White House Chief of Staff. The Department of Defense still refused to help, saying that: "The military appears inept. All advances in stopping aliens are the result of actions by civilians."

Even James Bond has become part of the Pentagon and Hollywood propaganda machine. In the original script of *GoldenEye* a US Navy admiral betrayed state secrets; in return for US army co-operation this was changed to a French admiral.

D NOTICES AND UK MEDIA CENSORSHIP

"ADVISORY, not for publication:
We have been asked by the secretary of the Defence, Press and Broadcasting Advisory Committee to publish the following:
FOR THE ATTENTION OF ALL EDITORS
FROM SECRETARY DEFENCE, PRESS &
BROADCASTING ADVISORY COMMITTEE
I understand that ..."

When a newspaper editor in Britain sees these words at the start of an email or fax, he or she will have just received a D Notice. The words following "I understand..." will give them details of a story that they should not publish.

The D Notice is usually the government's kiss of death to any news it does not want the public to know about. Although it lacks legal status, it takes a brave editor to ignore a D Notice and its "advice".

The first D Notice committee was set up during the First World War to ensure the press did not report anything that could damage the national interest. The "D" stood for defence and the notices were only advisory. The system continued after the war, becoming a way for the British government to exercise pressure on the press without having to prosecute them under the Official Secrets Act (a counter-productive action as it tends to generate additional attention).

The system was operated by the Admiralty and proved successful in encouraging widespread self-censorship by the British press of stories that the government considered sensitive and embarrassing as well as damaging to the defence of the country. In 1993, the old D Notice committee was renamed Defence, Press and Broadcasting Advisory Committee and for the first time included selected editors as well as Ministry of Defence and intelligence officials. It now issues DA Notices (Defence Advisory) but its meeting are held in secret and their decision-making process classified. The same cosy collusion by the press with the committee to keep the public in the dark remains in force.

Duncan Campbell, one of the world's leading investigative reporters and someone who has dared to ignore D Notices, has said he actually found them to be useful sources of leads for stories.

CRIME

7

"He who does not bellow out the truth when he knows the truth makes himself the accomplice of liars and forgers."
Charles Peguy

The police often ask the public to report liars and inform them of any secret illegal activity they have discovered, but in this section the position is reversed as the things they do their best to keep hidden are exposed to the public. From alliances with the Mafia and collusion with terrorists to efforts to suppress information on their flawed investigative procedures, there is a lot the bastions of justice do not want us to know about.

We expect criminals to be experts at keeping secrets and telling lies, but it seems that when it comes to crime they are rivalled by those entrusted with keeping law and order, those who have a lot to hide and are expert at generating falsehoods themselves.

Unless you are a career criminal or have been unjustly treated by those in the legal system, it is unlikely that you will share the above view of the police and judiciary. We are culturally conditioned to reject ideas such as the FBI and Scotland Yard regularly lying to us as crazy.

However, the more you uncover the truth about those responsible for delivering justice, the more it becomes clear that one of the biggest lies our society has bought into is the idea that those in the legal system would never deceive us because their only concern is protecting us from criminals. This widespread cultural myth has made it easy for corrupt elements to break the law and send many innocent people to jail.

JURIES HAVE THE RIGHT TO ACQUIT A DEFENDANT EVEN IF HE HAS BROKEN THE LAW

It has been called the most subversive secret of the judicial system and campaigners in American have been arrested for doing nothing more than telling people the information you are about to read. The truth is that many in the courts do not want the public to know that juries have a right to judge the law and can decide to acquit a defendant, even if the defendant has broken the law.

The knowledge that a jury can acquit even if all the evidence proves someone has broken a law – and can decide cases on grounds other than the facts involved – means they can effectively put a law itself on trial. The right to do this is known as jury nullification and it exists in both English and American law.

Members of the American Fully Informed Jury Association have been prosecuted for handing out literature containing quotes such as those of Lord Denham in the case of *O'Connell v. Rex* in which he said: "Every jury in the land is tampered with and falsely instructed by the judge when it is told that it must accept as law that which has been given to them, or that they can decide only the facts in the case." This directly contradicts the words used by almost every judge when instructing juries as to how to proceed with making a judgement on a case.

In 1969, the Fourth Circuit Court of the Appeal in the US judged: "If a jury feels a law unjust, we recognize the undisputed power of the jury to acquit, even if the verdict is contrary to the law given by the judge and contrary to the evidence."

Jury nullification has played a strong role in the history of the public refusing to accept unjust laws. It was used in the American Colonies to free people the British had brought to trial for speaking ill of the king. In recent years, some juries have exercised the right and refused to convict users of marijuana for medical purposes and anti-war protestors. No wonder some want the truth suppressed.

`below` They are the law and they might look intimidating in their wigs and gowns, but juries have the right to ignore a judge and put the law itself on trial.

DNA MATCHING EVIDENCE USED IN COURTS IS NOT ALWAYS RIGHT

It has become known as the "CSI effect" – after the TV crime drama "CSI: Crime Scene Investigation" – a belief by juries, judges, lawyers and detectives that DNA evidence is infallible and incontrovertible proof of guilt if produced by prosecutors in court.

Presented as the greatest revolution in forensic science since the introduction of fingerprints, DNA is seen by the public and the majority of forensic scientists as a magic bullet that is always capable of delivering an infallible verdict. It is meant to convict the guilty and free innocent victims of earlier miscarriages of justice. Experts have produced statistics that claim the chances of a DNA match occurring by chance are more than one in a billion. With those odds, no wonder it is a piece of evidence that is rarely challenged and a process that has inspired higher public confidence in the judicial process in rape and murder trials.

The truth is that public confidence in DNA evidence being an infallible indicator of guilt or innocence is highly misplaced. Independent tests into the forensic use of DNA showed that one in a hundred may give a false result, making the odds of a false DNA match considerably lower than the quoted one in a billion.

Researchers asked labs to match a series of DNA samples. They knew which ones were from the same person, but found that human error led to the wrong result in twelve in every 1,000 tests. In secret tests on 135 labs carried out by the College of American Pathologists they discovered that 14 of the labs completely botched the process.

In one year in just one US state (Seattle) 23 major crime investigations were shown to have been affected by misleading genetic evidence, including one where bungling scientists had accidentally contaminated the clothing of a 10-year-old rape victim with DNA from another case they were working on.

Despite such evidence, British government scientists say that errors are impossible and the UK's Forensic Science Service claims: "No mistakes are allowed to go to court."

HOW A KNOWN TERRORIST DISAPPEARED FROM A SWISS CELL WITHOUT ANY INVESTIGATION

When Osama Bin Laden is captured, the American authorities should hope it doesn't happen when he makes a trip to Switzerland to withdraw some funds from the bank accounts he has in Geneva. The last time Swiss authorities captured a known terrorist making a withdrawal, they allowed him to disappear from the cell he was being held in within 72 hours.

The disappearing prisoner was Licio Gelli, wanted by Italian authorities for his involvement in two of the major scandals that rocked Italy in the early 1980s. He was directly linked to the collapse of the Vatican Bank subsidiary Banco Ambrosiano and was the key player behind the P2 Masonic lodge's involvement in sponsoring terrorism. In particular, he was being sought for funding the bombing of Bologna Central Railway Station in 1980 that killed 80 people and left 200 maimed.

The bombing was initially blamed on Red Brigades but it soon emerged that far-right terrorists were really responsible. The bombers were part of the Gladio network set up by the CIA after the Second World War to ensure that Italy never fell under communist rule. Former SS *Oberleutnant* Gelli had been the man recruited to run Gladio. He also set up the P2 lodge.

Gelli, who had been on the run since 1981, was caught trying to withdraw $60 million from his Swiss numbered accounts. He had entered the country on an Argentine passport under the name Bruno Rizzi but was nabbed at the Geneva branch of the prestigious Bank of Switzerland. Taken into custody, Gelli was held for extradition to Italy on terrorism, conspiracy and fraud charges in the Champ-Dollon Prison. Within 72 hours he had disappeared from his cell and fled back to Argentina.

Despite the natural anger of the Italian government, Swiss authorities refused any inquiry into the matter except the local police investigation, which found no evidence that Gelli had been helped to escape. All documents relating to the escape remain classified. The Swiss authorities refuse any comment except that Swiss police are the most incorruptible in the world.

THE MAFIA HAVE BEEN WORKING WITH US INTELLIGENCE AGENCIES SINCE THE SECOND WORLD WAR

Intelligence agents are taught to develop relationships with those who will be useful sources of information. They are also taught that when doing this, they will often have to set aside their own moral concerns because the only criterion that counts is the asset's usefulness to the furtherance of the agent's mission. This viewpoint can be summed up as "the enemy of my enemy is my friend".

A perfect example of this philosophy in action is the liaison between the US secret services and the Mafia that began during the Second World War. The first recorded contact was in 1942 when the Office of Naval Intelligence (ONI) approached Meyer Lansky to ask his boss "Lucky" Luciano – imprisoned at that time for pimping – for assistance in getting the Mafia-controlled waterfront workers to watch out for enemy agent activity. It was the start of a beautiful relationship.

In January 1943, both the ONI and the Office of Strategic Services (OSS) – the forerunner of the CIA – approached Lansky again. This time they wanted a big favour: Mafia collaboration with the Allied invasion of Sicily. They were prepared to cut a deal. If the Mafia helped out, Lucky would be released from jail. The Mafia agreed and their intelligence, sabotage and other forms of assistance proved invaluable. However, Lansky used this new link not only to secure the release of his boss but also to get the case against prominent New York Mafioso Carmine Galante – caught red-handed while murdering an Italian newspaper editor – quietly dropped.

After the war, the relationship continued to flourish with the CIA's James Jesus Angleton using the Mafia in Italy as part of the anti-communist Gladio network he set up with former Gestapo agent Licio Gelli. In return, more gangsters were released in the US. The links between the CIA and the Mafia continued throughout the Cold War but details of arrangements remain classified. It is known, however, that in the early 1960s, the CIA found willing partners for several assassination attempts on Fidel Castro with those mobsters who had lost millions when Castro had thrown them out of Cuba.

left Mobster Lucky Luciano arrives at the Supreme Court flanked by detectives. He would later be freed in a secret deal between the Mafia and US intelligence services.

THE FBI'S COINTELPRO AND THE *BLACK PANTHER COLOURING BOOK*

The Federal Bureau of Investigation are meant to be the good guys. America's national police force, they exist to fight organized crime and terrorism and hunt America's "most wanted". If you check out their website you'll also discover one of their top priorities is "protecting civil rights".

Forgive me if I laugh in a hollow manner for a moment. It is hard to take this claim seriously if you have any knowledge of the secret history of the FBI and the activities of its ruthless COINTELPRO campaign against the Black Panther Party (BPP).

Starting out as a small, militant movement against police brutality on the streets of Oakland in California, the BPP quickly went from being six law students to having 40 chapters nationwide dedicated to resisting racism, bringing food, clothing, shelter and left-wing education to African-Americans. They wore black, had a neat line in moody sunglasses and leather jackets and carried guns. They also scared the hell out of white America.

FBI Director J Edgar Hoover described the Panthers as "The greatest threat to the internal security of the country,"
and dedicated the FBI to bringing the BPP down. The FBI had established COINTELPRO (standing for "counterintelligence programs") to "disrupt and neutralize any organization of a Black Nationalist Hate Group nature." It was a secret campaign to eliminate legitimate dissent.

When the BPP set up a free breakfast programme, the FBI mailed a *Black Panther Colouring Book* it had created to businesses such as Safeway who were donating food to the free breakfast programme. The book was full of offensive illustrations of BPP members killing policemen, who were depicted as pigs. The FBI also anonymously mailed it to thousands of homes across America to increase public resentment of the BPP. It worked.

Not content to leave it at that, the FBI then sent thousands of fake BPP Christmas cards to its agents. The images on the cards showed Black Panthers shooting and bombing white people who were celebrating the festive season. Agents were to follow instructions and "Anonymously mail these cards to all newspaper editors, public officials, responsible businessmen, and clergy in your territory."

below The Black Panthers were the coolest looking revolutionaries in 1960s America and the ones most feared by J. Edgar Hoover and the FBI.

LIE DETECTORS ARE NOT THOUGHT EFFECTIVE BY MANY INVESTIGATING AUTHORITIES

For most of us, when we lie our bodies give us away. Our heart rate, breathing and the electrical conductivity of our skin all increase (just as they do in a more pronounced way when we are sexually aroused).

The changes are minute and usually invisible to the person we are lying to, so there is practically no chance of being caught out this way. We can relax, the boss won't know about our trips to the stationery cupboard. However, the theory is that if we were hooked up to a polygraph machine and asked about taking stationery for personal use, those same signs would reveal us for what we really are, downright petty pilferers of the company's paperclips and pens.

In the US legal system, where polygraph tests are admissible in court, they call taking a lie detector test "going on the box". Many state prosecutors insist on tests being taken to prove innocence before they will drop charges, while an ever-growing number of employers use them to screen employees. Their use has expanded into domestic areas of life, with spouses using them to check their partner's loyalty.

With this level of judicial and public acceptance, it is surprising to learn that most scientists regard lie detection as "pure junk science". US military courts refuse to admit polygraph evidence, a position the Supreme Court backed them on, stating: "There is too much controversy about the reliability of lie detector test results and polygraph tests might undercut the role of the jury in assessing witness credibility."

In 2001, scientists at America's Department of Energy and national defence laboratories, including those at Los Alamos, refused screening tests on the basis that they were scientifically invalid and too unreliable. A Senate investigation backed their position. On top of all of this, FBI polygraph expert, Dr Drew Richardson, gave evidence to the Senate Judiciary committee on polygraphs claiming: "There is almost universal agreement that polygraph screening is completely invalid and should be stopped. The diagnostic value of this type of testing has no more value than that of astrology or tea-leaf reading."

HOW THE VATICAN BANK HELPED ORGANIZED CRIME GANGS TO LAUNDER VAST SUMS OF MONEY

If you cannot trust the Pope, whom can you trust? With its record of links to organized crime and proven role in laundering vast sums of money, you certainly can't trust the Vatican bank.

As the Vatican City is an independent state, it is only natural that it would have its own national bank – the Insituto per le Opere di Religione – the Institute of Religious Works (IOR.) Although it runs the ATM machines in the Vatican and maintains accounts for clerics and religious organizations, another part of the work of the IOR is that of being the Pope's personal bank.

Created in 1941, the IOR is a "for profit" organization that is charged with looking after the money of the Holy See money and generating additional revenue for the papacy. Even ignoring the incongruous notion of the Pope as Christ's representative on earth being the nominal owner of a bank and Jesus throwing the moneylenders out of the temple, the IOR has been at the centre of scandal from its earliest days.

In 1973 the Vatican bank was used by an American Bishop called Paul "the Gorilla" Marcinkus in an attempt to pass off counterfeit US banks with the face value of £14.5 million that had been obtained from the Italian mafia. Throughout the 1970s Marcinkus set up a network of "ghost banks" and front companies. FBI and Italian investigations proved these companies were being used to launder mafia drug money. Italian authorities asked the Vatican to surrender Marcinkus for trial. As a sovereign state, it refused. He was removed from the IOR and made President of Vatican City instead.

As an author of a specialist book on money laundering I have been personally surprised by how many high ranking FBI, Italian and Interpol investigators I have interviewed still expressed concern that the Vatican had not done more to prevent the IOR ever being used to launder money again. Of course, money laundering is not the official policy of the Vatican Bank. It is without doubt that Marcinkus was speaking in a purely personal role when he told *The Observer* newspaper in 1986: "You can't run the Church on Hail Marys".

THE MONSTER OF FLORENCE: SERIAL KILLER – AN INSPIRATION FOR HANNIBAL LECTER – MURDERED HIS VICTIMS ON BEHALF OF A SATANIC GROUP

Between 1968 and 1985, 16 people were murdered in Florence and the surrounding hills of Tuscany. They were all couples, executed with a .22 Beretta before the women involved were then mutilated with a surgical scalpel.

After the 17 years of terror, the killings stopped. In 1994, a semi-literate peasant, Pietro Pacciani, was tried for the killings. One of the spectators at the trial was the novelist Thomas Harris, who was so intrigued by some of the case that he set his third Hannibal Lecter novel in Florence and refers in the book to "Il Monstro" – the Monster – the name that Tuscans and Florentines gave to Pacciani.

When Pacciani was found guilty and sentenced it became a closed case for the Italian police. However, other investigators had huge doubts that the truth had been revealed in court. There was the unexplained matter of how a poor peasant had more than £50,000 in his bank account. No real investigation of Pacciani's claims that a mysterious Doctor Lotti had ordered the murders or that occult aspects had been involved. It appeared secrets were being kept and no one was prepared to ask any questions about them.

When Michele Giuttari became head of Florence's detectives in 2001 he discovered that the Sisde – the Italian secret service – had run their own investigation into the murders, paid for out of a secret "black fund". He raided the homes of the Aurelio Mattei, a secret service psychologist who had been part of the investigation, and of Francesco Bruno, Italy's top criminal psychologist who had been a consultant on the case.

Following revelations about the secret investigation, four wealthy and powerful individuals, including a top lawyer and a university professor, have already been charged with being part of a conspiracy to cause the murders. Police now publicly believe that they and other wealthy Tuscans were part of a satanic group which paid Pacciani and his accomplices to murder the couples so that their bodies could be used in their rituals. They also believe that Sisde is still keeping secrets regarding "Il Monstro".

FINGERPRINT EVIDENCE USED IN COURT IS OFTEN HIGHLY FLAWED

Before TV shows "CSI" and "Silent Witness" hit our screens, the humble fingerprint was the staple of every crime novel and TV cop drama. Ever since Scotland Yard obtained the conviction of Henry Jackson for burglary in 1902, fingerprinting has gone from strength to strength as an accepted detection technique. Open any textbook on the subject and you will always find one word: "infallible".

Fingerprint identification is a trump card for prosecutors. Juries tend to accept it as conclusive proof and it is rarely challenged. Lawyers often advise their clients to plead guilty to crimes they did not commit if they can't provide a solid explanation for the finding of their fingerprints at a crime scene.

Growing doubts about the reliability of fingerprint evidence used to obtain convictions have begun to surface in recent years due to the fact that identification is a subjective process. Law enforcement agencies including the FBI have attempted to scrap scientific reports into the reliability of fingerprint evidence.

A FBI case in which fingerprinting was exposed as flawed was that of Brandon Mayfield, a US citizen who was held for two weeks on suspicion of being involved in the al-Qaeda Madrid train bombings. Fingerprints from Spanish police were sent across the world. When entered into the FBI's fingerprint computer database they produced a match with Mayfield. Despite Spanish analysts rejecting the fingerprint match, the FBI believed their computer and human experts were right and detained Mayfield until it became clear that he had no connection at all to the Madrid atrocities. If the FBI cannot get it right, what chance do under-funded local police forces have?

Even police officers have been falsely charged on the evidence of flawed fingerprint comparison, including Scottish policewoman Shirley McKie, who was accused of perjury on the basis of a single fingerprint found at a murder scene. Four British experts positively matched her prints with one found at the scene and she was only spared prison by the intervention of an American expert witness, who demonstrated the flaws in their identification.

SCOTLAND YARD'S OWN CHIEF CLAIMED HIS POLICE FORCE CONTAINED 250 CORRUPT OFFICERS

Britain has a long tradition of crooked detectives and police officers. Most notable were some of the detectives from the now disbanded West Midlands Serious Crime Squad, which framed criminals and wasn't above suffocating suspects to gain confessions to crimes they did not commit. Another infamous example was exposed by the Operation Countryman investigation into Scotland Yard's Flying Squad in the 1970s that discovered a tangled knot of corruption between some of its officers and Soho pornographers.

Given this, no one suspected to bat an eye when Scotland Yard discussed in Parliament in 1994 the number of officers in its employ which it suspected of being corrupt. However, when the head of Scotland Yard, the Metropolitan police commissioner, Sir Paul Condon, told a House of Commons select committee they had uncovered "250 bent officers", and many were due for prosecution, many MPs and experts were shocked.

The announcement was a bombshell. No one had guessed that such a high number of officers could have potentially faced charges at the same time. Even the most cynical commentators who expected the Metropolitan Police force would try to suggest they had fewer corrupt officers than they really had saluted the breathtaking honesty.

Scotland Yard went on to officially praise its elite squad of detectives called the "Untouchables" (with an intelligence section known as the Ghost Squad) working for the Complaints Investigation Branch (CIB) to investigate police corruption. Officially the Untouchables were hailed as a huge success.

However, in 2000, Michael Gillard and Laurie Flynn, two investigative reporters from *The Guardian* managed to reveal a very different picture. After more than seven years of investigation costing several million pounds, the Untouchables had only managed to successfully prosecute nine low ranking officers.

Whilst there was no suggestion of any corruption or incompetence within the CIB or within anyone else prosecuting the matter, even Commander Andy Hayman, director of the CIB had to admit that after seven years and huge expense it was reassessing its methods in uncovering potentially corrupt officers.

Amongst the methods employed by the Untouchables and the Ghost Squad was planting the use of £500,000 of cannabis in a flat to lure officers into stealing it. An officer caught stealing was turned into a supergrass. Scotland Yard received criticism from leading politicians such as Lady Emily Blatch for its methods, secret deals it did with supergrasses and the results obtained in tackling the now legendary 250 bent coppers.

right Watching the detectives - Sir Paul Condon. The Untouchables failed to prosecute all of the 250 bent officers Condon claimed were under investigation.

OFFICIAL VERSION

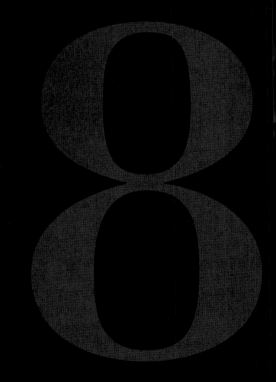

The basic truth that those in control often do not want you to know all of the facts has not changed throughout history. Governments of all types have a tendency not to play fair when it comes to manipulating the information that they are happy for you to have at your disposal.

Even before we entered the age of modern spin-doctors and media manipulation techniques with snazzy names such as "re-labelling", governments already had long established the technique of creating official versions of things they would rather the public did not know about.

Today we have digital retouching of photos, but airbrushing people from reality for propaganda purposes was a technique favoured from the first days of Stalin's rule of the Soviet Union. Tools of truth repression such as classifying information as sensitive to a nation's security or making official denials accompanied by censoring anyone who questions your version are even older and date back as far as the Roman Empire.

Many lies are repeated endlessly because nobody dares challenge the massive assumptions behind them. Some of the lies underpinning the official versions we are given are so stunningly big that it seems insane to doubt we are being told anything but the truth – surely no one in power tells such a blatant lie? However, the assumption that no one would dare tell such a whopper lies behind the powerful and basic technique of the "big lie" that many deceitful official versions, which are exposed in this section, are based on.

CLAIMS BY THE US MILITARY THAT PEOPLE DID NOT DIE FROM RADIATION AFTER THE ATOMIC BOMBING OF HIROSHIMA AND NAGASAKI

Today, the idea that atomic bombs do not produce radiation seems insane. When you discover that the people who actually dropped the first atomic weapons were behind claims that there was no radiation sickness, it's hard to know whether to laugh at their stupidity or be furious over their belief that they could get away with such a ridiculous lie as their official position.

In the wake of the bombings the US Army categorically denied reports of deaths caused after the bomb had been dropped and publicly ridiculed anyone who mentioned the possibility of "atomic sickness".

Ignoring the ban General Douglas MacArthur had declared on journalists entering Hiroshima, Australian reporter Wilfred Burchett went to the city to see for himself the aftermath. He wrote a harrowing account of the destruction he saw – tens of thousands dead, people reduced to shadows burnt on to walls, victims with the skin half-melted from their bodies, everything reduced to ash and rubble. He also wrote about survivors who were suffering fevers, hair loss and uncontrollable bleeding in the mouth and under the skin. The

Daily Express printed his story with the headline: "THE ATOMIC PLAGUE."

The article caused a worldwide sensation. To counter it, Major General Leslie Groves, director of the US atomic bomb project, invited journalists to New Mexico for a tour of the first atomic bomb test site. The reporters included William L Laurence of *The New York Times* who wrote a front-page story with the headline: "US ATOM BOMB SITE BELIES TOKYO TALES: TESTS ON NEW MEXICO RANGE CONFIRM THAT BLAST, AND NOT RADIATION, TOOK TOLL." (The *Daily Express* headline was much more eye-catching as well as accurate.)

Laurence received a salary from both *The New York Times* and the War Department – Major General Leslie Groves employed him to write press releases for the Manhattan Project. For his report on the tour of the site, Laurence won a Pulitzer Prize, while Wilfred Burchett was expelled from Japan as soon as he was well enough to travel after being hospitalized with a mild dose of the officially non-existent radiation sickness.

`below` Ashes to ashes, dust to dust – Hiroshima was reduced to a city of radioactive rubble marked by the scorched shadows of the dead by the US atomic bombing.

right Hot air - the US army lied when they claimed Roswell debris was a weather balloon.

THE UNITED STATES AIR FORCE'S VERSION OF THE ROSWELL CRASH

There has never been a better example of the lies behind an official version of events causing so much trouble for those behind the authorized account than that of the Roswell crash. By being secretive, putting out a series of conflicting explanations and then being exposed as liars, the United States military has turned an obscure small New Mexico town into a word synonymous with aliens and conspiracy theories across the globe.

The problems for the army began in 1947 when the headline "Army Captures Flying Saucer on Ranch in Roswell" appeared in a local paper. The story had been written from information given to journalists by Lieutenant Walter Haut, the press officer at the Roswell Army Air Field. Several major papers also picked up the information released by Haut. The next day, the most sensational press release of all time was replaced by a new official and much less exciting account of what the army had found at Roswell. A crashed saucer became the wreckage of a weather balloon.

Usually an official denial is the end of the matter, but UFO researchers are a strange group. Their mix of obsession, paranoia and willingness to believe in the impossible means they rarely give up if they think something is being covered up. Not willing to accept that senior army personnel would mistake a balloon for a spaceship they badgered politicians until "in 1994". New Mexico congressman Steven Schiff asked the US General Accounting Office to investigate any documents relating to the incident. Hearing about this new inquiry the army released a new official version in a 25-page report claiming that the weather balloon was now in fact a top-secret Mogul balloon and they had originally lied to hide this knowledge.

When this was challenged as not fitting the facts, the army released another report entitled "The Roswell Report: Truth Versus Fiction". This time the official version was that any bodies observed were the result of dummies being dropped from a high altitude balloon. With the army changing its version of events every few years, it's not surprising so many people believe the wilder Roswell stories.

THE MISSING COSMONAUTS OF THE SOVIET SPACE PROGRAMME

According to the official accounts, the Soviet space programme was a glorious triumph of superior technology. They placed the first artificial satellite in orbit with the launch of Sputnik 1 in 1957 and on April 12, 1961, Yuri Gagarin became the first human to travel into space.

All rumours of accidents, dead or missing cosmonauts and failings in the USSR's exploration of space were dismissed as, "Inventions of a few organs of the bourgeois press. No one can doubt the safety of our space vehicles except those who purposefully spread cosmic lies."

The Soviet claims were right about one thing: many of the accounts circulating in the western press detailing a "road of Soviet slaughter to the stars" were based on false names and information generated by the CIA. During the lifetime of the Soviet Union, details of its space programme were kept secret with the identities of their pioneering scientists never revealed and even the massive operation of its failed attempt to put a Russian on the moon completely hidden. This allowed rumours to flourish, but in the era of Glasnost, space historian James Oberg established most of these to be false.

However, the Stalinist practice of erasing people out of group photographs had been used extensively when it came to cosmonauts. The majority of these "phantom cosmonauts" could be explained, but not all. Some cosmonauts said to have been dropped from the programme for health reasons and returned to the air force appear to have disappeared completely – whether as victims of covered-up failures in the space programme or as prisoners in gulags it is impossible to tell. The fact that all of the early space successes of the Soviets were down to forced scientific labour camps remains the most ghastly secret of the era.

Even today the full history of Soviet space exploration is difficult to obtain but it certainly featured more deaths, crashes and setbacks than were every officially admitted at the time, although not as many as the "bourgeois press" believed.

THE DEATHS OF THE BAADER-MEINHOF GANG

With Andreas Baader and close colleagues Gudrun Ensslin and Jan-Carl Raspe in a high security block specially constructed to hold them at Stammheim prison, the West German authorities claimed an end to the Red Army Faction (or as they press called them, the Baader-Meinhof gang).

They were wrong. Inspired by the activities of the Baader-Meinhof gang and the deaths of imprisoned members on hunger strike, a second-generation sprang up with the aim of freeing the captured Red Army Faction. With their already existing links to Palestinian terrorists, the campaign to free them also took on an international dimension.

On September 6, 1977, former Nazi and now powerful German businessman Hanns-Martin Schleyer was kidnapped with a threat that if the government did not release the Stammheim prisoners he would be killed. The crisis was supervised by a secret government team headed up by Chancellor Helmut Schmidt. It dragged on into October when Lufthansa flight LH 181 was hijacked by Arab terrorists who included the release of Baader's group among their demands. On the night that GSG-9 officers – an elite German police unit – stormed the plane, Baader, Ensslin and Raspe are claimed to have committed suicide.

The official version is that Baader had somehow managed to smuggle a revolver into one of the most secure prisons in the world and shot himself after having made it look like there had been a struggle; that Raspe had managed to obtain a 9 mm Heckler Koch pistol and shot himself in the head; and that Ensslin had hung herself.

No explanation was offered as to why the electronic bugs in every cell were switched off that night, or how forensic evidence was destroyed, why papers in Ensslin's cell, meant to be given to a priest in case "anything happens to me", went missing and why no fingerprints were found on the guns used. Nor was any explanation offered as to why they had levels of sedatives in their bodies which would have rendered them insensible or how Baader shot himself from behind. Officially, none of these things are "significant of investigation or in any way odd".

above Back on the farm – even with key members such as Andreas Baader behind bars, the rest of the Baader-Meinhof gang remained a deadly threat.

BRITISH SUPPRESSION OF THE MAU MAU IN KENYA THAT INCLUDED THE USE OF TORTURE, NAPALM AND CONCENTRATION-STYLE CAMPS

In the murky history of Britain since 1945, almost no period stands out as more secretive and shameful than the eight-year-long Kenya Emergency and the bloody suppression of the Mau Mau insurrection.

The Kenya Emergency was first declared in 1952. It was a full-scale rebellion against British rule by 1.5 million Kikuyu – the country's majority ethnic group – resulting from seven years of growing anger at British refusal to allow native Kenyans the right to elect representatives to the council that governed the colony's affairs.

Officially, it was an "Emergency" rather than a war and according to government ministers such as Harold Macmillan no pattern of abuse or breach of British or international law was occurring. Facing a network of secret gangs, the British responded with a brutal crackdown against the whole of the Kikuyu people.

During the eight years of the "Emergency" more than 55,000 troops were deployed. Despite officially being a civil insurrection, the British resorted to using napalm and a range of worrying counter-insurgency tactics were used.

Brigadier Frank Kitson developed a policy of creating bands of renegade Mau Mau, led by heavily disguised white officers, that would pretend to be rebels and lure genuine rebels into ambushes. The British Army and colonial police summarily hanged more than a thousand Kikuyu. The use of torture in questioning was widespread.

Some 77,000 people were interned without trial, with many being forced to work as slave labour on the construction of the new Kenyan airport. Declassified files show that the then colonial secretary, Alan Lennox Boyd, sanctioned a policy of violence toward the interned. A report headed "Use of Force in Enforcing Discipline" said: "They are of the type that only understands and reacts to violence."

More than a million people were forcibly resettled into heavily policed new villages during which up to 50,00 people – mainly women and children – died from starvation and disease in what the British termed "holding camps". Official figures of Mau Mau deaths are 11,503. Research has shown that the real figure is above 30,000.

`below` Great British mistake - the brutal regimes at some containment camps in Kenya cost thousands of Kikuyu lives.

THE ISRAELIS' "ACCIDENTAL" ATTACK ON THE AMERICAN WARSHIP USS LIBERTY

above
The USS Liberty – does it look like an Egyptian horse carrier to you?

On June 8, 1967, the American intelligence-gathering vessel the *USS Liberty* was anchored 14 miles off the Sinai Peninsula in international waters. The sea was calm and there was just enough breeze to stir the Star and Stripes the ship was flying. Were it not for the on-going Six Day War, the progress of which the *USS Liberty* was monitoring, the day could have been described as perfect.

Then at just after 2 p.m. in the afternoon, unmarked Israeli aircraft began attacking the ship. For the next 75 minutes fighter aircraft and Israeli motorized torpedo boats attacked the *USS Liberty*. Five torpedoes were fired with one hitting the *Liberty* amidships, instantly killing 25 sailors. A total of 34 died in the attack and 172 were wounded.

The official Israeli account claimed: "Our air force attacked a vessel and half an hour later torpedo boats of the Israel Navy attacked the same vessel. During the attack by the torpedo boats, it became clear that the vessel, thought to be an enemy ship, was a vessel of the United States Navy. The

attack was immediately broken-off." Israel retains the official position that the *Liberty* was mistaken for an Egyptian horse carrier, that the attack was partially the fault of the US for operating in a war zone and that the *Liberty* did not fly a flag.

The *USS Liberty* displayed two flags – the bullet-ridden remains of both can been seen in US museums – and made repeated attempts to communicate with its attackers, the tape recordings of which make for harrowing listening. In recent years at least one of the Israeli pilots has admitted they knew it was a US ship but were still ordered to attack. Even given this, the official Israeli version has not wavered.

Dean Rusk, US Secretary of State at the time, subsequently said: "I was never satisfied with the Israeli explanation. I didn't believe them then, and I don't believe them to this day. The attack was outrageous."

THE NSA'S INVOLVEMENT WITH UFOS

"Regarding your enquiry about UFOs, be advised that the National Security Agency does not have any interest in UFOs in any manner."

As official denials go, the standard NSA line on UFOs is as unequivocal as you could ever expect from an arm of the intelligence services. It was a denial that the NSA had stuck to ever since members of the UFO research community threw the question at them. Even in the face of such a categorical statement, many refused to believe it. Investigators reasoned that as the largest of the intelligence agencies handling all global and domestic communication and electronic intelligence there must something. They asked again, the denial remained.

It was Peter Gersten, an attorney with an interest in UFOs, who revealed that the NSA's official account was a falsehood. Obtaining CIA files on UFOs under the 1974 Freedom of Information Act (FOIA) passed in the wake of Watergate, he found the CIA material referred to material held by the NSA.

Caught in an outright lie that it could no longer sustain (what would an organization with no interest in UFOs be doing keeping files on them?), the NSA then refused Gersten's request under the FOIA to release its UFO-related material. Doing an about turn from having no interest to having a national security interest that prevented them from releasing them, Gersten started to progress his request through the courts.

When the case reached the Supreme Court, the judges announced their decision not to hear the case on the basis of information given to them in an affidavit from the NSA Director of Policy, Eugene Yeates. Gersten was able to obtain a heavily censored version of the document – 412 out of 582 were blacked out – which revealed that the NSA had admitted to the judges it had 156 classified UFO files. However, when another researcher asked the NSA about these files, the information officer's response was: "The NSA do not have any interest in UFOs in any manner." Proving, if nothing else, that when the NSA lie, they at least do it consistently.

PEARL HARBOR AND HOW TOP HISTORIANS WERE REMOVED FROM SCHOOL TEXTBOOKS BECAUSE OF THEIR VIEWS ON IT

Just before dawn on Sunday, December 7, 1941, a massive sneak attack by Japanese forces was launched on US forces in Hawaii, sinking 18 ships, destroying 188 aeroplanes and killing 2,403 Americans. The following day, President Franklin D Roosevelt addressed a joint session of Congress and delivered his famous "a date which will live in infamy" speech.

The official version of Pearl Harbor is well known and taught to schoolchildren across America. It is the one that never deviates from the basis that the attack came as total a surprise. This is despite the fact that every piece of evidence that has emerged since December 1941 suggests that, as an army board of 1944 reported, "Everything that the Japanese were planning to do was known by the United States."

Despite the overwhelming proof that the existing account is wrong it is rarely challenged and certainly not in school textbooks. Prior to the war, Professor Charles Beard was one of America's most respected historians. He and his wife wrote the acclaimed two-volume *The Rise of American Civilization*, a work later historians claim "did more than any other book to define American history for the reading public". It was also required reading in schools and colleges until Charles Beard published work attacking the official version of Pearl Harbor. After that, textbooks containing his quotes were removed from approved lists and his books were removed from the academic curricula.

This set a pattern that continues right through to today. Another example is that of famed historian, Harry Elmer Barnes. A prolific writer of textbooks on world civilization and sociology, he also authored seminal works aimed at an audience of scholars. When he published a history book that pulled apart the existing myth, his books were removed from schools and taken off of college reading lists – even those that had nothing to do with history. It seems that the need to ensure that a new generation grows up learning what officially happened is so strong that even an historian can find himself or herself written out of history.

CLAIMS THAT THE US DOES NOT BREACH INTERNATIONAL LAW WITH ITS 127 CHEMICAL AND BIOLOGICAL WARFARE RESEARCH PROGRAMMES

Hans Blix and his team of UN weapon inspectors hunting for chemical and biological weapons of mass destruction in Iraq made a critical error: they went to Iraq. Blix's team should have gone to a country where they would have been guaranteed to find not only massive stocks of chemical and biological weapons, but would have also been able to find on-going illegal research programmes. They should have gone to the USA, as it has the largest stock of biological and chemical weapons in the world. It also runs 127 chemical and biological warfare programmes.

Since 1969, the United States has claimed to renounce all methods of biological warfare, promising it would eliminate its arsenal and support an international ban on the development and possession of biological and chemical weapons. Its official position is that such weapons pose a significant risk to unprotected civilian populations and are not useful on the battlefield. In 1972, the USA signed a new Biological Weapons Convention. The treaty forbids any development, retention or transference of these weapons.

As a result of a lawsuit, the Department of Defense was forced to divulge that it operates 127 chemical and biological warfare research sites in America. Officially these are all bio-defence programmes. However, a leaked memo from 1994 detailed a range of biological weapons being researched including what it labelled a "gay bomb" that would make enemy soldiers "sexually irresistible to each other" alongside projects such as a weapon to make skin burn when exposed to sunlight.

In 2002, anti-biological weapons campaigners unearthed patent 6,523,478 held by the US Army. It was for a hand grenade to deliver biological weapons. The development of biological weapons delivery devices is prohibited "in any circumstance" by Article I of the 1972 Biological and Toxin Weapons Convention, to which the US is a party. There is no exemption from this. Equally serious, in the wake of 9/11, when anthrax was being posted throughout the US, it emerged that both the US Army and CIA had secret anthrax programmes considered illegal under the Convention.

THE REPUBLIC OF IRELAND BEING NEUTRAL DESPITE ALLOWING THE US MILITARY TO USE SHANNON AIRPORT

The Irish have a tradition of neutrality dating back to the eighteenth century when the United Irishmen urged that Ireland remain out of a potential war between Britain and Spain. With the establishment of the Republic of Ireland, the belief in remaining neutral has become such an established part of political life that many of its citizens actually believe it is part of their constitution.

During the Second World War, more than 70,000 of its citizens volunteered to join up with the British forces, while at the same time many Irish Republicans were actively collaborating with the Nazis. Neutrality has delivered benefits over the years ranging from the safety of its citizens from foreign terrorists to Irish delegates regularly receiving the most votes from other countries to be elected to senior UN positions. No wonder then that the official position is that Ireland remains neutral.

In 2003, Irish troops had to be deployed to guard the buildings, runways and seven miles of perimeter fencing of Shannon Airport in County Clare, Ireland, from more than 2,000 protestors who objected to it being used as a part of the US Army's troop and arms supply route for the invasion and occupation of Iraq. Up to 150,000 US troops passed through Shannon in both military and civilian planes while US Hercules C 130 warplanes, carrying equipment and ammunition (including armour piercing depleted uranium ammunition) also used it as a refuelling base. US tankers also travelled up the Shannon estuary to deliver aviation fuel for the flights.

It is a good job for Ireland that Saddam Hussein did not have any weapons of mass destruction. Under International Law it would no longer be classed as neutral and he would have been within his rights to attack the Republic for what would be classed as military support, which it was giving – and continues to give – to the USA.

Even given this, the official position of the Irish Prime Minister Bertie Ahern is that Ireland remains neutral and withdrawing the facilities for the US military at Shannon Airport would be "seen as a hostile act".

above Irish police hold back protestors outraged that the long cherished ideal of Irish neutrality has been wiped out by the US military use of Shannon airport

MISSING EVIDENCE

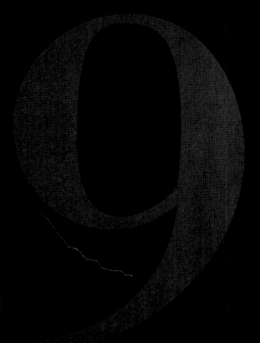

*"No one ever confides a secret to one person only.
No one destroys all copies of a document."*
Renata Adler

The weapons for keeping things secret are many. One of the best tricks in the secret keeper's toolbox – even more effective than the lies of an official denial or classifying something "Top Secret" for 30, 50 or even 100 years – is the technique of destroying the incriminating evidence.

Shredded documents are much harder to leak. Permanently deleted emails cannot be forwarded to journalists or be printed off and submitted in a court case. A convenient fire that destroys all records is often a politician's best friend. The best way to guarantee that there is no smoking gun for anyone to find is to ensure the weapon is sitting at the bottom of a deep river.

It does not take an overly paranoid state of mind for a professional journalist or other researcher to become worried about just how often critical government documents appear to have been accidentally lost when you make a request under the Freedom of Information Act, or to wonder at just how many fires and floods there have been at national record centres.

You can make a pretty good guess that you have been lied to and that secrets are being kept when crucial, incriminating evidence goes missing. However, without the hard proof it is usually impossible to take investigations further and expose someone's lies or an insidious conspiracy. All you are left with is the mysterious coincidence that bits of the picture which would have landed someone in jail and resolved all the unanswered questions are nowhere to be found.

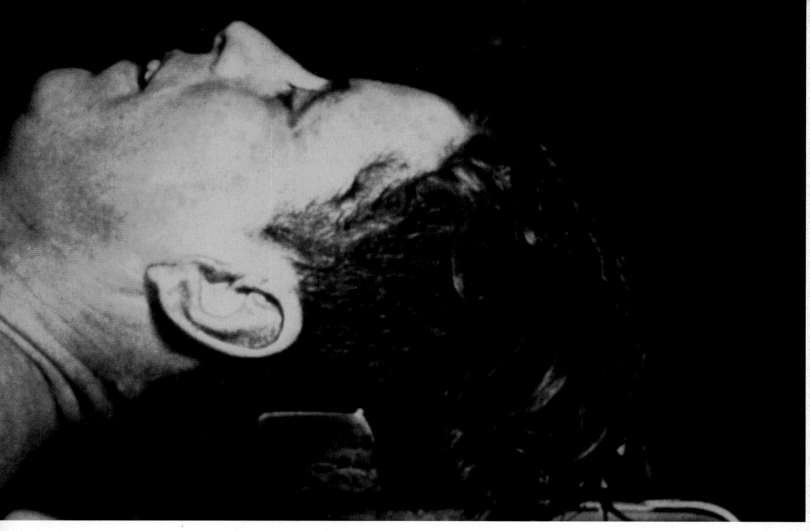

THE PRESIDENT'S BRAIN IS MISSING

Bill Hicks was not the type of comedian to have catchphrases. The closest he came to one was: "Back and to the left. Back and to the left." It was a reference to one of the key controversies surrounding the assassination of President John F Kennedy. As Bill Hicks put it: "How come if he was shot from behind, the laws of physics get suspended and you can see his head slam back and to the left in the Zapruder film?"

The official version answered Hicks' question by suggesting it was a neurological spasm that made Kennedy's head move backward and give the appearance he had not been shot from the direction of the Texas Schoolbook Depository. It is an answer that does not satisfy many doctors. There is, however, an easy way to settle the matter conclusively. By examining the brain of JFK, it should be easy to determine from which direction he had been shot and once and for all resolve decades of wild speculation.

Despite the fact that a naval medical technician testified on oath that Kennedy's cranial cavity was empty when the body arrived for autopsy at the Bethesda Naval Hospital in Washington, the official records show that it was sectioned and fixed in formaldehyde – the standard pathological processes that you would expect to happen. An examination of the X-rays, slides of the brain section or the brain itself by a competent forensic expert would determine how many shots hit the president's head and from which direction they were fired.

The only problem is that the president's brain is missing. As are the X-rays, tissue samples and other elements of the autopsy report that could settle the matter. The controversial nature of the disappearing presidential grey matter is heightened by the fact that the doctors who first saw JFK's body when it was rushed to the Parkland Hospital in Dallas testified that all the evidence they saw supported the fact that he had received a frontal shot. This directly contradicts the naval pathologist who produced the official autopsy report.

THE GUN THAT KILLED ROBERT KENNEDY

obert Kennedy was more idealistic, charismatic and talented than his brother John F Kennedy. If he had not been assassinated as he left the Los Angeles Ambassador Hotel after triumphantly accepting the Californian nomination for Democratic presidential candidate in 1968, there are few historian who doubt he could have gone on to eclipse his brother's rather mediocre record as president.

Unlike the assassination of his brother, the killing of Robert F Kennedy looked like it was a much more straightforward case. The gunman – Sirhan Bashira Sirhan – had appeared in front of RFK, fired eight shots from his gun and then been wrestled to the floor by assorted security men and civilians, including professional football players, who were shocked by the almost superhuman strength the scrawny gunman possessed. The only problem was the forensic evidence.

The autopsy of Robert F Kennedy was performed by Dr Thomas T Noguchi, a world-renowned pathologist. He testified under oath that the fatal shot which entered RFK's body just behind his right ear was fired from a distance of no less than one inch and no more than three inches away. All of the witness reports never place Sirhan and his gun as being any closer than one to five feet directly in front of him.

The only other person at the murder other than Sirhan who was holding a .22 pistol was private security guard Thane Eugene Cesar who was walking with Kennedy on his right side, holding on to his elbow. After being confronted with witness testimony that he had been seen drawing his gun, he admitted that he did own a .22 pistol but that it had been sold before the assassination. He then changed his story, claiming that he had the pistol on the night of the assassination but had sold it soon afterward.

When investigators tracked the new owner of the pistol to Arkansas, he claimed that it had been recently stolen, therefore preventing any forensic testing that would have settled the question as to whether it was the gun that was used to shoot RFK.

below and right American tragedy – the brutal assassination of Robert Kennedy robbed the United States of one of its potentially greatest ever presidents.

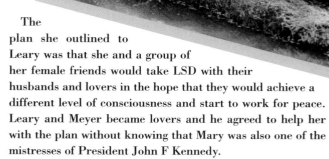

THE DIARY OF A PRESIDENT'S MISTRESS WHO PLANNED TO SAVE THE WORLD WITH LSD

A few years ago, an actor asked me to research Mary Pinchot Meyer for a film script he was developing. When he read the material I'd accumulated he decided to develop a different story. "No one would buy this, even though it's true," he said. "One person with all that going on is just not believable."

The established facts of Mary Pinchot Meyer's life do make for incredible reading. She came from a wealthy Washington family and had the reputation for being one of the most beautiful women in the American capital. A talented painter and doyenne of the city's party circuit, she was married to Cord Meyer, one of the CIA's top men.

In 1962, Mary visited Timothy Leary, who was at the time conducting his pioneering LSD research at Harvard University. Her first words to him were: "I've come from Washington to discuss something important. I want to learn how to run an LSD session." Mary had already had her own LSD experiences and believed that "the world would be a better place if men in power had LSD experiences".

The plan she outlined to Leary was that she and a group of her female friends would take LSD with their husbands and lovers in the hope that they would achieve a different level of consciousness and start to work for peace. Leary and Meyer became lovers and he agreed to help her with the plan without knowing that Mary was also one of the mistresses of President John F Kennedy.

When Mary was shot while out walking in Washington in 1964, one of her friends asked her sister Tony to find Mary's diary. When Tony and her husband went to Mary's studio to look for the diary they found the CIA's Director of Counterintelligence James Angleton already looking for it. Finding it later, Tony discovered it contained details of Mary's affair with JFK, so she decided to give it to the CIA. The CIA has told researchers trying to obtain the diary that Angleton must have destroyed it and therefore all evidence of Mary's LSD plan for world peace.

PROJECT BLUE BOOK REPORT 13

Project Blue Book was the most important study of unidentified flying objects undertaken by the United States Air Force, running in various forms between 1952 and 1970. Its aim was to determine whether UFOs were a potential threat to US national security. During the course of its investigation, Project Blue Book collected, analyzed and recorded more than 13,000 sightings.

Originally all of the reports written as part of Project Blue Book were classified, but over the years all files and reports have come into the public domain. The only officially acknowledged exception to this was a document called "Estimate of the Situation" which, when it crossed the desk of Air Force Chief of Staff General Hoyt Vandenberg, was ordered to be destroyed. Vandenberg believed that the document's conclusion that UFOs were extraterrestrial craft was flawed and lacking in proof.

As Project Blue Book's findings were published in a series of reports numbered 1 to 14, it seemed as if there was something else missing – Special Report 13. Researchers

were bemused when there was a gap in the numbering sequence, jumping from Blue Book Special Report 12 to Blue Book Special Report 14. When the air force was first asked about the apparently missing report they explained that the reason why there was no Special Report 13 was the same reason some skyscrapers don't have a thirteenth floor – the belief that the number is unlucky.

Finding it hard to believe that scientists and members of the air force suffered from triskaidekaphobia – the irrational fear of the number 13 – UFO researchers tried to find the missing report. One of the most reliable and professional researchers investigating UFOs, Stanton Friedman, was able to find evidence that the report had been written and was still classified. Faced with this evidence, the air force changed the official story and said that Report 13 did exist but only in a draft form. Whether or not the air force were being honest at last, the report is still missing and 13 remains an unlucky number for those wanting to know the truth.

THE MISSING POLICE NOTEBOOKS FROM THE LOCKERBIE CRASH INVESTIGATION

On the night of December 21, 1988, Pan Am Flight 103 exploded over the Scottish border town of Lockerbie, killing 270 people, including 11 on the ground. It later emerged that the plane had been brought down by a bomb placed in a suitcase in the cargo hold, making it the largest act of terrorism against the US before 9/11.

The Lockerbie bombing was also Britain's worst air disaster and resulted in Scotland's largest ever murder investigation. After a three-year joint investigation by the Scottish police and the FBI, Libyan intelligence agent Abdel Basset Ali al-Megrahi was charged with the bombing and in 1996 was eventually convicted of murder and sentenced to 27 years in prison.

Nagging doubts remain over the case, especially when it emerged that key elements of the evidence had been destroyed. Many police officers were disturbed by the presence of Americans at the crash site and were told by senior officers that they were not to enter material about American activity in their notebooks. In 2000, Labour MP Tam Dalyell revealed that a former constituent, WPC Mary Boylan, had come to him to express her concerns over the destruction of police notebooks belonging to officers involved in the initial stages of the Lockerbie crash-site investigation.

Almost 11 years after the event Boylan had been asked to give evidence to an inquiry over Lockerbie, so the retired WPC had phoned Livingston police station to ask for her notebook. She was told it had gone missing, despite the legal requirement to keep it safely stored. She then learned that the notebooks of Lothian and Borders Police who had been at the crash site had been destroyed.

In the House of Common Dalyell asked: "Who gave the instruction for the destruction of the notebooks in the biggest murder trial Scotland?" It was a question that was not answered. What happened to the remains of a suitcase belonging to Joseph Patrick Curry – a member of the US Army special forces – which Boylan recovered from the crash site also remains a mystery. Like the police notebooks, it too is "missing".

THE MISSING FILES OF DANNY CASOLARO

Danny Casolaro has become a legend among investigative journalists. A former part owner of Computer Age Publications, he sold his share in the company to give himself a source of funds to allow him to pursue a full-time career as an investigative reporter.

He began his new career with an investigation of a piece of software called PROMIS which, its developers claimed, had been stolen from them by the US Justice Department. What started out as a business dispute escalated into a much larger story when one of his sources, Michael Riconosciuto, told him that he had personally programmed PROMIS with a backdoor. This meant that the software the Justice Department was selling could be hacked into and therefore the information collected by those US and foreign law enforcement agencies using PROMIS could be accessed by outsiders.

As his investigation continued, Casolaro took to taking all of the evidence he had accumulated with him in a large, accordion-style file case. It never left his side. Friends joked that the computer buff has gone all "Luddite", putting more trust in paper than computer disks. On more than one occasion, Casolaro turned up for a meeting with the accordion-style file handcuffed to his wrist. Friends also joked that the case even went with Danny when he went on dates.

Evidence continued to be added to the file as Danny's investigation began to move away from his familiar world of computing and into the murky world of secret service intelligence gathering. Casolaro's state of mind became increasingly paranoid, believing in a conspiracy he called the "Octopus", but everyone who saw the papers he had gathered testified that the contents of his file would support prosecutions in the criminal courts.

Casolaro's naked body was found in a bathtub full of bloody water in a Virginia motel room on August 10, 1991. When the room was searched the police found a four-line suicide note, but not his file, despite the fact that he was seen carrying it when he checked into the hotel. His case file and all evidence of Casolaro's year-long investigation remain missing.

WHITE HOUSE EMAILS THAT COULD HAVE FORCED FORMER PRESIDENT BILL CLINTON OUT OF THE OVAL OFFICE

The idea that the US president would not have his emails archived and backed up strikes most people as somewhat surprising – especially when those emails could have forced him out of power.

Yet this was the problem facing members of a Justice Department task force when their investigation into the campaign finances of President Bill Clinton and Vice President Al Gore led them to request to see emails sent to and from the White House. Despite subpoenaing the electronic communications they were told that they could not be handed over due to technical problems.

A malfunction meant more than 100,000 emails from key members of the White House, including President Clinton himself, had been lost. When investigators tried to talk to employees about the lost emails, the White House threatened the staff who ran the email system with jail if they talked about the problem.

A former computer contractor who ran the White House's systems – told a House Government Reform and Oversight Committee that "I was told there would be a jail cell with my name on it", while another employee, Betty Lambuth, told the Committee that the technical problem was to be kept so secret it was named (rather unimaginatively) "Project X".

In an affidavit Lambuth stated that many of the lost emails contained information regarding matters under investigation either by Congress or the Justice Department, including Clinton's relationship with Monica Lewinsky as well as campaign finance matters. Lost emails included more than 500 messages exchanged between Clinton's secretary Betty Currie and Lewinsky and a similar number between Vice President Al Gore and the Democratic National Committee regarding financial irregularities.

A former White House employee said "the emails contained 'smoking guns' to several contentious issues" while other colleagues claimed "top people would have gone to jail" if the emails had been seen by the Justice Department. We will never know whether that is right because the evidence, yet again, has been "lost".

below The look of lust - Clinton's adulterous office romance nearly cost him the presidency.

EIGHTEEN MINUTES OF TAPE RECORDINGS MADE IN THE WHITE HOUSE BY PRESIDENT NIXON DURING THE WATERGATE SCANDAL

<u>above</u> Explekive deleted - E. Howard Hunt - convicted Watergate burglar, member of CREEP, long-time CIA agent and participant in the Bay of Pigs invasion of Cuba.

The Watergate scandal remains a pivotal moment in US history. Not only did it result in Richard Nixon becoming the only President who has been forced to resign, it was the point when no one in America could rely on its leader to tell the truth, even if he swore that "I am not a crook".

Nixon's downfall is largely credited to two reporters from the *Washington Post* – Bob Woodward and Carl Bernstein. Their investigation of a burglary at the offices of the Democratic Party in the Watergate Hotel by members of the Committee to Re-elect the President (CREEP), including former Nixon aide and CIA agent E Howard Hunt, became headline news. It led to the US Senate forming a Select Committee to look into the matter.

The hearings discovered that Nixon had installed bugging equipment in the White House to record his conversations in secret. The Senate pressed for the release of the tapes, which showed Nixon knew about the break-in and ordered a cover-up. Known collectively as the "smoking gun", the recordings were the evidence that cost him the presidency.

However, on one crucial tape there is gap of 18 minutes and 30 seconds between conversations. The White House claimed that the missing conversation had been erased accidentally by Nixon's secretary, Rose Mary Woods, who had allegedly left her foot on a pedal on the far side of her desk – an unconvincing gymnastic stretch for that length of time. Audio experts examined the tape for the Senate and claimed it had been deliberately wiped.

What was wiped – and why – remains a topic of intense speculation. It seems to have been more sensitive than the rest of the material that cost Nixon the presidency. In passages before the critical gap, Nixon calls the Warren Commission "the greatest hoax that has ever been perpetuated", and refers to "The whole Bay of Pigs thing" – his phrase for the Kennedy assassination. We will never know what he so desperately did not want us to hear as the evidence remains lost to us.

THE MYSTERIOUSLY BURNT FILES THAT COULD HAVE PREVENTED LYNDON B JOHNSON FROM BECOMING PRESIDENT OF THE USA

When Lyndon Baines Johnson became president in the aftermath of the assassination of JFK, he was already shrouded in the type of rumour and insinuation of shady dealings that would have ended a lesser politician's climb up the ladder of power.

In 1948, LBJ won a place in the Senate by just 87 votes in an election that was notorious for voting irregularities – such as 202 ballots in one county all being cast in alphabetical order and all for Johnson. He earned the ironic nickname "Landslide" Johnson but it did not stop his political ascent.

Neither did appointing Malcolm E Wallace as his Washington aide, despite the fact that Wallace had been convicted of murdering John Douglas Kinser, a professional golfer who was dating Senator Johnson's sister Josefa at the time of his death. Wallace had been represented by LBJ's lawyer and only received a five-year suspended sentence for his crime of shooting Kinser five times with a handgun. Making the murderer of your sister's lover your aide is odd even by Texan political standards.

One thing that did seem to threaten Johnson's political career was an investigation into breaches of election law over campaign contributions he had received and irregularities in his tax dealings with the Internal Revenue Service (IRS). Focusing on his relationship with the Texan construction company Brown & Root (now a subsidiary of Halliburton), Austin District Collector for the IRS Frank L Scofield amassed a huge collection of evidence on paper.

Scofield files showed that Brown & Root had been subsidizing Johnson's salary since he achieved office and had made significant cash donations to his various campaigns. An exposure of this would have called into question the highly lucrative federal contracts LBJ had secured for the company.

At one point in the investigation, all of the paperwork Scofield had amassed was transferred to a prefabricated Quonset hut. Within days, the hut had been burnt to the ground. The police suspected arson. With the evidence missing in the fire, the IRS case against Johnson was shelved indefinitely.

THE BLACK BOX FROM THE CRASH OF US COMMERCE SECRETARY RON BROWN'S PLANE

In April 1996, *The American Spectator* magazine contained an article titled "Why Ron Brown Won't Go Down". The US Commerce Secretary, Brown was a close ally of President Bill Clinton. A few days after the article came out, the embattled politician and his T-43 military transport plane both went down, crashing as he headed toward Dubrovnik airport in Croatia.

At the time of the crash, Brown was under investigation from the Commerce Department Inspector General, the Justice Department and the Senate Judiciary Committee for his part in a scandal involving illegal campaign contributions. Before leaving for Croatia he had told independent counsel that he was prepared to negotiate a plea bargain where he would divulge full details of the fundraising activities of the Clinton-Gore White House campaign in return for leniency.

Time Magazine, Newsweek and major newspapers reported his plane had come down in the Adriatic in the "worst storm in a decade". Dubrovnik airport, however, reported only light scattered rain. With weather ruled out as the cause of the crash, the recovery of the craft's black box recorder was the best way to determine what brought it down. The air force announced the plane had not been fitted with a black box recorder, despite the fact that it is illegal to transport government officials without the equipment installed.

When the Croatian government found a black box at the crash site in the hills 10 miles from Dubrovnik, the US government declined to inspect it as they said Croatian investigators had only recovered some instrumentation that looked exactly like a flight recorder. Whatever was found, when independent researchers tried to examine it, the evidence had gone missing.

Joining it in the lost file were the control tower tape, the backup cylinder of the control tape and X-rays and photos of Ron Brown's body. These became important when two members of the US Armed Forces Institute of Pathology – Lieutenant Colonel Steve Cogswell and Lieutenant Colonel David Hause – claimed that Brown's skull had a large hole in it that was consistent with a gunshot wound.

SUPPRESSED DATA

10

"All truth passes through three stages. First, it is ridiculed. Second, it is violently opposed. Third, it is accepted as being self-evident."
Arthur Schopenhauer

One of the biggest lies we have drummed into us in school is that everything we are being taught about science and nature is based on all the facts available. However, as anyone who has studied the works of Charles Fort can tell you, academics have a long history of excluding a vast range of amazing data just because it does not fit in with their neat theories.

This suppressed data tends to reveal that we live in a much more mysterious universe than we are led to believe. The problem is that if evidence of a puzzle is hidden and we are deceived into thinking the correct answer has been established, the mystery is lost to us and no one can ever attempt to find the real truth.

As pioneering rebel scientist Dr Jack Sarfatti has pointed out, the public is not told the truth by many scientists because they themselves are unaware of the evidence that discredits the theories they continue to peddle. Once an orthodox view in science has been established, all you usually need to do to keep it dominant is to make life unpleasant for anyone who challenges it – as happened to Wilhelm Reich and Dr Rupert Sheldrake.

The established orthodoxy has suppressed open-minded questioning and free thought on subjects as familiar as Darwinian theory and General Relativity to the much stranger frontiers of quantum physics, because some scientists seem to value being right much more than wanting to know the actual truth.

STRANGE LIGHTS OBSERVED ON THE MOON BY ASTRONOMERS

The official and orthodox scientific view of the Moon is that it's a lifeless, unchanging satellite composed of rock. Despite the central role it occupies in myth, religion and folklore throughout humanity's history, we are led to believe that it is actually rather dull.

If you pick up almost any reference work on the Moon, you won't find mention of strange lights observed on its surface. It seems that one of the biggest lunar mysteries – the recording of everything from coloured flashes to pulsating spots – is not a topic astronomers want to discuss with the public. The causes of Transient Lunar Phenomena (TLP) remain unknown and therefore details are swept under the scientific community's carpet like a dirty little secret.

TLP have a long history. In 1787, Britain's Astronomer Royal Sir William Herschel recorded prominent TLP and showed them to King George III through a telescope in the grounds of Windsor Castle. In the months before Neil Armstrong first set foot on the Moon, NASA ordered a catalogue of TLP to be undertaken. Excluding all reports that could be viewed as dubious, the report listed 579 mysterious lunar events. Many of these were witnessed by world-renowned astronomers and included red strips of light seen on crater floors, patches of violet glow and white streaks.

On July 19, 1969, with Apollo 11 in orbit, astronomers reported transient phenomena in a crater called Aristarchus. NASA asked the astronauts to check the observation and Neil Armstrong reported he could see "an area that is considerably more illuminated than the surrounding area. It seems to have a slight amount of fluorescence to it." Armstrong thought it was coming from the region of Aristarchus.

Despite confirmed observations, NASA and other space agencies continue to downplay the existence and importance of TLP. Manned and robotic exploration of the Moon seemed to rule out previously suggested causes such as volcanic activity. Many lunar geologists have attacked the very existence of TLP, suggesting that everything can be explained by occasional rock falls and meteor impacts – even pulsating, coloured lights observed over a period of several hours.

left The light side of the Moon – the scientists have yet to come up with a coherent explanation of strange lights observed on the lunar surface.

THE "WOW!" SIGNAL – EVIDENCE THAT ET HAS ALREADY CALLED EARTH

At 11:16 p.m. on August 15, 1977, the Big Ear radio telescope situated in Ohio picked up what could be the most important radio transmission in the history of mankind. Lasting for up to 72 seconds and of a non-terrestrial and non-solar system origin, the narrowband signal was at the scientifically significant frequency of the hyperfine transition of hydrogen. Seeing the computer printout and a signal so strong it went off the device's recording chart, Big Ear astrophysicist Jerry R Ehman circled it and wrote "Wow!" next to it – giving a name to the signal that has stuck ever since.

Ehman's excitement is easy to understand. The manner in which the "Wow!" signal rose and fell over 72 seconds helped rule out any possible terrestrial source. The signal had all of the predicted elements of a beacon pointing to an alien civilization. It seemed as if scientists involved in SETI (the Search for Extraterrestrial Intelligence) had found the proof they had been looking for.

Astronomers around the world were quick to attack the significance of the signal. While many acknowledged that it looked impressive, they suggested the fact that it had only been recorded once was proof that it was not an attempt at communication from an alien source. Scientists who back the "Wow!" signal as evidence of ETs point out that no more than an hour has ever been devoted to trying to trace it in any given position and it could be that the signal is on at other times, when no one is listening

Many orthodox scientists continue to ridicule the "Wow!" signal and the whole process of scanning the heavens for significant signals as a branch of "pseudoscience". Using the arguments that had got Congressional funding for Big Ear and other SETI facilities cancelled, they claimed it had no credibility because the only form of testing SETI researchers did was to try and find proof of a theory, rather than testing the theory itself. More than 25 years on, the media continue to report the scientific orthodoxy that no credible sign of extraterrestrial life has ever been discovered.

THE MYSTERIOUS BLACK KNIGHT SATELLITE OF 1960, FOUND ORBITING THE EARTH EVEN THOUGH NO ONE THEN HAD ROCKETS LARGE ENOUGH TO LAUNCH SOMETHING OF THAT SIZE

On a clear night you can look into the sky and see dozens of artificial satellites journey across the heavens. The miracles of rocketry have made GPS, global communications and satellite TV so commonplace that we no longer possess a sense of wonder where they are concerned.

In 1960, just three years after the USSR had won the first heat of the space race by putting Sputnik 1 into orbit, satellites were far from routine. When, in February 1960, one of the stations that formed the North American Air Defense System picked up a radar echo of a new satellite it sent panic throughout the US military.

Not only did the intelligence agencies have no idea that the USSR had launched a new satellite, nothing in their reports on Soviet space activity suggested they had the capacity to place an object into a polar orbit or to launch something that was estimated to be in excess of 15 tons. The military scientists were horrified, since they were at least four years away from achieving polar orbits and getting payloads that large into space.

The Soviets were also panicking. They had not launched the satellite and knew they were years away from being able to accomplish such a feat; they also knew the Americans could not do it either. The Americans nicknamed the satellite "Black Knight" after the British rocketry programme – even though they knew it could not have been a UK-launched object either. No one knew where it came from, but it was definitely there.

Scientists in the US, USSR and other countries such as Sweden tracked the mystery object for three weeks before it disappeared without a trace. The Black Knight satellite was a secret that could not be cracked, so no record of it was placed in the almanacs that record known satellites launches, and no further scientific research was carried out. The only people who continued to speculate over its origins were writers such as Philip K Dick, who wrote stories about it, renaming it VALIS or ZEBRA.

SUPPRESSION OF FLAWS IN THE EVIDENCE SUPPORTING DARWINIAN THEORY

The quickest way to commit professional suicide in today's scientific world is to challenge any aspect of Darwinism. The theory is so entrenched as the bedrock of all biological and zoological science that anyone who examines it is attacked with a frightening degree of professional hostility.

There is no doubt that the evidence for evolution is conclusive, but elements of Darwin's theory of mutation combining with natural selection appear to be flawed. Logically, if Darwin's theory of gradual genetic change was accurate, more evolved creatures should contain complex genetic structures. Comparing the complexity of DNA by looking at the number of chromosome bases shows that humans have 23 pairs compared to a snail's 56. It is an anomaly that orthodox science has not explained.

An example of the suppression of any scientist who questions any aspect of Darwinian theory is that of British biologist Warwick Collins. In 1976 he wrote a paper on sexual selection as an anomaly in Darwinian theory. As he was about to speak at an international conference to explain his paper, renowned geneticist Professor Maynard Smith stood up and attacked Collins in front of the audience. He told him he would use his influence to block publication of any further papers he wrote. Smith seems to have been true to his word as Collins continues to have his papers rejected for publication for no given reason.

Respected science journalist and author Richard Milton encountered another form of pro-Darwinist suppression when he was commissioned by the *Times Higher Education Supplement* to write a critique of Darwinism. It was trailed in the publication the week before with the line "Next Week: Darwinism – Richard Milton goes on the attack". This led scientists to write to the editor to try and stop the article's publication, claiming the Milton was a "secret creationist" (which he is not, his criticisms are purely scientific objections), "loony" and "in need of psychiatric help". Milton has since been attacked by scientists such as American geologist David Leveson merely for asking questions of the theory.

right Monkey's uncle – powerful voices in the scientific establishment have adopted scary tactics to suppress the views of any who question elements of Darwinian theory.

right Space monkeys are go! Astrochimp Ham is an example of apes being used in science.

EVIDENCE THAT CHIMPANZEES HAVE THE ABILITY TO MAKE UP WORDS

Of all the differences that scientists hold up to draw a distinction between animals and humans, language is the most cherished and most often used one. The orthodox scientific view is that humans have language, animals do not.

On the basis of this, scientists have built up careers claiming that they have isolated the genetic mutation that gave us language. Everything from the explanation of why Neanderthals died out (some researchers claim they lacked the language gene) to the moral justification for experimenting on animals has been advanced on the basis that even our closest genetic relative – the bonobo or pygmy chimpanzee – does not have our ability to use language.

Against this background, it was always inevitable that when a bonobo chimpanzee called Kanzi, kept at Georgia State University, Atlanta, came up with four distinct sounds for the things closest to his heart – banana, juice, grapes and the word "yes" – without being taught to do it, scientists would be quick to try and reassert the orthodox lie that it is impossible for apes to speak or use words like a human.

Previously, when another chimpanzee called Washoe learnt American Sign Language, scientists redefined language as being the ability to use syntax and not just words. However, not content with making up his own words, contrary to the leading theories of many primatologists, Kanzi went on to demonstrate his ability to construct sentences (another ability he should not have had according to the majority of scientists) by selecting words from among 3,000 symbols stored on a touch-sensitive computer screen to build such basic sentences as: "I would like some grapes."

Accepting apes have language would not only affect what it means to be human, but also whether we have the right to experiment on fellow sentient beings. One of the more generous denigrators of the work carried out at Georgia State University was Dr Tom Sambrook who said: "I doubt it signifies all it appears to. Were a four-year-old child to use language in the way a chimpanzee uses it, we would consider it disturbed."

CALLS BY THE SCIENTIFIC ESTABLISHMENT TO BURN THE BOOKS OF DR RUPERT SHELDRAKE, PIONEER OF THE MORPHIC FIELD THEORY

When scientists want to keep a theory or anomalous piece of evidence out of the view of the mainstream world, their usual tactic is to ignore it and hope it will go away. This usually works, as the non-scientists cannot ask questions about evidence they know nothing about. Once in a while though, a scientist breaks rank from the orthodox view and brings into the open a theory so controversial that a very public attack seems to be the inevitable consequence.

When, in 1981, Sir John Maddox, the editor of *Nature* – one of the most important scientific magazines in the world – wrote an article titled "Fit for Burning" about a book, it was a sure sign someone had got the white coats all riled up. The book he suggested burning was *A New Science of Life* by Dr Rupert Sheldrake, a British biology professor at Cambridge University.

Maddox went on to describe the book as "an infuriating tract not to be taken seriously" and "an intellectual aberration". It was Sheldrake's theory in the book about what he called "morphic fields" – an invisible form of information that exerts an influence on biology and plays a key role the development of self-organizing systems – that caused Maddox to launch such an astonishing attack on a fellow scientist.

Sheldrake packed his book with numerous examples of phenomena that backed his theory. However, his suggestion that there are intangible fields that help determine animal instinct and play a role in telling DNA what it should develop into only drew ridicule from his colleagues, despite fitting the observed facts far better than the previously established theories.

One of Sheldrake's critics, Professor Steven Rose of the Open University, described morphic fields as "rubbish and unnecessary". Sheldrake agreed to perform learning experiments on day-old chicks to back his claims, but Rose refused to accept results that seemed to back his opponent. In the face of scientific rejection, Sheldrake left his position at Cambridge. Ironically, in the years since, almost all of the experiments into his work have proved that his theory has a high degree of validity.

SUPPRESSION OF EVIDENCE THAT CONFLICTS WITH EINSTEIN'S THEORIES

The Michelson-Morley experiment has gone down in history as the one that led the way for Einstein's Special Theory of Relativity, but the account of it in science books is a lie.

The version taught to generations of students is that when Albert Michelson and Edward Morley performed their experiment in 1887, it proved there was no such substance as the previously theorized "ether". (The ether theory postulated that, just as sound waves require a medium to move through, light waves must have a mysterious invisible medium – "ether" – in order to travel through space.)

Michelson had invented a piece of equipment called an interferometer that could measure the velocity of a beam of light. Together with Morley, he tested to see if there was a drag factor being exerted by the ether on the speed of light. Textbooks claim the experiments showed there was no measurable ether drag.

However, that was not what the pair discovered at all. Their experiments actually showed a small, anomalous deviation from the expected value. When another scientist, Dayton Miller, performed the same experiment over an extended period during the 1920s and 1930s with even more accurate equipment his results consistently showed an ether drag effect. In 1988, French Nobel Prize winner Maurice Allais repeated the experiments of Michelson-Morley and Miller and secured the same results.

As Miller's results conflicted with the new Special Theory of Relativity put forward by Einstein they were not accepted even though they could not be refuted. However, the very existence of the results cost Einstein the Nobel Prize for his relativity theory. When Miller died in 1941, his former student Robert S Shankland took over his professorship and attacked his work as worthless. Within weeks of this, Einstein granted Shankland a series of financially lucrative interviews.

Prior to the denigration of Miller's work, the spelling "ether" was used and accepted by scientists such as Michael Faraday and Albert Einstein. However, after Miller's death, scientific journals began referring to "aether", an obsolete medieval spelling that conjured up images of alchemy and other psuedosciences from history.

above Back to the blackboard – no one doubts the genius of Einstein, but his supporters have worked to discredit and misrepresent the results of experiments that conflict with his theories.

THE SUPPRESSION OF WILHELM REICH'S THEORY OF ORGONE ENERGY

Wilhelm Reich is the only scientist to have been condemned as mad by both Sigmund Freud and Albert Einstein. He is certainly the only scientist to have been described by Freud as "my most brilliant pupil" and to have the result of one of his experiments verified by Einstein. He is also the only scientist in the twentieth century whose books were burned by both the Nazi and American governments.

Having trained with Freud as a psychoanalyst, Reich split with his former teacher and went to work in Germany. In 1933, he fled the country after his books, including *Character Analysis*, *The Function of the Orgasm* and *Mass Psychology of Fascism*, were seized by Nazi stormtroopers and burnt on a public bonfire. Settling in the USA in 1939, Reich coined the phrase "Hoodlums In Government" to show the similarity between the Nazis and the American government agents who seized several tons of his books in 1956 and had them incinerated.

The heretical view that caused Reich's books to be confiscated and burnt by the US Food and Drug Administration was that he believed he had discovered evidence for a biological form of energy, which he named "orgone". The idea of bioenergy was not new, but Reich carried out a large number of experiments that he claimed gave scientific proof to the idea that the energy could be detected in the atmosphere and all living matter. He also believed that the energy could be manipulated to treat disease.

In 1941, he even got Einstein to confirm his experimental findings (though they disagreed on the explanation of what they showed) and renegade scientists have been able to duplicate his work. In 1987, Dr Robert Dew published papers containing detailed photographic material backing Reich's assertion that decaying vegetable matter showed tiny pulsating particles forming spontaneously. With conventional scientists having proclaimed Reich's theories "worthless junk", their approach to such confirmation has been to ignore it completely and veto its publication in many scientific journals. It seems that pretending something isn't happening tends to draw less attention to it than old-fashioned book burning.

above Orgasm addict – Wilhelm Reich faced constant state suppression for his ideas, with his books burnt by both Nazi stormtroopers and US government agents.

HOW SCIENTIFIC TESTS SUGGEST THAT THE BLIND CAN SENSE EMOTION

According to orthodox scientists, there is no such thing as a "sixth sense". As humans, our only source of information about the world we inhabit comes from what we can touch, taste, smell, hear and see. Renowned sceptic James Randi even offered to pay out $1 million to anyone who can demonstrate psychic powers.

If Randi was not as obsessed with his belief that all claims of psychic phenomena are "simply standard magic tricks being used to accomplish allegedly paranormal feats", he might be writing out a large cheque to Dr Alan Pegna of the School of Psychology at the University of Wales.

Under rigorous laboratory conditions, Dr Pegna tested a blind man who possessed a "sixth sense" that allowed him to recognize the emotion on faces. The 52-year-old test subject, known only as "Patient X", had suffered two strokes, which damaged the brain areas that process visual signals and left him blind. He was able to tell if a face was happy, sad, fearful or angry.

While not able to determine the sex of a face, he consistently scored a much higher than chance success on guessing the emotion depicted on human faces. Neural scans showed the information was registering in an area of the brain other than the visual cortex. Patient X displayed neural activity in the right amygdala, an almond-shape structure situated deep within the brain's temporal lobe that is known to be involved in the processing of non-verbal signs of anger, defensiveness and fear.

The startling implications of the results of Dr Pegna's experiments – that there is a secret process by which the brain receives information not related to the five senses – quickly triggered a backlash from certain other scientists who were not prepared to accept such a possibility. Attacks ranged from the media reporting of the results to suggestions that Patient X is not actually blind, despite the results of test on his eyesight having been conducted by the Department of Neurology at the University Hospital, Geneva.

HOW PROMOTERS OF ALTERNATIVE THEORIES MISLEAD THE PUBLIC ABOUT EVIDENCE IN THE SAME WAY AS THEY CLAIM THE ESTABLISHMENT DOES

The Sphinx and the Great Pyramid have made the Giza Plateau in Egypt not only a place of extreme historical significance but also the focus of intense debate between those holding alternative theories about the purpose of the ancient monuments and those established historians and archaeologists who hold conventional views.

The claims of the alternative camp make sensational reading, suggesting there are undiscovered underground chambers under the Sphinx. Some even suggest that conspiracies exist linking the Sphinx and the "face on Mars".

The claims have started to gain ground in the public's mind and spawned a vast number of best-selling books and several television programmes. Alternative researchers have claimed that the Director of the Egyptian Council of Antiquities, Dr Zahi Hawass, has lied about evidence found on the Giza Plateau and was suppressing details of secret archaeological work in the area.

One alternative researcher, Tom Danley, claimed to have found evidence of a clandestine tunnelling operation in the Great Pyramid – a serious charge as this type of structural damage would be a breach of Egyptian law and international laws protecting a world heritage site. Another proponent of alternatives theories, Richard Hoagland (who believes that Ancient Egypt was linked to life on Mars) reported on his website and in radio interviews that evidence from an investigator he had sent to the site proved "someone was secretly driving a new tunnel deep into the pyramid" and that there was "elaborate and obviously clandestine tunnelling activity". These claims fanned the flames of conspiracy and caused outrage in the archaeological community.

When English researchers Chris Ogilvie-Herald and Ian Lawton visited the Great Pyramid to check what was happening, they discovered there was no evidence at all of secret tunnelling and that the public had been totally misled by the statements made by Hoagland. They even found that one of the supposedly "new secret channels" was the exact match of one excavated in the early nineteenth century. If alternative investigators are willing to mislead the public in the way they claim the authorities do, it will always be hard for people to believe any aspect of their research.

CELEBRITIES – BEYOND THE GOSSIP

"When whole races and peoples conspire to propagate gigantic mute lies in the interest of tyrannies and shams, why should we care anything about the trifling lies told by individuals?"
Mark Twain

It is a hard life being a celebrity – the money, the fame and the need to cover up any embarrassing details about your life that could end the adulation you receive and cost you your glamorous lifestyle.

Even though we know deep down inside that there are more important things to worry about, in our celebrity obsessed culture we always find it hard not to be curious about the secrets of our favourite film stars, musicians and writers. We know that it cheapens us to have a prurient interest in what happens in other people's private lives, but that doesn't stop us taking in the copious celebrity coverage provided by the media.

Given this, it is understandable why so many celebrities feel the need to lie and cover up aspects of their personal lives when questions about their sexuality, recreational habits and political orientation can cost them their careers. Even those celebrities whose secrets may not see them end up in court on murder or child molestation charges will go to incredible lengths and tell the most fabulous lies to ensure that their fans do not know what is going on behind closed doors.

One of the biggest secrets in the world of stardom is that the apparently adversarial relationship between journalists and celebrities is regularly full of incidents of media collusion to perpetuate certain celebrities' images and keep their secrets from the public. Even the most cynical journalist has heroes he or she we will always cover for.

above The devil not only has all of the best tunes, he has all of the coolest followers, if Sammy Davis Jr. is anything to go by.

SAMMY DAVIS JR WAS A SATANIST

For anyone currently trying to rack his or her brains for another famous person called Sammy Davis Jr who might just be a Satanist – because the facts of this entry are so shocking to their established world view, let me clarify: the Sammy Davis Jr to whom I'm referring is none other than the coolest of the cool cats, the legendary entertainer and member of the Rat Pack.

Aside from his acting, singing, dancing and trumpet playing, Davis is most well known for his friendship with Frank Sinatra and for his stance on refusing to play venues that practised racial segregation – which led to the integration of many nightclubs and Las Vegas casinos. When asked whether the prejudice he faced had been a handicap he would often quip: "I'm a black, one-eyed Jew in America, what more of a handicap could I face?"

Despite the fact that Davis had converted to Judaism after the 1954 car crash that cost him an eye, his actual adherence to any religious faith seems to have been wonderfully erratic. When, in 1970, Davis wed for the second time, the Reverend Jesse Jackson conducted the ceremony, while three years later Davis joined the Church of Satan.

Formed by former circus performer Anton LeVey, the Church of Satan had come to prominence thanks to media savvy publicity stunts such as LeVey performing the satanic baptism of his own daughter. A consultant to several Hollywood films, including *Rosemary's Baby*, LeVey had written *The Satanic Bible* – a plagiarized mix of magic and Ayn Rand's *Atlas Shrugged*, with added attacks on Christianity. He then founded his own take on a satanic religion and declared himself the "Black Pope".

After he had officially joined the Church of Satan in April 1973, Sammy Davis Jr began to hold grand and well-attended satanic orgies at his Los Angeles home. More than one associate of Davis has suggested that it was the prospect of orgies that led him to become a satanist in the first place.

The words written on Davis's gravestone seems a profoundly apt comment on his spiritual life as it reads: "The Entertainer. He tried everything."

JOHN WAYNE HELPED FUND THE IRA AND PLANNED TO OVERTHROW THE GOVERNMENT OF PANAMA

The declassified elements of John Wayne's FBI file are very different from those of his contemporaries. While other stars were under investigation for being communist or supporting left-wing causes, he received praise for his vociferous anti-communist views and work he did in support of the House Committee on Un-American Activities (who were blacklisting any actors or film-makers with leftist views).

Wayne had helped found the rabid Motion Picture Alliance for the Preservation of American Ideals in 1944, which had begun working to exclude "Reds" from Hollywood even before the House Committee on Un-American Activities was formed. Wayne was not all talk when it came to fighting what he perceived as the communist threat.

The fabled man of action was happy to dig deep into his pockets to help fund anti-government forces in Panama who were planning a coup against the officially elected government of Ernesto de la Guardia. Although de la Guardia was a conservative businessman in the eyes of his people and the rest of the world, the Duke thought that his insistence that Panama had some rights over its famous canal and should be treated with more respect by the US made him a "pinko-commie bastard".

It was actions like this and the Duke's outspoken political views that so enraged Soviet dictator Josef Stalin that he ordered a plot to kill Wayne. Stalin was a big fan of cowboy films, including Wayne's first blockbuster *Stagecoach*, but thought he was "a threat to the cause". At least one attempt was made on his life when two Soviet agents, posing as members of the FBI, attempted an assassination in Wayne's office at the Warner Brothers studios in Hollywood.

Wayne and his long-time friend, collaborator and director John Ford were close friends of Ernie O'Malley, a leading Irish Republican Army (IRA) figure during the Irish revolution. Wayne and Ford employed O'Malley as a consultant on their movie *The Quiet Man*, but both had already been providing strong financial support for the republican gunman in his work as a key fundraiser for the armed nationalist cause.

below Gung ho on screen and even more gung ho off screen, John Wayne's freedom fighters are seen by others as gun-wielding terrorists.

DAVID BOWIE WAS OBSESSED WITH THE NAZI JOSEPH GOEBBELS AND BELIEVED THAT FELLOW ROCKER JIMMY PAGE WAS OUT TO HARM HIM BY THE USE OF OCCULT POWERS

There are times when however objective an author wishes to be, his personal opinions influence his writing. In a book dealing with the truth, it is only fair to tell you I am a huge David Bowie fan before you read the rest of this entry.

In 1976 Bowie was at the cutting edge of rock, but his sanity was suspect. His interest in the occult took strange turns. Aside from practising magic himself, he had his house in LA professionally exorcized and then began storing his urine in a fridge so that no wizard could steal his bodily fluids.

The wizard Bowie feared most was Led Zeppelin guitarist Jimmy Page. Bowie and Page had worked together in the 1960s with Page contributing to Bowie's 1965 song *I Pity The Fool*. The guitarist was known as one of the world's greatest collectors of material connected with diabolist Aleister Crowley, but Bowie believed that Page was a master occultist who was using his magic to curse Bowie.

It was also during 1976 that Bowie's obsession with Nazism came to the fore. Talking to journalist Tony Parsons, Bowie admitted: "Goebbels intrigued me more than the other Nazis because of the way he used the media. He was an extraordinary guy. I was fascinated by his quest for the Holy Grail – he had come to Glastonbury Tor in England looking for it. The Nazis took the swastika and turned it around so it became dark. That fascinated me. Who was the Nazi black magician?"

When Bowie returned to England later in the year, he stood in the back of a car at Victoria station and gave a Nazi-style salute and predicted a new rise in fascism. After the resulting public backlash, Bowie sobered up, went to Berlin to paint, study art and make music with Brian Eno.

In his defence, it must be pointed out that during this period not only was Bowie daily taking quantities of cocaine that would have felled most elephants, he was also making some of the most brilliant music of the twentieth century.

right Cracked actor? The thin white duke went through a period of extreme cocaine abuse and an obsession with the occult and Nazism.

WALT DISNEY WORKED FOR THE FBI

Walt Disney is one of the few creative pioneers who left a lasting legacy on western culture. Ignoring the theme parks and globalization of the brand that carries his name, Walt Disney's true legacy is the feature length animated film and the magic of his creations such as Mickey Mouse.

During the latter part of his life, Walt Disney was careful to project, as well as protect, his avuncular image as the keeper of the keys to the magic kingdom. After his death, it is an image that the Walt Disney Company has been passionate about preserving and promoting, realizing that the warmth people associate with Walt is a key part of their corporate image. This is one of the reasons so many people at Disney are keen to push the theory that Mickey Mouse was their founder's alter ego.

The truth is that Walt Disney was a man with dark secrets, and the only representation of corporate spirit he brings to mind for many ex-employees is that of George Orwell's Big Brother – due to his culture of spying, informing and invasion of privacy. He had a hatred of unions after the 1941 strike by his artists and took the opportunity to give evidence to the House Committee on Un-American Activities to denounce many of his employees. He regularly spied on his staff and developed a close relationship with the FBI to help him with this process.

His FBI file reveals that he was "approved as a Special Agent in Charge", meaning he had the status of a major informant. In return for his help, the Bureau assisted him with finding his long-lost biological mother. Walt not only fed them information about his staff, but about other film-makers and stars he believed to be subversive. A kiss-arse of the first order, Disney regularly changed scripts of his movies to show the FBI in a good light, allowed the free use of Disneyland for FBI agents and even promoted working in the FBI crime lab as part of a Mickey Mouse Club "future careers" spot.

`below` Walt Disney's magic kingdom had the air of an Orwellian nightmare for those workers Walt spied on for the FBI and Senator McCarthy.

CARY GRANT USED LSD

At the height of his popularity as Hollywood's most popular and debonair leading man, Cary Grant could easily be forgiven for saying: "Everyone wanted be Cary Grant. Even I wanted to be Cary Grant." Idolized by millions of women, many men also looked up to Grant as a model for masculine behaviour.

However, behind the persona of Cary Grant the movie star hid the tortured man born Archibald Alexander Leach in Bristol, England. His mother had been incarcerated in a mental asylum when he was nine – a fact that he did not discover for another 20 years – and despite his film career success, he was deeply insecure, commenting: "I probably chose my profession because I was seeking approval, adulation, admiration and affection."

Seeking a way of tackling his problems, he turned to pioneering psychiatrists Dr Mortimer Hartmann and Dr Oscar Janiger, who were leading the way in the use of the drug lysergic acid diethylamide (LSD) as a way of tackling deep-rooted neuroses. Hoping to resolve the problems that had led him to say, "I have spent the greater part of my life fluctuating between Archie Leach and Cary Grant, unsure of each, suspecting each", Grant began a course of LSD therapy that would see him take more than 60 trips.

In the book *Cary Grant: A Touch of Elegance*, he is quoted on the experience: "I have been born again. I have just been through a psychiatric experience that has completely changed me. It was horrendous. I had to face things about myself that I never admitted. I was an utter fake, a self-opinionated bore, a know-all who knew very little."

It wasn't all tough face-yourself style trips for Grant. He also told of how: "In one LSD dream I shit all over the rug and shit all over the floor. I imagined myself as a giant penis launching off from Earth like a spaceship."

I don't know about you, but I will never watch *North By Northwest* or *To Catch A Thief* in the same light ever again.

right Hollywood heartthrob and psychedelic psychonaut Cary Grant took more than 60 LSD trips in an attempt to sort himself out.

BURT LANCASTER WAS INVESTIGATED BY THE FBI FOR POTENTIAL LINKS TO COMMUNISM AND ATTENDING GAY ORGIES

When you hear the word "butch" used in the same sentence as Burt Lancaster, it is not the gay connotations of the word that usually spring to mind. Whether in his personal life or on the cinema screem, Lancaster appeared as the apotheosis of masculinity. In his roles he was often cast as the tough but gentle, brave, virile and resolutely heterosexual hero, while in his private life he was known as a serial womanizer. There was no irony when one casting director called him "a man's man".

It comes as shock then to discover that the FBI kept secret surveillance files on Lancaster that detailed his attendance, along with his friend Rock Hudson, at a gay orgy that boasted more than 200 US marines. When the Office of Naval Intelligence heard about the report, they took it so seriously that they organized a raid on the mansion where the orgy had taken place.

The FBI had Lancaster under close watch because they believed he was a communist after he spoke out against the Hollywood blacklists and House Committee on Un-American Activities. While some argue that the FBI lied about Lancaster's attendance at the orgy as part of a campaign to denigrate him for his liberal views, others point to reports from his personal life and strict rule of only appointing homosexual secretaries (when asked about this he simply said: "They're the best.").

Lancaster would not have been the first and certainly is not the last leading man in Hollywood to have had to hide his sexual orientation. Even today, there are several male stars whose homosexuality or bisexuality is hidden from the public in the belief that it would damage their box office credibility.

No secret in Lancaster's closest will eclipse his reputation for doing the right thing – such as being the first to offer public support to Rock Hudson when it was announced he had AIDS – or being one of the few stars in Hollywood who would work for almost free if he shared the liberal values of the film or its director.

CHARLIE CHAPLIN PREYED UPON UNDERAGE GIRLS

Few truly great iconic cinema images come close to that of a small man with a comic moustache, bowler hat and a cane, making a funny walk across the silent screens of early Hollywood. Charlie Chaplin was the first global movie star. His rags to riches story of a poor working class boy from South London becoming the first actor to negotiate a $1 million deal in 1917 is the stuff of legend and is reflected in his most famous cinematic creation, *The Little Tramp*.

It may have been the character that earned Chaplin the nickname "The Little Tramp" but the name was appropriate in more ways than one. Adored by millions as the funniest man alive, Chaplin's private life revolved around his obsession with underage girls.

When he was 29, he married his first wife – 16-year-old Mildred Harris – but divorced her two years later after several affairs with young girls. His next high profile conquest was actress Lillita McMurray, who was only 12 when Chaplin cast her in his film *The Kid*. Renaming her Lita Grey, Chaplin was forced to marry her or face a statutory rape charge when she became pregnant at 16. His comment on this was: "It's better than the penitentiary."

Lita's 42-page divorce petition to finish their two-year marriage was so lurid that "The Little Tramp" gave her an $825,000 settlement (the largest ever awarded at the time) to keep details of his serial seduction and affairs with jailbait out of court and out of the press. In 1992, Grey said: "Charlie liked to see a young girl awakened."

It was Chaplin's left-wing politics and refusal to condemn communism that led the US government to expel him in 1952. Recently declassified British secret papers showed that his leaning to the left also prevented him from being given a knighthood until two years before his death.

Chaplin would not survive in today's Hollywood. The combination of his leftist politics and preference for pubescent girls would have had him in court faster than Michael Jackson and probably fleeing the country Roman Polanski-style.

above Occult and gadget obsessed comedian Peter Sellers enjoys the sun on holiday with his secret lover Princess Margaret

PETER SELLERS BELIEVED HE COULD TALK TO THE DEAD, AND WAS ONE OF PRINCESS MARGARET'S LOVERS

If you want a prime example of celebrities living vast, bizarre and secret lives that the press do not report on until they are dead, there is none better than the life of Peter Sellers. Not a word on his interest in occultism, cocaine use or sex sessions with a member of the British royal family went reported while he was alive, despite all of these activities being well known to Fleet Street reporters.

Hints may have been dropped about his superstitious nature, his mood swings and close friendship with Her Royal Highness Princess Margaret, but nothing was written about what was really going on behind the celebrity mask.

After a serious falling out of favour in Hollywood in 1964, Seller's "died" of a heart attack. His heart stopped beating briefly and he was rushed to hospital where his heart had to be re-started a further seven times. It became apparent after his recovery that Sellers was a changed man. His knowledge of the occult elements of Freemasonry, previously one of his many interests, became a key interest. He constructed an

altar to his dead mother, whom he believed he was in communication with, and regularly conducted magical rituals. Sellers believed that he was in contact with the spirit of his dead dog and performed further magic rituals on the cliffs at Hastings.

Seeing less of old friends such as ex-Goons colleagues Spike Milligan and Harry Secombe, his adoption of a much more mystical view of life coincided with becoming an almost Austin Powers-style figure renowned for a succession of affairs with beautiful women, owning bizarre gadgets and maintaining a fleet of more than 50 sports cars. After separating from his second wife Britt Ekland in 1968, he became the lover of Princess Margaret and even entertained the idea that they could marry. Despite boasting of marathon sex sessions with HRH, and hinting that they were also joined by one of Margaret's lesbian lovers, Sellers made the mistake of introducing the Princess to Warren Beatty, whom she also welcomed into her bed.

ELVIS WANTED TO BE AN FBI INFORMANT

If the King were alive today, as many of his fans (or believers, given that there are now registered churches of Elvis) think he is, surely he would make his comeback in the law courts and sue those who have been lying about him since his death in 1977.

The most notorious lie told about Elvis Presley is that he made the racist comment: "The only thing black people can do for me is shine my shoes and buy my music." Many have wanted to prove that the performer who took black music and made it acceptable to white audiences said this, but there is no evidence he uttered the words. (That doesn't stop mainstream papers and mainstream journalists repeating it as fact.)

One area where the secret side of Presley's life and the belief that he is living in hiding come together is over his relationship with the Federal Bureau of Investigation. Even though most children grow up knowing that no one likes a snitch, Elvis wanted nothing more than to spy secretly on his show business colleagues and then betray their trust by ratting to the FBI.

When the King travelled to Washington in 1970, he asked President Nixon to make him a FBI agent, a favour Nixon was happy to grant, giving him a badge and making him an honorary agent. A few days later, Elvis asked to meet the Director of the FBI, J Edgar Hoover. While Hoover's aides decided the meeting was inappropriate (due to the entertainer's "wearing of all sorts of exotic dress") the King was given a tour of the FBI headquarters.

During this visit Elvis asked if he could become an informant, ratting on celebrities who were using narcotics and "poisoning the minds of young people with their politics". An FBI report of the visit recorded that: "In this regard he indicated that should the Bureau ever have need of his services he can be reached under the pseudonym of Colonel Jon Burrows, 3764 Highway 51, South, Memphis, Tennessee."

below The King Fu-using, crime-fighting king of rock 'n' roll comes face to face with criminal mastermind President Richard Nixon.

BRITNEY SPEARS – A CAREER BASED ON LIES

One of the differences between celebrities of earlier years and today is that those in the past had a modicum of talent and were known for more than scantily clad dancing in promotional videos. Seizing on a zeitgeist that allows mediocre dancers to achieve star status, the management team behind Britney Spears has made her one of the globe's most recognized faces.

Her management has turned her Warholian 15 minutes into a long-lived career and got her the type of stardom where her record company feels no sense of shame in describing her as an "American cultural icon".

However, Britney's carefully crafted image has been built on a series of lies designed to win her a strong fan base and media coverage. The most famous lie – and one that won her support from the Catholic Church – was: "Yes I am a virgin and I do not want to try to have sex until I'm married." Such statements made her a role model with the influential US abstinence movement and deflated criticism of her raunchy image that was limiting her airplay. After several years of pretence, former boyfriend Justin Timberlake exposed the fraud that had been perpetrated on fans and cardinals alike.

Spears maintains an image of a committed Christian while studying the Kabbalah, a Jewish mystical system, which makes her a heretic in two religions. When criticized for her role in the sexualization of pre-pubescent girls, Spears said she was not trying to generate a sexy image; her next video featured her kissing Madonna. Spears also said: "I don't believe in drugs or even smoking," yet later she was photographed drinking scotch and smoking.

Spears spoke out publicly against pressure on teenage girls to have perfect bodies and took an anti-plastic surgery stance. When challenged over her own implants, she claimed that her radical change in bra-size was purely the result of "a growth spurt" despite the photographed telltale signs of surgery.

There is something very wrong with a culture that not only rewards mediocrity, but offers no censure for a career created on the back of a series of ridiculous lies.

right Oops! She did it again. Regarded as a heretic in two religions and an American cultural icon by her record company, Britney Spears has faced allegations of mendacity.

NOTHING TO SEE

*"We dance round in a ring and suppose,
But the Secret sits in the middle and knows."*
Robert Frost

In our digital and interconnected age it is easy to be fooled into thinking every secret can be found somewhere on the Internet. It is also easy to imagine that satellite surveillance means there is no longer anywhere capable of being hidden from view.

These widely held beliefs make the idea that governments and others still tell lies about a raft of locations seem ridiculous and even quaint. However, beneath our feet and under our noses are a host of secret buildings deeply connected to those in power. We are often told downright lies about the real nature of places that sometimes drop off official maps. This section will give you the chance to learn the secret locations and true purposes of a host of sensitive places.

The right to privacy is not a right to secrecy or an excuse to tell lies about issues of genuine public interest – even for our governments. The age of denying where government laboratories and military complexes are actually based did not end with Cold War paranoia and neither the public nor foreign nations are to be trusted with real facts of what occurs within their walls.

Many other groups have good reasons for not revealing where certain places are located and what happens at those places. After all, if they did not make a supreme effort at secrecy and obfuscation of the truth, they might have curious authors sneaking into their underground courtrooms or gate crashing their secret shindigs.

LISTENING TO THE WORLD VIA MENWITH HILL

In 1999, comedian, investigative journalist and political activist Mark Thomas did something risky, brave and exceptionally funny. To help expose the lies surrounding illegal spying operations, he flew a hot air balloon over RAF Menwith Hill.

Thomas was in no danger from aircraft traffic as the RAF part of the title of the base on the moors of North Yorkshire is a fiction to disguise the fact that it is run by America's National Security Agency (NSA). What appears to be an area of English countryside spoilt by a bizarre collection of white golf-ball-like structures is in fact 562 acres of American soil and Thomas risked being shot for invading US airspace.

Officially known as NSA Field Station F83, Menwith is the European base of ECHELON operations that allow for the interception of more than eight million phone calls, faxes, emails and text messages per hour. Despite being highly computerized, more than 1,200 NSA staff work at the site, while British military forces under the command of an American officer provide security.

Without the approval of Britain's Parliament, the site was given to America in 1956 under terms that remain highly classified. The territory given to the USA has become home to the largest regional intelligence station in the world. More than 27 golf-ball-like objects up to 62 metres in diameter (officially called radomes) are scattered across the landscape, along with assorted satellite dishes and microwave installations, giving it the appearance of a futuristic sci-fi outpost.

Menwith Hill also plays a crucial role in America's "Star Wars" project. Among the equipment employed at the site is some for the Space Based Infrared System designed to give enough advance warning for the use of space-based weapons. Linked directly to US Space Command, Menwith and the US-controlled Pine Gap base in Australia are crucial to America's military domination of space.

MP Alice Mahon criticized the secrecy surrounding Menwith, stating: "Despite many attempts to get answers to questions, it is quite clear that Menwith Hill is not accountable to MPs and therefore not accountable to the British people."

`below` Many see the radomes that blot the Yorkshire landscape as visible signs of a secretive evil empire of Star Wars installations that are spread across the globe.

BOHEMIAN GROVE – SECRET PLAYGROUND OF THE RICH AND POWERFUL

Situated among the beautiful redwood forests of Sonoma County, California, is the home of a secretive playground for rich and powerful men, known as Bohemian Grove. Hidden away in the privately owned 2,712-acre estate of forested hills, whitewater rapids and rocky cannons is a network of wooden lodges and an open-air arena by a lake where prime ministers, presidents, soon-to-be-presidents, military chiefs and some of the world's most important businessmen come for a special "summer camp".

Originally set up under the auspices of the San Francisco Bohemian Club at the end of the nineteenth century, the week-long camp attended by political leaders, financiers and key global figures has evolved into an unofficial high-level summit. The camps have proved politically influential in the past with the go-ahead for the development of the US atomic bomb research, stemming from ideas discussed at Bohemian Grove. Among those known to have attended in recent years include President George W Bush and his father, Donald Rumsfeld, David Rockefeller, former UK prime minister John Major, Arnold Schwarzenegger and Henry Kissinger.

Cloaked in secrecy (there is no official published lists of attendees), with a phalanx of secret service agents to ensure privacy, there is no mainstream media coverage of the camp. In the information void that has developed, rumour has run rife.

Until US researcher Alex Jones and British author Jon Ronson managed to infiltrate a meeting in 2000, no one had taken seriously talk of giant owl statues being burnt, mock human sacrifice and druidic rites. They had always been dismissed until Jones and Ronson came back with the video evidence.

Some researchers have tried to suggest that Bohemian Grove is no different from the week-long Burning Man festival held on the playa of the Black Rock Desert in Nevada, 120 miles north of Reno. Comparing a radical, open community of 35,000 people committed to self-expression and self-reliance who come together to form a temporary city to a secret, male-only group of the world's rich and powerful – just on the basis that they both burn statues – is exceptionally misguided.

ROOM 801 – THE PLACE WHERE BRITAIN'S "X-FILES" WERE HOUSED

In the seminal TV series "The X-Files", Mulder and Scully's work solving the mysterious and UFO-related cases of the FBI was carried out from cramped office space hidden in the basement of the FBI headquarters. The team working on Britain's "X-Files"-style UFO reports also worked out of cramped office space, hidden away in Room 801 of the old Metropole Hotel building in Northumberland Avenue in the heart of London's Whitehall area.

The ornate hotel had once been used by members of the British royalty (including King Edward VII), when indulging in hanky-panky before it was taken over by the Ministry of Defence in 1936. By 1952, the building was almost exclusively used by the Air Ministry, so when the rash of UFO sightings over Washington that year panicked world leaders, it was natural that the reports would be housed in the Metropole.

Commander Myles Formby and his two staff, whose job it was to collect and analyse UFO reports, were crammed into the small attic room, numbered 801, fighting for space among thousands of files. Reporting to the Deputy Director of Intelligence at the Air Ministry, from this confined and concealed office they oversaw the UK investigation of some startling UFO sightings. The quality of incidents investigated was high and usually involved military personnel, a classic example being the report by RAF pilot Flight Lt J R Salandin on October 4, 1954. He reported nearly colliding his Meteor jet with "a huge metallic object shaped like two saucers pressed together" over North Weald in Essex.

The 10,000-word secret report based on Formby's work written in 1954 is still classified, and his team's responsibility for investigating UFOs moved elsewhere into the MoD. It is believed that the current base of operations is situated at RAF Rudloe Manor. It is open to speculation whether the MoD official policy remains (as they reported to the USAF in 1965): "To play down the subject of UFOs and to avoid attaching undue attention or publicity to it. As a result we have never had any serious political pressure to mount a large scale investigation."

HOW THE VATICAN SECRETLY HOUSES A HUGE LIBRARY OF SATANIC, OCCULT AND PORNOGRAPHIC BOOKS

It is hard to imagine that the Pope reads anything other than the Holy Bible, but if he did wish for some more exotic bedtime reading, the Vatican Secret Archives could provide him with more satanic, occult, pornographic and heretical works than any other library in the world.

While elements of the Vatican Library have been open to the public since the fifteenth century, the cardinal in charge of the endeavour ensures that all of the juicy stuff is kept hidden. The Catholic Church started the library at the beginning of the fourth century, recording not only its own details but also those of heretical Christians and Gnostic sects. Although it officially claims that everything before the ninth century was lost "for reasons not entirely known", the majority of the material still exists but access is strictly controlled.

The Papal Inquisition brought many new titles into the clandestine collection, but it was the creation of Index Librorum Prohibitorum (Index of Forbidden Books) that gave the biggest boost to the Vatican Library's secret section. Under the Index, copies of any heretical, satanic, occult or pornographic works discovered were immediately lodged with the Pope's librarians. Even legitmate Catholic scholars find access to many of the classified books difficult. One Jesuit working in the Vatican explained: "Control is achieved through not indexing material because you cannot request what you do not know exists."

On another side of the library are the archives of Papal and Church papers. It takes real confidence in your power to keep buried what you do not want others to know, to call your repository of suppressed papers documents something as blatant as the Vatican Secret Archives. Headed up by a cardinal in the same way that the Vatican Library is, the Secret Archives are home to everything the Church wants kept in the dark, including Nazi collaboration and scandals dating back to the earliest periods in its history. Vast, purposefully disorganized and running to more than 24 miles of shelves, the Archives are only open to those with direct approval from the Pope.

right The Papal Inquisition's Index of Forbidden Books means that the Vatican Library has an unrivalled secret collection of pornographic and occult books.

A different type of aircraft carrier – a USAF C-5 Galaxy flew into Boscombe to collect the wreckage of the ultra-secret craft that had crashed there.

RAF BOSCOMBE – THE UK'S ANSWER TO AREA 51

It is no coincidence that the areas in the UK generating the most reports of UFOs are in the vicinity of the two most secretive Royal Air Force bases currently in operation. Scotland's RAF Machrihanish at Campbelltown on the Mull of Kintyre boasts a two-mile runway and regular sighting of mysterious flying craft, while RAF Boscombe Down, in spitting distance of Stonehenge in Wiltshire, produces so many UFO sightings that it has been nicknamed "Britain's Area 51".

Covering an area much larger than any nearby towns, the Boscombe Down complex (which includes a series of underground buildings) has been located in such a way that it is effectively shielded from public view. Security at the base is at the highest levels seen in the UK. Even before 9/11, anyone anywhere near the base could be met by force from the constant security patrols. More than one innocent holidaymaker has been confronted with a guard waving a gun in their faces simply for being lost.

Run by the Defence Evaluation and Research Agency (DERA) – the arm of the military responsible for testing experimental weaponry – Boscombe Down is the home of several highly classified programmes. One of the aircraft currently being put through its paces at the airbase is the UK's secret project entitled HALO (High Agility, Low Observability), thought to be responsible for many of the UFO sightings.

On September 26, 1994, the secrecy surrounding Boscombe was almost exploded by the downing of a US black project vehicle. Within an hour of the crash, units from both the SAS and SBS were patrolling the base. They were soon joined by a phalanx of CIA agents (according to one of my sources, "There were more agents than when a President comes to town") who flew in on a special Boeing 737. The wreckage of whatever crashed was retrieved when a massive C-5 Galaxy (usually used as "Space Program Outsized Load Carrier") landed at Boscombe.

The Ministry of Defence refuses to comment on the incident or the nature of the craft being tested at the airbase.

AN UNDERGROUND MASONIC COURTROOM IN THE HEART OF LONDON'S WEST END

If any part of London is the beating heart of London's West End, it is Piccadilly Circus, an intersection of some of the most famous streets in the world. With its neon apocalypse of advertising signs and the famous statue of Eros (whose real name is The Angel of Christian Charity) it has become a tourist attraction in its own right.

Thousands of people pass over Piccadilly Circus every day and yet none are aware that beneath their feet lies a secret Masonic temple, also used as London's Freemason Court, where Masonic judges and lawyers put on trial their Brothers in the Craft who have broken Masonic law. Outside of Freemasonry, few people know of its existence, though it was used as a location in Alan Moore's influential novel *From Hell*. Its status as a real place has been questioned. It should not be. It exists and is part of a larger collection of Masonic temples in the Piccadilly Circus area.

In the late Victorian period, a series of above-ground and underground temples was constructed to cater for Freemasons whose other gentlemen's clubs were located in the West End and Westminster. Although not in use today, there is still a Masonic temple on the top floor of the famous Lillywhites store, though similar temples at the top of the Regent Palace Hotel, the Trocadero and 7-11 Coventry Street (now an HMV record shop) are no longer in use.

A similar number of temples was constructed underground. At least two remain in full operation, including the one in the basement of the Café Royal, which is entered through a secret door in a cloakroom. The courtroom could be entered from the old Criterion restaurant and through another location (which I cannot reveal for legal reasons as this was the route I used to investigate it). The Freemason Court also functioned as the Masonic temple connected to the lodge that drew its members from the Hardwicke Society (a debating club for London's judges, lawyers and barristers), which provided the judges of the court.

FORT HALSTEAD – THE MOST SENSITIVE AND SECRET LABORATORY IN THE UK

There have only been a few times in my career as a journalist when I have been told: "Don't look into that, it will get you killed." Of course, hearing this is a red rag to a bull for any curious author. I was warned that I risked being shot when I began looking into Fort Halstead, the UK's most secretive scientific establishment.

Walking on the public footpaths in the countryside near the base is an eerie experience, as you are constantly aware of being tracked by numerous CCTV cameras. If you leave the paths, you quickly trip hidden electronic surveillance systems, and few are brave enough to try further investigation after the warning klaxons sound.

Built on the site of a fort that was part of the English defences against Napoleon, Fort Halstead in Kent is hidden near the inside of the South East boundary of the M25 orbital motorway. The base is one of the three research facilities that the UK Defence Science and Technology Laboratory (DSTL) network did not place in the hands of the private sector because it is far too sensitive.

Labelled on ordinance survey maps of the area simply as "works", Fort Halstead comprises a complex of 181 buildings above ground, two helipads and a major underground complex (whose existence was confirmed to me by an employee of a firm contracted to refit at the base). The site has always been at the forefront of British secret weapon research. The UK's first atomic weapon was assembled there in 1947 under the supervision of Lord Penney, who had helped develop America's atomic weapons at Los Alamos.

Recruited from all scientific disciplines, but never below PhD level, researchers at Fort Halstead work on sensitive programme. These range from world-leading development of improving the yield of weapons using depleted uranium (the amount that is used and stored at the base, along with other nuclear materials, is surprisingly high) and military applied magnetic mapping to exotic and almost unbelievable research into invisibility, electromagnetic weaponry and applied genetics.

MOUNT WEATHER – HOME OF THE US UNDERGROUND GOVERNMENT SYSTEM

In the minutes after the second plane hit the World Trade Center on the morning of 9/11, as George W Bush sat reading *My Pet Goat* with schoolchildren in Florida, Vice President Dick Cheney and National Security Adviser Condoleezza Rice were sitting in the Presidential Emergency Operations Center – a hardened bunker buried beneath the East Wing of the White House. The thing uppermost in their minds was deciding where to go next.

They had two options. Mount Raven or Mount Weather – the two secret bases built to ensure "Continuity of Government" (CoG) in the event of nuclear war or other national emergency. Sitting in the White House bunker, big Dick ordered everyone designated as a successor to the president – from the Speaker of the House of Representatives to the entire Cabinet – into Marine Corps helicopters that are always kept ready exclusively for this purpose. They were then flown to the Federal Emergency Management Agency's bunker, known as the High Point Special Facility, inside Mount Weather near Berryville, Virginia, 48 miles from Washington DC.

Mount Weather was started in the 1950s and finished in the 1970s at a cost of more than $1 billion, and there is little visible above ground to be seen, except a few small office buildings and a network of satellite and microwave dishes that keep it in constant contact with the White House. However, behind an eight-foot-thick door built deep into the mountain's granite is a small secret city complete with its own power plant, radio and television studio, hospital, cinema, private reservoir, crematorium and sleeping spaces for thousands of people.

The veil of secrecy over Mount Weather has never been fully penetrated. In 1975 Senator John Tunney tried to get to the root of why it held files on more than 100,000 Americans and what was stored on the arrays of "bubble-domed computer banks". However, officials stonewalled the two Senate hearings he managed to hold on the issue. The list of those who make up the 6,500 strong "survivor's list" to be taken to Mount Weather also remains a guarded secret.

RUDLOE MANOR – THE UK'S SECRET MILITARY NERVE CENTRE

I first heard rumours about Rudloe Manor while investigating claims made by a former member of the UK's Special Boat Squadron that he had been taken to the RAF facility there for debriefing after coming across something strange during a mission in Antarctica.

Although the original story collapsed under rigorous investigation, it did lead me to make further study of RAF Rudloe Manor – one of the UK's most important secret bases. Situated a few miles southeast of the town of Bath, Rudloe Manor is the name of an above-ground installation that forms part of an intricate network of linked underground sites collectively known as the Corsham Complex.

Officially, RAF Rudloe Manor is purely administrative and the home of No. 1 and No. 6 Signals Units, the MoD Communications Network, Provost and Security Service (special military police) and Headquarters Defence Fixed Telecommunications Systems. However, it has an established secret history as one of the bases where UK UFO sightings were investigated by the military and as an often brutal centre for internal security interrogations.

The Manor looks like a standard English stately home but is linked by tunnels to the rest of the labyrinthine Corsham Complex.

Originally the underground rock quarries and mines at Corsham were used for ammunition storage during the Second World War. A branch line of the main London-Bristol railway ran directly into what was known as Tunnel Quarry, which meant that not only did the military have access to miles of underground tunnels and storage areas, they had a means of transporting arms with ease. These characteristics ensured that during the Cold War Corsham was redeveloped as Britain's key military nerve centre in the event of nuclear war.

Powered by a nuclear reactor, Corsham has developed into a vast underground city fed by a secret rail route. It is now home to what is euphemistically referred to as the Corsham Computer Centre – a "black project" that has transformed the underground base into a back-up seat of government (and royalty) in the event of a national emergency.

CHEYENNE MOUNTAIN – HOME OF THE SPACE COMMAND

From *War Games* to *Stargate*, whenever you see a road disappearing into a secret mountain base in a Hollywood movie, it's based on military facilities at Cheyenne Mountain situated near Colorado Springs in the Rockies.

Built in the 1950s in anticipation of the growing Soviet nuclear capability, the road passes through the iconic visual entrance and makes for a strange journey. Once past the 25-ton blast doors, the two-lane highway, complete with traffic lights, continues for more than a mile into the rock. The base was built using 1.5 million pounds of dynamite at a modern-day cost of $18 billion. Given its exposure in movies, it is not exactly confidential that Cheyenne Mountain is the HQ of the North American Air Defense Command (NORAD), the arm of the US military responsible for watching the skies for enemy aircraft and missiles.

However, the really hush-hush operations undertaken by the 1,300 people living and working in the subterranean city mounted on thousands of steel springs (to help it withstand a nuclear blast better), revolve around US Space Command,

which is also based there. Formed in 1985, the space capabilities of the US army, navy, air force and marines are brought together under the central control of Space Command. Linked to the nearby Space Warfare Center at Schriever Air Force Base, its official duties are monitoring the 8,200 manmade objects in orbit and maintaining military satellite capability. Space Command does much more than that though.

Unofficial duties of Space Command include the training and maintenance of America's space marines (an elite force trained to fight in zero gravity and whose existence is denied), the tracking of any unidentified UFOs entering the Earth's atmosphere (but not thought to be a missile) and the monitoring and maintenance of all space surveillance and weapons systems (including all of the black project-funded ones that are not meant to exist). Cheyenne Mountain is also home to the Space Battlelab facility that undertakes pioneering work on space-based weapons, including the development of firearms designed for use in zero gravity and pressurized craft.

`below` Beyond the iconic entrance to Cheyenne Mountain, immortalized in many films, lies the secrets of both NORAD and US Space Command.

DRUGS AND MEDICINE

13

The discovery that you are being lied to and information is being kept from you always hurts more when those that you trust most are doing it. Our politicians and security services have proven so duplicitous we are almost immune to the outrage that should naturally flow from exposure of their many falsehoods. We are in such a sorry state that those in the intelligence agencies who compile dodgy dossiers get promoted while those politicians who use them to deceive us in order to start a war get re-elected rather than booted out of office.

However, there are many groups in our society that we generally still trust. One of them is the medical profession. This is natural. You have to have a degree of belief in those in whose hands you may have to place your life. The discovery that these gods in white coats have suppressed the truth and lied to us over the years as much as anyone else to protect their profession's reputation can come as a painful shock.

If we cannot trust those who prescribe legal drugs to cure our ills to tell us the truth, it at least means that it is less of a surprise to discover that those leading the war against illegal drugs have plenty of hidden agendas and hushed-up facts that the public would be horrified to uncover. Neither doctors nor government drug tsars seem willing to trust the public with full, open knowledge about the drugs taken for either medicinal or recreational purposes.

DOCTORS INFECTED 400 PRISONERS WITH MALARIA WITHOUT TELLING THEM WHAT WAS BEING DONE

When Dr Alf Alving died, the obituary columns all noted the role he had played in medicine by developing the first standard preventive pill for malaria. Many were gushing in their praise. If you check the University of Chicago website, they still proudly boast of him on their "Distinguished Chicago Scholars" page. The obituaries fail to mention – and the university continues to fail to mention – the fact that many people regard Dr Alving as a war criminal.

In 1942, while working for the US Army's Office of Scientific Research and Development, Dr Alving led the team whose aim was to gain, in his own words, "a better profile of malaria and develop a treatment for it". To aid in his research, he experimented on 441 predominately black convicts from the Statesville Penitentiary, Illinois.

At the Nuremberg trials, when Nazi doctors were being tried for the war crime of experimenting on patients without their consent, their defence lawyers cited the work of Dr Richard P Strong, a Professor of Tropical Medicine at Harvard, who had infected and killed convicts with bubonic plague (survivors were rewarded with cigars). They also cited the work of Dr Alving.

The convicts had not been told what was going to be done to them, only that they were "helping with the war effort". The defence lawyers argued that without knowing they were being given transfusions of malaria-infected blood, they could not give informed consent (especially as many of them were mentally subnormal) and that Alving should also be on trial for the resulting deaths.

The response by the US authorities was that many prisoners had volunteered (although some had to be coerced) and that the Nuremberg Code was to apply in cases of "barbarism", not research undertaken by "normal doctors in the civilised world". No charges of any kind were ever brought against Alving.

The *British Medical Journal* recorded comments from a British scientist who had worked with the American doctors. The scientist reported that one doctor had said: "Criminals in our penitentiaries are fine experimental material – and much cheaper than chimpanzees."

`below` The friendly face of medical care - some US doctors during World War Two fell well short of the ethical standards displayed by those doctors fighting malaria today.

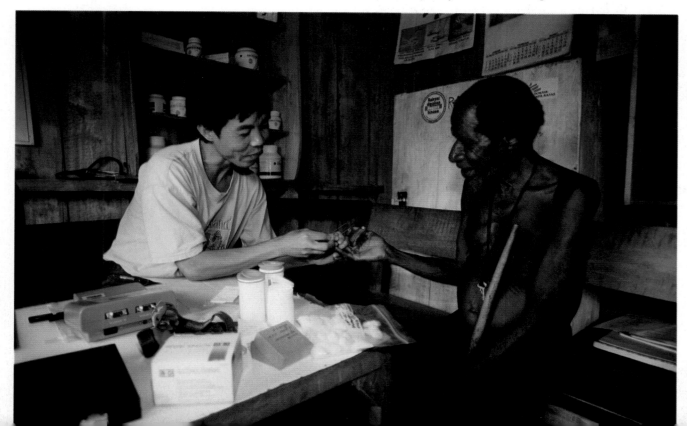

above Members of the cult of Bwiti prepare to consume iboga - the sacred drug that both cures addiction and seems to allow users to catch glimpses of their past lives.

CIA RESEARCH INTO PSYCHEDELIC DRUGS HELPED IN THE DISCOVERY OF IBOGAINE, A DRUG THAT APPEARS TO CURE A RANGE OF ADDICTIONS

In 1953 the CIA began MK-ULTRA, a secret programme dedicated to brainwashing and mind-control. A strong focus of the project was research into drugs that could be part of the process of breaking someone down.

Building on the work of Nazi scientists recruited to MK-ULTRA, one of the first drugs investigated was Ibogaine, a psychoactive indole alkaloid derived from the rootbark of the African plant *Tabernanthe iboga*. The plant is used in central Africa by the Mitsogo and Fang people as part of their religious ceremonies to induce visions in which they believe they step outside of time and are able to view their lives from a different perspective and meet a deity called Bwiti.

When the head of MK-ULTRA learned that Ibogaine could induce a 36-hour trip, he prioritized experiments with it, believing the length of the drug experience made it ideal for brainwashing. He was disappointed that even when combined with torture, those who took Ibogaine reported a spiritual experience that let them reassess their lives. Several agents quit the CIA after taking the drug. Author

Philip K Dick suspected the CIA might have dosed him with Ibogaine at one point when he began having visions of past lives and came into what he believed was telepathic contact with an entity from the future called VALIS.

It was through CIA links to the underground science community in the early 1960s that Ibogaine came to be discovered by researchers such as Howard Lotsof, who recognized those with addictions of any kind came out of the experience cured of their need for cocaine, heroin, alcohol or nicotine.

Today, more scientists are confirming that the drug-induced experience of stepping out of time, reviewing your life and meeting some form of "intelligence" (which often echo the descriptions of Bwiti) does cure addiction. Dr Deborah Mash, professor of Neurology and Molecular and Cellular Pharmacology at the University of Miami, has said: "I didn't believe it when I first heard about Ibogaine. I thought it was something that needed to be debunked but it is effective for blocking opiate withdrawal, diminishes the desire to use alcohol and blocks cocaine cravings."

TWO POPES AND VARIOUS MEMBERS OF EUROPEAN ROYALTY, INCLUDING QUEEN VICTORIA, REGULARLY USED TO ENJOY WINE LACED WITH COCAINE

Ange-François Mariani was a genius. The Corsican-born inventor may have been a mediocre chemist, but he excelled at marketing the product that bore his name – *Vin Mariani* ("Mariani's wine").

In 1863 he began researching the properties of the coca plant and its extract cocaine. Having become a keen user of the substance, he hit upon the idea of mixing it with a Bordeaux red wine. Not just trusting in the potency of his product, Mariani began aggressive advertising. He also had the savvy to recognize the power of celebrity endorsement and began sending cases to leading figures. Once hooked on the cocaine-laced wine, it was not hard to get testimonials from presidents, popes, members of various royal families and even "Buffalo Bill" Cody.

Although Mariani tried to keep the exact balance of ingredients secret, other chemists at the time recorded that *Vin Mariani* contained 0.12 grains of cocaine per fluid ounce. Given that the recommended daily intake of the drink was a "claret glass full before and after every meal",

drinkers could be taking up to 2.16 grains of cocaine per day. This type of cocaine usage was more than enough to justify the ads' claims to "chase away fatigue" and "make you feel good" more than justified.

Among the high-profile drinkers of Mariani's wine were Queen Victoria, Pope Pius X and Pope Leo III, President Ulysses S Grant, the Shah of Persia and inventor Thomas Edison. Science fiction writers H G Wells and Jules Verne were both fans, as was novelist Emile Zola. When Louis Bleriot became the first aviator to cross the English Channel, Mariani's ads were able to truthfully claim he did it with the help of a flask of *Vin Mariani*.

Angelo became the world's first cocaine-based millionaire as the success of *Vin Mariani* led to an explosion of other products containing cocaine, including John S Pemberton's invention – Coca-Cola – which was designed to appeal to teetotal drinkers who wanted a bit of extra vim in their beverage. Public concern over growing cocaine addiction led to *Vin Mariani* being withdrawn from sale in 1914.

PATIENTS WHO HAVE HAD MEDICAL SCANS CAN SET OFF RADIATION ALARMS

A lot of things changed in America after 9/11. One of them was an incredible increase in the number of radiation detectors in use. It is now estimated that there are more than 12,000 in operation at airports, train stations, tunnels and bridges along with the small portable scanners given to those working in roles such as border patrol.

The introduction of the record number of detectors was not only to prevent al-Qaeda smuggling and transporting radioactive materials, but also to allow the emergency services called to any terrorist bombing to know if a radioactive "dirty bomb" had been used. It quickly became apparent that there was going to be a problem: so many radioactive people were walking around that a ridiculously high number of false alarms was being triggered.

Treatments from iodine therapy used to treat thyroid cancer to cardiac exams and CAT scans were reported to be setting the alarms off. In Santa Fe, California, a full-scale alert was sounded – with the highway being shut down – while

a search for a nuclear device was carried out, purely because a man who had a scan walked past a fire engine with its radiation monitor switched on. Radiation is measured in rems and millirems and the monitor was set to detect 75 millirems (five times the naturally occurring radiation level).

The spate of false alarms exposed the lack of information given to many people having medical scans. The benefits of a necessary scan outweigh the increased risk of cancer by exposure to radiation, but even some doctors are concerned that their colleagues order unnecessary CAT scans without telling patients the full facts. None mention that a CAT scan gives a radiation dose of 1,300 millirems, the equivalent of being at a distance of 1.5 miles from the Hiroshima explosion.

Surveys in America have shown that seven per cent of CAT scans are not needed (scans that cost patients up to $16 billion per year) and that 78 per cent of doctors do not know the level of radiation involved in a scan. How can patients have informed choice when their doctors are so ignorant?

UNTIL THE MID-1980S, DENTAL PORCELAIN USED TO CONTAIN URANIUM

Many of the official bodies regulating dentistry continue to tell us that there is nothing harmful about the use of mercury in amalgam fillings. Not everyone believes them that a filling containing half a gram of a toxic substance with links to infertility and immune system problems is safe. In the state of Maine in the USA, Governor Angus King introduced a law requiring dentists to inform their patients fully about the potential negative effects of mercury.

King is not alone in believing that the exapmple of the use of mercury is not the first time that dentists have not told their patients all of the facts about what they are having placed in their mouths. From the 1940s right through to the mid-1980s, uranium was widely used in dental porcelains to give a natural colour and fluorescence to dentures and crowns. Dentists tended not to tell their patients that their new teeth were radioactive.

Uranium in artificial teeth was introduced in 1942. Up until 1945, there was little public concern over radiation, with products containing traces of radium such as radium water and radium soap promoted as health remedies. However, the atomic devastation of Japan had alerted people to the dangers of radiation, so the dental ceramic manufacturers decided not to reveal what the special ingredient was that helped make their teeth glow. The US Atomic Energy Commission aided them in this by giving them an exemption to continue using uranium.

Although the amount of uranium used in dental porcelain was small, for many users it was bombarding the oral tissue with 600 rems per year (rems are the standard radiation measurement unit). Depending on the amount of dental porcelain someone had, they could get an annual dose more than 20 times the level of normal background radiation. Manufacturers phased out uranium in the 1980s when the alternative elements for generating fluorescence became cheaper than uranium. We can only hope that future scientists do not discover that the cerium, terbium, dysprosium and samarium now used pose any health risk.

`below` Open wide – visiting the dentist has always filled most people with horror; in the past it might have also meant they were filled with uranium as well.

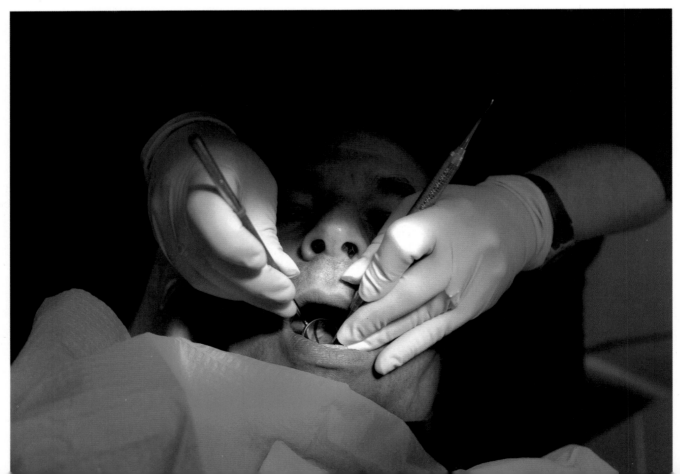

THE AWARD-WINNING MENTAL HOSPITALS DESIGNED BY ARCHITECTS WORKING ON LSD

In the war against some drugs (because as more than one wise man has said, alcohol and tobacco have not yet had "shock and awe" declared on them by any drug tsar) the propaganda battle means that the potential benefits of substances are kept as secret as possible. Suitably reviled for its abuse, lysergic acid diethylamide, commonly called LSD, has a clandestine history of use in science, engineering and architecture.

Though the use of LSD as a source of inspiration by renowned scientists and mathematicians is now starting to be exposed, the public has been kept unaware of its role in architecture. One rare instance where it is acknowledged that a prominent architect took the substance to help him design a building is the case of Kyoshi Izumi's work on the Yorkton Mental Health Center in Saskatchewan, Canada.

Wanting to understand how mentally ill people perceived their surroundings so that he could create a more positive environment for their treatment, Izumi began to take LSD on visits to old mental asylums. He found himself terrified of the glistening tiles, the bars on the windows and the endless corridors. Using the insights he gained while on LSD, Izumi went on to develop what has been called the "ideal mental hospital".

The American Psychiatric Association presented the hospital with a special award to acknowledge its revolutionary design. They admitted that: "Izumi is a pioneer in psychiatric architecture. The result of his work must rank among the most attractive and architecturally advanced buildings constructed for psychiatric services." Using the principles he established to make mental hospitals less threatening for patients, several other award-winning buildings have been constructed across America.

It is not only hospitals that have been built with the use of LSD. In the drug's 1960s heyday, it was the inspiration for a number of public buildings. The designer of one shopping centre recalled: "I was blank about what to do until I took LSD. Suddenly I saw the finished project. I began to draw, trying to keep up with the images. Within minutes I had completed four sheets of comprehensive sketches."

THE US GOVERNMENT'S INDIAN HEALTH SERVICE CARRIED OUT MASS STERILIZATIONS ON NATIVE AMERICAN WOMEN

The American government's relationship with the Native American tribes has not been a happy one and is characterized by the abuse of trust and power by the US authorities. One of the worst abuses of trust that happened relatively recently was carried out by US government doctors, and it echoes much older policies designed to reduce the numbers of Native Americans.

In the 1970s, Dr Connie Redbird Uri Pinkerman, a Choctaw Indian physician, was working for the Indian Health Service (IHS) – a healthcare programme for Native Americans living on reservations. She was going through records and noticed that a large number of sterilizations had been performed, including abnormal numbers of hysterectomies. She was concerned because as she later commented: "In normal medical practice, hysterectomies are rare in women of child bearing age unless there is cancer or other medical problems." There were no such problems in the cases she uncovered.

Investigating further she discovered that many of the operations had been performed after the patients had been coerced by IHS workers into signing consent forms. Typically this was done by telling the woman involved that she was a bad mother for having too large a family and that her children would be taken into care unless the operation was undertaken. Some women were actually told that the operation would still allow them to give birth.

Dr Pinkerman persuaded South Dakota senator James Abourezk to instigate an inquiry by the investigative arm of Congress – the General Accounting Office – into the number of sterilizations performed and the pressure being used to force women to have hysterectomies. Looking at just four areas covered by the IHS, they found 3,406 women had been sterilized in a four-year period. The statistics for just one tribe, the Navajo, showed that the rate of sterilization had more than doubled from 15 per cent to more than 30 per cent. They also discovered that the consent forms did not comply with regulations. After their report, IHS policy on sterilization was changed, but it had already left lasting scars on the women's lives and government-tribal trust.

MANY VACCINES GIVEN TO CHILDREN CONTAIN ADDITIVES SUCH AS MERCURY

For many parents, the first hint they had that their children may have been getting more than modern medicine's miracle-like protection with their vaccinations came with the controversy over possible links between the MMR vaccine and autism.

Although there is still division among scientists over whether MMR has a role in the onset of autism (with the majority of the medical establishment still believing that there is insufficient data to establish a causal link between the two) it did highlight the secrecy surrounding vaccine additives.

Vaccines are usually produced by weakening a toxic bacterium or a live virus by passing it through animal tissue such as chicken embryos or monkey kidneys. In addition to the primary ingredient that provides the protective immune response, many vaccines given both to children and adults contain small amounts of metals such as mercury, chemicals such as formaldehyde, thimerosal (a mercury derivative), ethylene glycol (aka anti-freeze) and proteins known to cause allergic reactions.

Alternative health campaigner Jock Doubleday offered a $20,000 challenge to the head of any major pharmaceutical company if they would "publicly drink a mixture of standard vaccine additive ingredients in the same amount as a six-year-old child is recommended to receive".'To date, no chief executive of any pharmaceutical company has taken him up on the chance to claim the cash.

While the medical establishment claims that the preservatives and additives "pose little risk", on the basis of wanting informed choice, many parents and patients' rights groups have started petitioning for pharmaceutical companies to provide full lists of all vaccine ingredients to the public in open and accessible ways. Naturally, the companies have opposed this move.

The irony is that the drug companies' attempts at secrecy in the listing of ingredients may be unnecessary. Most parents will not buy a product in the supermarket without checking the ingredient list on the back. However, most fail to ask to see the list of ingredients and manufacturers' warnings on the vials of a vaccine that will be used on their child. Laziness and the fear of challenging authority win out again.

ITEMS COMMONLY FOUND IN OUR KITCHENS, SUCH AS LETTUCE AND NUTMEG, CAN ALTER CONSCIOUSNESS IN THE SAME WAY DRUGS DO

If it were widespread knowledge that many entirely legal foods and spices are capable of producing altered states of consciousness, the drug tsars might have to move their war into the kitchens of millions of homes.

It would be grossly irresponsible to provide the information needed for anybody to experiment with the substances detailed in this entry (that is what the Internet is for), so the following is written purely to reveal the truth of the secret life of some legal, innocent-looking vegetation and food flavourings. It is strongly recommended that you do not use the substances detailed as they could seriously jeopardize your health.

Although the properties of nutmeg, lettuce and saffron and other substances are known about by the select band of their regular users, you will not find mention of their more interesting properties in any cookbook or gardening manual. The authorities have actually gone as far as to suggest in drug advice booklets designed for teenagers and on websites that it is an "urban myth" that they "produce any kind of buzz".

The use of such a ridiculous and easy-to-verify lie gives an indication of how strongly the drug tsars do not want anyone knowing about them.

In no standard recipe book will you discover that if the stem a lettuce is cut it will ooze a milky liquid which, when dried, is called lactucarium – lettuce opium. Used by the ancient Egyptians, it mimics many of the properties of opium though at much lower levels. Nor will you read that if taken in the right amount, nutmeg produces extreme mellowness and mild waking hallucinations. The amount needed to produce these effects also brings with it a risk of heart palpitations and vomiting. A safer spice is saffron. However, as one of the most expensive spices in the world, it does not provide a cheap alternative for those wanting to experience its narcotic effects. Also, if you have ever wondered why cats go mad for catnip, it may have something to do the fact that if dried and smoked with tobacco it produces an effect similar to having a weak marijuana spliff at much lower levels and with less side effects.

DOCTORS STILL DO NOT UNDERSTAND HOW ELECTROSHOCK THERAPY WORKS BUT CONTINUE TO USE IT DESPITE THE RISK IT POSES TO SOME PATIENTS

When the word electroshock is mentioned, the images that spring to mind usually come from *One Flew Over The Cuckoo's Nest* and the brutal use of the treatment on Jack Nicholson's character. The depiction of the anarchic human spirit being crushed by having electricity passed through the brain is horrific and haunting. However, the portrayal of forced electroshock is accurate for many patients today, and a series of lies are told by the psychiatric profession to justify it.

Electroshock – also known as electroconvulsive therapy (ECT) – was developed in the 1930s after Italian psychiatrist Ugo Cerletti saw pigs in a slaughterhouse being stunned with electricity to make them docile before having their throats cut. Cerletti then pioneered passing electricity through the brain to induce an artificial seizure as a treatment for schizophrenia. Despite scientists not understanding how it works (they still admit they don't, but they have some interesting guesses), by the 1950s ECT was widely used to treat everything from depression to obsession, homosexuality and truancy.

Many who have experienced electroshock treatments report long-term damage to their memory. The American Psychiatric Association (APA) claimed only 1 in 200 people receiving shock treatment suffered trouble with their memory. When faced with reports showing 50 per cent of patients complained of memory problems, they admitted the figures were "impressionistic" (PR spin for made-up with no factual basis). The APA also claimed only one death in 10,000 persons after ECT, but they were forced to admit this was also "impressionistic" after studies showed the rate was closer to 1 in 200.

Naturally, many people do not want ECT treatment. Despite this, doctors in the UK have the power to force patients to have ECT. While the APA claims there is no forced use of ECT in America, the government's Center for Mental Health Services states that the practice continues. Novelist Ernest Hemingway was devastated by the electroshock treatments he received. He told a friend: "What is the sense of ruining my head and putting me out of business? It was a brilliant cure but we lost the patient."

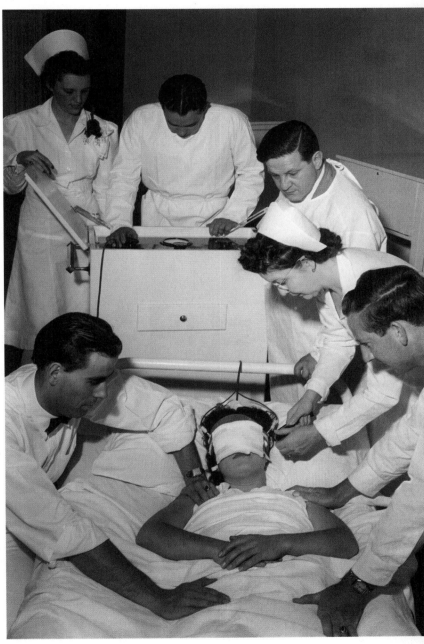

above Shock treatment - electroshock has been inflicted on some of the most creative minds of the twentieth century, including Ernest Hemmingway and Lou Reed.

TECHNOLOGY

14

While today we enjoy greater access to information than ever before, we also have never lived in an age with greater secrecy. Despite a Freedom of Information Act, both in America and the United Kingdom, there has never been a time when more is classified, restricted or deemed sensitive and therefore hidden from us. One of the biggest areas where governments keep the lid on what is going on is in their research and use of cutting edge technology.

When you research the area, it becomes clear that not only are enemy nations being misled about what is being developed, our elected officials often have no idea what the R&D budgets they vote for are spent on.

Researched in secret laboratories, funded by government agencies that do not officially exist and lied about when companies are asked what they are really making, this section will expose the frightening and bizarre side of new technologies being developed today across the world. It will also unravel the facts about those technologies that have been developed, used and continue to be used that we still have not been told the full truth about.

The research and development of new technologies has always had a clandestine element, especially in the cut-throat world of business where there is a fear that rival companies could learn valuable commercial secrets. However, when technology is being developed for military and intelligence agency purposes, the secrecy and misinformation surrounding it reaches outstanding and even deadly levels of control over information.

above NSA Fort Meade HQ in Maryland – ECHELON allows its intelligence analysts to intercept millions of emails and phone calls every hour or every day.

ECHELON – THE SECRET SERVICE COMPUTER SYSTEM THAT SPIES ON ALL OF YOUR EMAILS, FAXES AND PHONE CALLS

They are listening. They are watching and their intelligent computer systems are text mining every electronic communication. This is not paranoia, it's the secret job of the American National Security Agency (NSA), and the codename of the programme illegally monitoring communications on a global level is "Echelon".

There is no doubting that Echelon is the largest electronic spy network ever established. Although run by the NSA, agreements with the UK, Canadian, Australian and New Zealand governments mean that it has posts across the globe linked to a network of 120 satellites. It captures telephone calls, faxes, SMS text messages and emails from anywhere in the world. The system intercepts almost three billion communications daily.

The vast amount of information captured from radio, microwave, fibre-optic, cellular and satellite traffic is then processed through a series of the most sophisticated and powerful supercomputers on the planet, which are called "dictionaries". These then use a series of key words, phrases and names to filter out relevant possible intelligence to be passed on to human NSA agents for further analysis.

Privacy protestors have tried to jam Echelon by using "spookwords" – words known to figure in Echelon's dictionaries – in all communications. The jamming failed because Echelon's text mining and scanning abilities are so sophisticated they can only be triggered by complex word relationships. In other words, it is not enough to use spookwords such as "Artificer", "Theorem", "Barnacle", "Blacker", "Fastlane", "N-TIS", "Vortex-II", "Heritage", "HAARP", "Quicksilver", "Exdrone", "EKMS" or "Darts". You need to use them in a context that makes them meaningful. The software would quickly work out that "MAGIS Bush al-Qaeda DCS" is a meaningless string of words. However, an email, text, or fax that read "George J Tenet, Director, is telling SBU about plateau d'Albion station due to activist sending Solenzara CMSRR logs to al-Qaeda" would be much more likely to pique their interest.

Journalist Duncan Campbell, author of a report on Echelon for the European Parliament, recently revealed that the new NSA codename for Echelon is Magistrand. Don't forget to add that to the spookwords you use.

THE GUN THAT FIRES A MILLION BULLETS A MINUTE

When we see the coverage of the Third Gulf War in a few years time, expect to see terrible new US military weapons ranging from the mysterious flying back triangles being tested in our skies today to "Metal Storm" – an electronic firing system that allows for the building of a gun that can shoot a million bullets a minute.

Developed by Australian Mike O'Dwyers, the technology behind the Metal Storm guns is the most radical and scary development in ballistic weapons for a century. Instead of using mechanical firing pins to shoot bullets, O'Dwyer's guns hold multiple bullets in the barrel which are set off electronically at fractions of a second apart. This allows the bullets to be fired in such rapid succession that they actually push those in front and increase bullet velocity. In one test, a multi-barrel gun was able to deliver a firing rate of one million bullets a minute. For anything in the line of fire it was like walking into a wall of molten lead.

Most of the prototype Metal Storm guns that O'Dwyer is developing for the US and Australian military are highly classified. However, one project under development by O'Dwyer and the US Defense Advanced Research Projects Agency is "Metal Storm Weapons for Urban Environments". This features a combination of a Metal Storm prototype 40mm grenade launcher system attached to a robotic unmanned ground vehicle. It will eventually allow US generals to send in robots firing the fastest guns ever developed into urban areas without risking American lives. (Imagine how much scarier the still secret projects are.)

In his PR, Mike O'Dwyer likes to portray himself as an inventor who has done something worthwhile by creating Metal Storm. He has the *chutzpah* to say: "Part of my motivation came from the fact that my family understands loss in times of war." When Alfred Nobel created his famous prizes, it was because the inventor of dynamite had seen an accidentally published obituary that labelled him "the angel of death". Mr O'Dwyer, whatever you say, you are an angel of death.

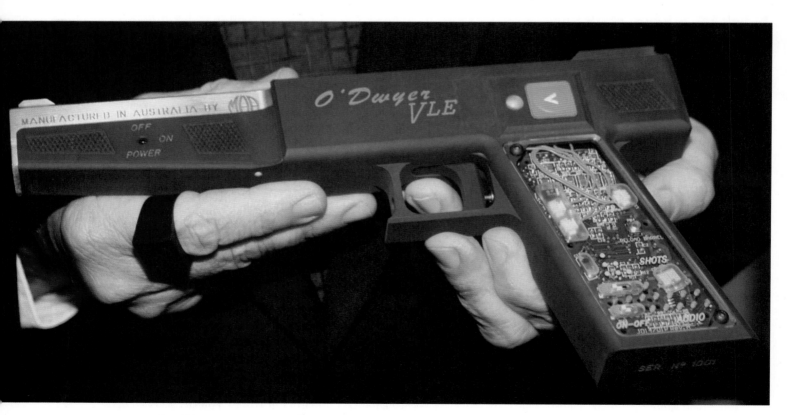

above Metal Storm – The world's first electronic handgun is the perfect weapon for an assassin.

SECRETS OF THE CIA BRAINWASHING PROGRAMME

Having touched upon how CIA brainwashing programme MK-ULTRA used ex-Nazi scientists, saw CIA agents spiking people with LSD and discovered a cure for most addictions, it might be thought there were no more secrets to divulge. However, the CIA knew the project contained even more embarrassing material, which is why it illegally destroyed all of its files on MK-ULTRA in 1972.

However, shredding all of the paperwork was not enough to keep some of the worst excesses of the project hidden. When CIA director Allen Dulless set up MK-ULTRA in April 1953 – in response to Soviet and Chinese experimentation on American prisoners captured during the Korean War – he granted it 6 per cent of the CIA's entire operating budget without any oversight.

One strand of research this funded – without questions being asked – was the work of world-renowned psychiatrist Ewan Cameron. Aside from his clandestine role with the CIA, his acknowledged claims to fame included being the first chairman of the World Psychiatric Association and a member of the Nuremberg medical tribunal. Travelling to Canada to conduct his experiments for MK-ULTRA (the CIA was less squeamish about killing Canadian citizens), Cameron used unwitting patients in Montreal psychiatric institutes who had been placed in his care.

Cameron was intent on erasing all existing memories and rebuilding a person so they could be used as the perfect double agent or unwitting pre-programmed assassin. Using techniques hinted at in the movies *The Manchurian Candidate* and *The Ipcress File*, he attempted to "depattern" his patients by putting them into month-long drug-induced comas and playing them tape loops of electronic noise and simple commands. He also used electroconvulsive shock treatment at 40 times the normal power. One of his surviving patients, a promising 19-year-old student, ended up returning home to her family with the mental age and bladder control of an 18-month-old child.

In 1976 the CIA promised the Church Committee – which was investigating the intelligence agencies – that it had stopped the programme and would never do anything like it again. Excuse me if I find that hard to believe.

THE HIDDEN REALITY OF MICROWAVE WEAPONS

When US President Jimmy Carter met Leonid Brezhnev as part of the Strategic Arms Limitation Talks he had no idea what the Soviet leader meant when he suggested they should outlaw the development of "new weapons more frightful than the mind of man has ever conceived". A presidential aide later explained to him: "He meant the microwave weapons."

For civilians, microwave technology has meant two things – faster food and mobile communications. For the military, microwave technology has offered the possibility of new ways to deliver pain, and "voice to skull" devices that allow the broadcast of sound and messages directly into the brain.

An example of the type of classified research into pain-centred microwave technology is the "Vehicle-Mounted Active Denial System" (nicknamed "the zapper") – a microwave beam device that heats up the skin from a distance to create "a burning sensation similar to a hot light bulb pressed against flesh". Colonel George Fenton, Director of the Department of Defense's Joint Nonlethal Weapons Program said the device was intended to "influence behaviour". Not officially deployed yet, it has been reported that it has been secretly "live tested" on protestors outside of America.

Microwave technology plays a key role in "manipulation weapons" such as those that allow military commanders to beam voices straight into their soldiers' or the enemies' heads. The disconcerting sensation of hearing voices could also be used by intelligence agencies to harass victims and plant subliminal information. To quote from a US military familiarization report on the technology: "Voice to skull devices are nonlethal weapons, which include (1) a neuro-electromagnetic device which uses microwave transmission of sound into the skull of persons or animals by way of pulse-modulated microwave radiation; the sound modulation may be voice or audio subliminal messages."

In 1999, the European Parliament passed a resolution calling for an "international convention introducing a ban on all developments and deployments of weapons which might enable any form of manipulation of human beings". Tony Blair refused to adopt this and the British Government does not deny it has manipulation weapons.

above Street fighting men – Pulsed Energy Projectile weapons may make riot control easier for the authorities, but it won't mean any less pain for those confronting the police.

THE ANTI-RIOT WEAPON THAT CAN DELIVER PAIN FROM TWO MILES AWAY

In 2007, the US military will get its first chance to try out a weapon that can deliver a bout of intense, debilitating pain from a distance of more than two miles away. It is a prospect that has already got some military commanders slavering in anticipation. The ability to hurt and incapacitate the enemy from such a distance has been a long cherished dream for many military strategists who believe that such a weapon could have a huge impact on the tactics used in war.

However, the originally intended victims of the weapon are not enemy soldiers, but rioters, both foreign and domestic. The existence of the programme to develop the new pain projection weapon was uncovered by the anti-weapons research organization, the Sunshine Project. They discovered that the University of Florida had been awarded a research contract to develop Pulsed Energy Projectiles (PEPs) that, according to a document they obtained, would have the ability to "induce pain suitable to disarm and deter individuals or to form barriers to the movement of large hostile groups".

The weapon works by firing a laser pulse that generates a burst of expanding energy when it hits a target. According to the document, PEPs hitting a person would activate the skin receptor cells that transmit pain without the need for heat or chemicals. The project built on earlier work undertaken by the US Naval Studies Board that found that PEPs produced "temporary paralysis" in tests on animals. One of the aims of the work at the University of Florida is to be able to do this without creating any tissue damage. The US Army has other research programmes not associated with University of Florida that are looking into the possibility of developing the lethal applications of PEPs.

When details of the project emerged, scientists working to control pain for medical reasons were outraged that their research was being manipulated into a pain-generating weapon. Some, such as John Wood of University College London, were also worried that its ability to create excruciating pain meant that it would be used for torture. Such concerns are obviously not enough to stop the dreams of the military.

BALL LIGHTNING WEAPONS – SECRET WEAPONS RESEARCH INTO THE POWER OF THE GODS

From Odin's spear, Gugnir, which could strike the gods themselves with lightning, to the deadly bolts of Zeus, mankind has associated lightning with a weapon belonging to the most powerful beings of his imagination. This connection has always made the idea that the searing power of nature could be harnessed as a weapon seem like pure fantasy.

It turns out that the world of pure fantasy made a very good cover for developing ball lightning weapons in secret at the height of the Cold War, as did the fact that scientists cannot agree on exactly what causes the phenomenon. Until recently, many meteorologists dismissed ball lightning as a myth and eyewitness reports of it as lies. However, recent study has established that ball lightning – a floating, moving ball of plasma which can occur naturally during a thunderstorm – is very much a reality.

Since electrical engineering pioneer Nikola Tesla claimed to have generated ball lightning in 1904, weapons developers have been excited by the prospect of creating searing balls of heat and electricity that could be projected at the enemy. In the Soviet Union during the Cold War, scientists secretly developed high-power microwave generators that allowed beams to intersect at high altitudes to create a stable ball of plasma. Details of the technology only emerged in 1993 when President Bush offered to share the American "Star Wars" project with the Russians.

The US followed Soviet research into using microwaves to create ball lightning. Experiments led to them being able to create a system where intersecting microwave frequency beams generated a glowing sphere of light. However, the US Air Force, following a different tack, produced the first device capable of firing ball lightning.

In the USAF's Phillips Laboratory in the early 1990s, a project called MARAUDER (Magnetically Accelerated Ring to Achieve Ultra-high Directed Energy and Radiation) managed to achieve doughnut-shaped rings of plasma and small balls of lightning that exploded when hitting a target. The project's initial success led to it becoming classified and no more details of how it developed after 1993 are available.

left Great balls of plasma – soon the legendary lightning power of the gods could be at the disposal of the United States military.

SCIENTISTS HAVE BEEN DEVELOPING TSUNAMI BOMBS SINCE THE SECOND WORLD WAR

On December 26, 2004, the world got an apocalyptic reminder of the devastating power of a tsunami when a massive undersea earthquake generated a destructive wave in the Indian Ocean. It killed at least 310,000 people across several countries, some as far as 5,000 miles away from the epicentre of the quake.

The tsunami was one of the deadliest disasters in modern times, but it brought out some of best characteristics of humanity, as private citizens across the globe responded with amazing generosity. The tsunami also recalled some of the worst instincts of mankind for anyone who was aware of the secret history of research into "tsunami bombs".

Military interest in wave weapons started in 1915 when the explosion of a bomb-carrying ship resulted in a small tidal wave in the English Channel. Recalling the devastation that a tidal wave caused after Krakatoa erupted, the possibility of generating similar phenomena through the explosion of underwater devices began to be discussed.

During the Second World War, a top-secret programme called Project Seal saw a series of experiments with tsunami bombs carried out off the coast of New Zealand. Under the direction of Auckland University professor Thomas Leech, a series of underwater explosions in 1944 successfully triggered mini tidal waves. His work was considered so promising the US and UK governments believed Project Seal could potentially be a devastating alternative to the atomic bombing of Japan.

Leech's experiments, which involved laying a pattern of explosives underwater to create a tsunami, led to him being made a Commander of the Order of the British Empire in 1947. Details of why the award was given were kept secret because development was still going on in the US. Papers relating to the wartime experiments have only recently been declassified and details of research after 1946 are still secret. However, evidence emerged after the fall of the Soviet Union to show that the Russians had carried out research into using a tsunami bomb to devastate southern England and Holland without the radiation problems generated by a nuclear attack.

above The devastation wreaked by the tsunami on December 26, 2004, at places such as Banda Aceh in Indonesia provides a frightening example of what a T-bomb could do.

RESEARCH INTO WEATHER CONTROL

Of all the unsung heroes of the Second World War, one unlikely to get its own blockbuster movie (with attendant rewriting of history where Americans play the major roles) is the English weather. However, if it had not been for the atmospheric conditions in the English Channel during late September and October 1940, the planned German invasion of southern England, codenamed "Operation Sealion", would have gone ahead, Churchill would have been deposed as PM and replaced with Lord Halifax (a known appeaser of Hitler), and history would be very different indeed.

The role of weather in determining conflicts can never be underestimated. From the thwarting of the Spanish Armada by storms to ending Napoleon's invasion of Russia, the weather has regularly decided the fate of nations and even whole empires. It is certainly something that the highest ranking military strategists in the Pentagon know the value of, hence the massive funding they have put into projects with the potential to control the weather.

Officially, Project HAARP (High-Frequency Active Auroral Research Program) is merely a US Air Force and Navy funded investigation to "understand, simulate and control ionospheric processes that might alter the performance of communication and surveillance systems", but many scientists have attacked its secret use in weather control research. Built near Gakona, Alaska, at an initial cost of $30 million in 1993, it has continually grown in size and now boasts 180 aerial towers that can transmit massive amounts of energy which can heat the atmosphere of the planet.

Patents for the technology involved in its construction mention that: "Weather modification is possible by, for example, altering upper atmosphere wind patterns by constructing one or more plumes of atmospheric particles which will act as a lens or focusing device." Scientists such as world-renowned weapons control specialist Dr Rosalie Bertell have confirmed that HAARP has weather modification applications and that: "US military scientists are working on weather systems as a potential weapon. The methods include the enhancing of storms and the diverting of vapor rivers in the Earth's atmosphere to produce targeted droughts or floods."

right Dr. Rosalie Bertell – she might look like your granny, but the Grey Nun is one of the foremost non-military experts on nuclear and exotic weapon systems such as HAARP.

THE PENTAGON'S ROLE IN ANTI-SHOPLIFTING RFID TECHNOLOGY

Radio frequency identification (RFID) is a method of storing and retrieving data using devices called RFID tags. The tag can be the size of a grain of rice and can be attached or built into any item. The in-built transmitter allows it to broadcast data such as location information or specifics about the tagged product (such as price).

The technology is being increasingly adopted in the retail sector as it allows stores to track a product from the moment it leaves a depot all the way through to it going on a shelf and eventually being bought by a customer. It allows for much tighter stock control and is an easy way of preventing theft from a shop as the technology will trigger an alarm if someone tries to steal an item.

Like the Internet and the barcode before it, RFID is a spin-off from the needs of the Pentagon. The massive investment they have made in it (more than a $100 million over the last few years) is driven by a logistical desire to track stores and equipment in fine detail. The Pentagon's role as the largest customer in the USA for many items has allowed them to demand that manufacturers use the technology and its own RFID standards, leading to its rapid take-up. Many civil liberties groups in the USA and elsewhere believe RFID will allow manufacturers and retailers to track their customers through what they buy.

When I was the chief spin-doctor for the organization representing British retailers (the British Retail Consortium), major efforts were made to get me to publicly back RFID. I was even told by one of the PR companies representing an RFID manufacturer that there were no civil liberty concerns and that I should help persuade retailers to back the technology beyond the point of sale. When I pointed out this was a lie, the tack changed and "generous sponsorship" was mentioned. It was an offer declined, but it gives a good indication of how a lot of expert opinion you read and hear about is generated through a combination of lies and money.

CHINA'S CYBER-WARFARE ATTACK ON US TELECOMMUNICATIONS

In 1997, China committed an act of war against the USA. It was an act of cyber-warfare that, according to sources within the CIA, was a live exercise by Chinese military hackers against the US telecommunications system. Luckily, for both sides and the rest of the world, America decided to pretend it didn't happen.

At 5 a.m. one morning in January 1997, a leading pager service sent out a "call me back" message to more than 100,000 of its customers. Foggy with sleep and wondering what the emergency was, thousands of people tried to call back. Most thought it was a local number, while hundreds of calls were received at a San Franciscan theological college. Three dozen people thought it was the pager number of another pager network customer and sent their telephone numbers back to the network to be passed on to the mystery person they thought was trying to page them. Those 36 telephone numbers were then sent to the original 100,000-plus people who got the false "call me back" message. One of those 36 was still receiving more than 300 calls an hour on the evening of the same day.

The pager network apologized to all of its customers for the technical error, but the *Wall Street Journal* ran a story suggesting the problem had been caused by Chinese military hackers engaged in an exercise. The company did not sue the paper. (This illustrates a very good way of knowing whether something you read in a newspaper is true. If someone doesn't sue over a story it is for one of three reasons: either the story is true; the person or organization involved doesn't want the publicity of a court hearing; or the person who has been libelled has no money.)

Pagers, SMS messaging and cellular phones are all vital to contacting military and emergency service personnel in times of terrorist attack. The technology is also increasingly used in combat situations, so the fact that a dry run by the Chinese successfully caused so much havoc is highly worrying.

CULTS AND SECRET SOCIETIES

15

"The very word 'secrecy' is repugnant in a free and open society; and we are as a people inherently and historically opposed to secret societies, to secret oaths, and to secret proceedings."
John F Kennedy

Every cult and secret society has things they do not want the uninitiated to know about. After all, it is their nature to keep things hidden from those who are not part of the "in-crowd". However, aside from the passwords, handshakes and rituals, they also tend to conceal the truth about their strange inner beliefs and real reasons for their existence – even from some of their own members.

The compartmentalized structure of secrecy employed in most cult and occult societies means that even those who join an organization at its lower levels will have no idea of its inner teachings and origins. For example, Freemasons at lower grades – known as the Blue Degrees – are intentionally misled, although it is intended that they will believe they have discovered the truth about the Brotherhood.

This need-to-know approach means that few individuals in the following organizations know the truth about what is really going on and what the genuine history of their organization actually is. Even some of those inside the organizations detailed in this book do not know the secrets you will learn in the next few pages. Knowledge is power and those in control of these groups are loathe to tell many members – let alone the general public – what they genuinely believe and intend to do.

Secrets are easier to keep if few people know them, but as we shall see, the truth leaks out, even from the most clandestine and tightly controlled cult or secret society.

THE RITUAL AND OATH THAT ALL MEMBERS OF THE MAFIA HAVE TO UNDERTAKE

Due to its incredible success as a organization which still leads the world in areas such as extortion, drug smuggling, gambling and money laundering (though they have begun to lag behind in prostitution, terrorism and assassination), it is easy to forget that the Mafia is a secret society.

Anyone who tells you they can give a definitive origin of the Sicilian Mafia is a liar. Although the current form and nature of the organization were laid down in the nineteenth century, the first elements of the Mafia came into existence during Sicilian resistance to the occupation of the island by the Moors. The word Mafia itself may come from a corruption of the Arabic *mu afah*, meaning either "a refuge" or "to protect".

The Mafia is not one uniform organization with a central structure, but is rather a collection of secret societies with a similar history and cultural background organized into "families" that work alike. The rituals of the Mafia have similarities with Freemasonry and may derive from the same source, the rites used by medieval military orders such as the Knights Templar.

Despite their depiction in relatively accurate films such as *The Godfather* and *Goodfellas*, many rituals, oaths and secret code words used by the Mafia remain unknown to anyone outside of the various families and the law enforcement agencies trying to combat them. Although members of the Mafia are practising Roman Catholics, the secret initiation of a member begins with their symbolic death and resurrection into organization. They then cut their hand and offer the blood as a sacrifice and a sign of their intent. A picture of the Catholic saint associated with the Mafia family (originally a local village saint) is held in the hand and burnt while the following oath is spoken: "I enter this organization to protect my family and friends. I swear not to divulge the secret words I am given and promise to obey with love and *omerta*. As burns this saint so burns my soul. I enter alive and I will leave it dead."

`below` The blood of another victim runs reds and stains the already damned reputation of the Sicilian Mafia

THE INNER TEACHING OF SCIENTOLOGY THAT CAN COST THOUSANDS OF DOLLARS TO DISCOVER

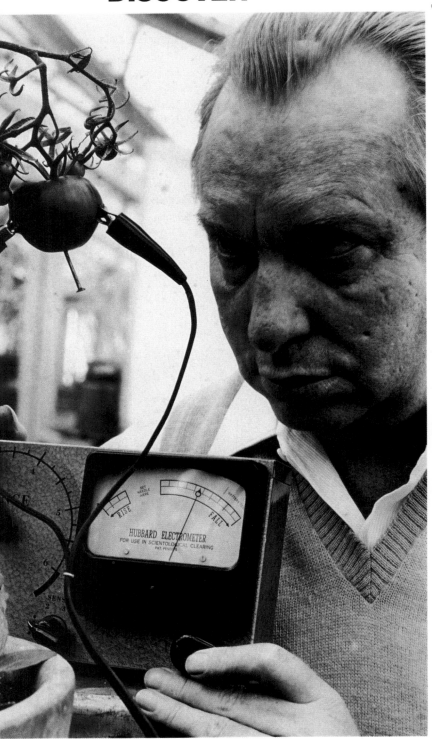

This is one of the entries that has scared me the most to write about. It is not because I find the inner teaching of Scientology (the religion created by sci-fi author L Ron Hubbard) the most inadvertently hilarious thing ever written. It is not because I find the prospect of people like John Travolta actually believing in it so depressing. I'm always worried typing Scientology because of their track record of suing and because former members have taken criminal actions against those they don't like.

In a memo to a judge deciding sentences on nine Scientologists who pleaded guilty to burglaries, forgeries, infiltration, obstruction of justice and other crimes against more than 100 US agencies, including the Department of Justice and the Department of Defense, a federal prosecutor wrote: "The crime committed by these defendants is of a breadth and scope previously unheard of. No individual or organization was free from their despicable conspiratorial minds."

The inner teachings of Scientology can set you back at least $120,000 to $150,000 as you progress through a seemingly endless series of courses and sessions where you are audited. The ultimate aim is to become "Clear" and once you have become "Clear" to move up to the level of an Operating Thetan. At the inner levels of Operating Thetan, you learn a secret that is meant to be kept from those who have not gone through the necessary auditing. Also, achieving the higher Operating Thetan levels is meant to give the person psychic powers such as telekinesis.

The inner secret that would usually cost you thousands of dollars to learn is that humans are made of clusters of "thetans" formed from 76 galactic races banished to earth 75 million years ago by a cruel space ruler named Xenu, who then had the exiles on earth thrown in volcanoes and nuked with bombs. This is the root of all of your problems. Aren't you glad I saved you the money?

left Founder of the Church of Scientology L Ron Hubbard tries to demonstrate that his E-meter measures the pain of a tomato that's been subjected to hearing his dire sci-fi stories.

THE FALSE CLAIMS ABOUT KWANZAA – A HOLIDAY INVENTED BY A FORMER CONVICT AND NOW CELEBRATED BY MILLIONS OF AFRICAN-AMERICANS

When Bill Clinton took up his second term in the White House, he became the first to support the celebration of the African-American religious festival Kwanzaa. Speaking about it he said: "The symbols and ceremony of Kwanzaa, evoke the rich history and heritage of Africa. It is a vibrant celebration of African culture that transcends international boundaries."

Kwanzaa is in fact nothing of the sort. It is an invented festival for a religion based not on African culture but upon Marxist principles and created by Ron Karenga, a man who used to be a radical advocate of black separatism and who tortured women.

A seven-day festival starting on December 26 is promoted as an African-American alternative to Christmas. It is claimed that it is based on seven ancient African principles – said to symbolize the seven principles of blackness – and that it takes its name from a Swahili harvest festival. First created in 1966, it is now celebrated by more than 12 per cent of African-Americans, who may be surprised to learn that the principles, including *Kujichagulia* (self-determination), *Ujima* (collective work and responsibility) and *Ujamaa* (cooperative economics) derive from Marxism not African culture, that no African people celebrate a harvest festival in December and that some of its symbols, such as *muhindi* (ears of corn), are not even native to Africa.

Before coming up with the spurious festival and its accompanying religion, Kawaida, Karenga had been a member of The United Slaves Organization, a radical black power group that was in violent conflict with the Black Panthers. In 1971 Karenga was convicted of felonious assault and false imprisonment after torturing two women from the United Slaves who he thought were trying to poison him. During his trial the prison psychiatrist reported that: "This man presents a picture which can be considered both paranoid and schizophrenic with hallucinations."

Quite understandable then that George W Bush continues to follows Clinton's tradition and give a presidential Kwanzaa message. It's rumoured that fans of the cartoon *Peanuts* are now lobbying for a similar recognition of the tradition of the Great Pumpkin, distributing gifts to good children on October 31.

above Ron Karenga – controversial former felon and a key member of United Slaves created Kwanzaa using well-known Marxist principles.

HOW APARTHEID WAS CREATED AND FINALLY ENDED BY A SECRET SOCIETY CALLED THE BROEDERBOND

If you listened to some conspiracy theorists you could be easily believe secret societies were behind every significant political event in history. However, when these claims are properly researched there are few facts that wholeheartedly back them up. To most people, this lack of objective proof just means the world is filled with a frightening number of delusional, paranoid nutcases. Almost always, most people are right.

One genuine secret society rarely talked about and yet undeniably behind some of the most momentous events in twentieth-century African history is the Broederbond. Formed in 1919 as an open political group, it evolved into a secret society determined to ensure that Afrikaners gained control of the South African government, economy and military.

By the 1930s, one of its political front organizations subverted and took over an existing political party – the Reunited National Party – giving it a firm political base while it members worked their way to stronger positions within the business community and South Africa's military

and judicial systems. By 1947 it was clandestinely in control of a number of arms of government, including the South African Bureau of Racial Affairs, which developed the idea of the apartheid system.

When the Reunited National Party came to power in 1948, they used their control of government to place Broederbond members in key positions, managing to take control of BOSS, South Africa's secret service organization. They also brought apartheid into legal force. Operating behind the scenes, their existence was doubted by many outside of the country despite revelations by former members, such as leading Afrikaner cleric Beyers Naude.

In the 1980s, the Broederbond decided the current system was unsustainable and opened up secret talks with banned organizations such as the African National Congress. This eventually led to the dismantling of the white state in the country. Not only are the Broederbond the only secret society proven to have been running a country behind the scenes, they are also the only secret society to have given up power voluntarily when the job got too difficult.

THE SECRET ORIGINS AND INNER BELIEFS OF THE NATION OF ISLAM

The strongest images of the Nation of Islam (NOI) in most people's minds come from the sight of its smartly dressed members in their unofficial uniform of black suits, white shirts and black ties or that of its most famous former member, Malcolm X.

NOI publicizes itself as a Muslim religious movement believing in radical black empowerment. This explains why it suppresses its real origins and some of its beliefs, which are certainly not part of standard Islamic doctrine. Although claiming that the movement started with Elijah Muhammad, they don't mention that the man Elijah claimed was god – Fard Muhammad – was in fact a convicted criminal, Wallace Dodd Ford, born of mixed European and Polynesian parentage. Wallace Dodd Ford took his ideas on black history and religion from a former carnival magician called Timothy Drew.

Wallace worked as Drew's chauffeur in the late 1920s when Drew was calling himself Noble Drew Ali and running a cult called the Temple of Moorish Science. Drew claimed to have

been initiated into an occult order in the Great Pyramid in Egypt and to have learned the secret history of the Black race and how they and the Irish shared a common ancestry in the Old Testament prophetess Ruth. He allowed anyone of Celtic descent to join the cult alongside African-Americans as "Moorish brothers". When Drew died, his chauffeur took over the cult and transformed it into the current NOI. Aside from the fact that the man their prophet called god believed red hair and blue eyes were a sign of "blackness", members of the NOI are reluctant to talk about statements made by Elijah Muhammad that white people were created by an evil scientist named Yakub and that a spacecraft is waiting in orbit to destroy all white people. Louis Farrakhan, the current leader of the NOI, claims to have been taken by aliens to meet with Elijah Muhammad who, as you read this, is orbiting Earth in a giant spaceship.

If anyone can find mention of this in the Koran, I'd be glad if they would let me know.

THE RITUALS THAT MEMBERS OF THE INFAMOUS SKULL AND BONES SOCIETY – INCLUDING GEORGE W BUSH – HAD TO UNDERTAKE WHEN THEY JOINED

The Skull and Bones Society is everything a secret society should be. It has powerful members, including the current president of the USA, a history dating back to 1833, its own private island and a macabre initiation ritual. With all of this, how could it not be one the most inaccurately speculated about organizations on the Internet?

Established at Yale University in New Haven, Connecticut, in the first half of the nineteenth century, the Skull and Bones Society has achieved prominence because of its incredible track record of producing members who go on to have dazzling careers in business, law and politics. In the 2004 presidential contest, both President Bush and his challenger Senator John Kerry were "Bonesmen" (the name given to those who are in the club). However, even the best secret society is only as good as its least drunk or loose-lipped members, so it's time to reveal just what George W Bush and his father before him had to do become Bonesmen.

Also known as Lodge 322, the rituals used to initiate members are a bastardization of much older Freemasonry initiations. Walking into the "tomb", their attention is drawn to the fact that all clocks inside run five minutes faster than those in the outside world – to symbolize that Bonesmen are ahead of the rest.

They are then taken down the "crypt" under the "tomb", where all of the current Yale Bonesmen wait in a room decorated with genuine skulls and bones (including those of various Native Americans and Mexicans). Brought before three symbolically dressed figures – the Grand Knight, the Pope and Lucifer – an elaborate ritual is then carried out in which the initiate kisses a skull and lies naked in a coffin to recount his full sexual history. After this he is reborn and made to kneel before the Grand Knight, who takes his sword and dubs him "a Knight of Euloga". Afterwards a meal is eaten using some of Hitler's old cutlery. Frankly, I was disappointed to learn this. I expected a touch more overt black magic in the Bush family history.

right George W Bush is only the latest in a long line of Bonesmen who go on to achieve positions of power after being initiated into the mysterious Skull and Bones Society.

LIES TOLD BY THE UFO AND SEX CULT THE RAËLIANS ABOUT CLONING

On December 26, 2002, French scientist and bishop in the Raëlian UFO sect, Brigitte Boisselier, announced that the cult organization Clonaid had cloned the first human baby, saying in a press conference: "I have created life."

Refusing to reveal details of where the mother and alleged baby were, she promised that proof and independent testing of baby "Eve" would be allowed in the future to prove her claims. It later emerged that former French journalist Claude Vorilhon founded Clonaid. He claimed a UFO experience in 1973 had led him to rename himself Raël and form the Raëlian religion. Despite offering to create a clone for a fee of $200,000, evidence surfaced that the company had only two staff and had never cloned a sheep let alone a human being.

The big attraction of the Raëlian movement, aside from cloning and being able to believe that humanity was created by aliens who chose to pass on their message to a former writer on motor racing, is its teachings on sex, which are hedonistic to say the least. Before becoming the chief liar of the Clonaid hoax, Brigitte Boisselier was more infamous for her role of helping initiate people into the cult, which usually involved her leading groups of both male and female new recruits in exploring their darkest sexual fantasies. These often seemed to revolve around having group sex in candlelight accompanied by a soundtrack of whale song and chanting.

When confronted by a Montreal newspaper with proof of a hoax, Vorilhon responded by saying: "If it's not true, she's making history with one of the biggest hoaxes ever, so it's wonderful because, thanks to what she is doing now, the whole world knows about the Raëlian movement. I am very happy with that." This means that a man asking us to believe he is telling the truth when he says his father was an alien and that he was taken in a flying saucer to meet Jesus and Buddha (who gave him a religious mission) is also saying it is fine to lie if it brings you publicity. Irony doesn't even begin to cover it.

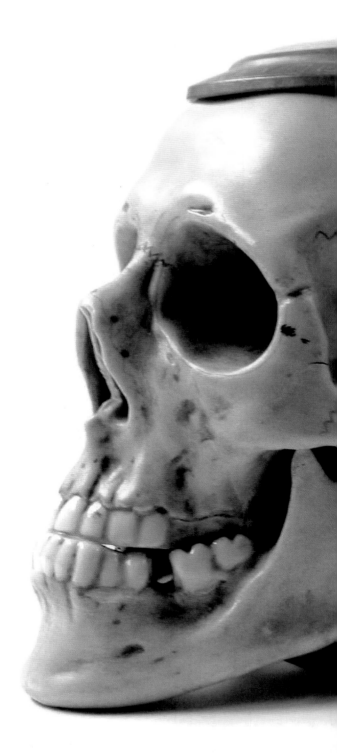

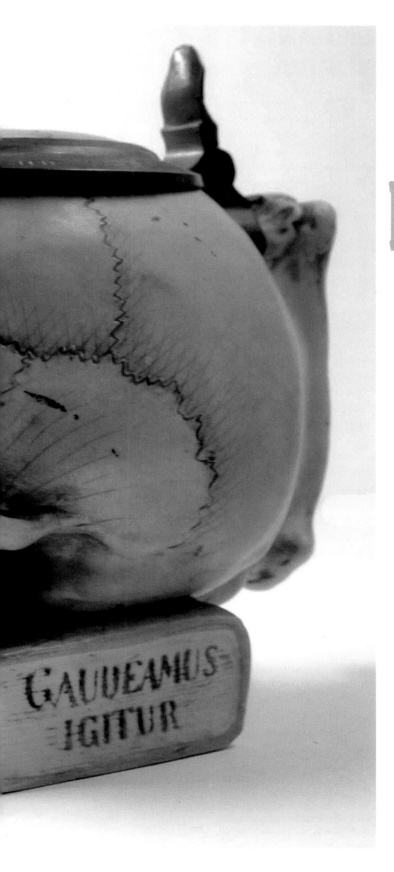

THE SECRET NAME AND THE SIGNIFICANCE OF THE CENTRAL CHARACTER IN MASONIC TRADITION

I have always felt sorry for Freemasons. Of all of the secret societies that exist, none has been more misunderstood than the Freemasons. Whatever else is said about them, established facts show that members are joined together by shared metaphysical interests and participation in certain occult rituals.

This had led to the existence of the most persistent lie put about by the critics of Freemasonry: that the central figure in their rituals is Lucifer. Given that Freemasons have to take fearsome oaths involving the removal of their tongues, hearts and burial "beneath the sea-mark" if they ever reveal what goes on in their rituals, it's a criticism that many have found hard to defend.

As I'm not a Freemason myself, I can reveal that the central character that forms the basis of Masonic mythology and ritual (certainly for the first three degrees of Masonry) is not Lucifer, but a chap called Hiram Abiff. Also known as "the widow's son" (charitable acts undertaken by Freemasons are always said to be done "for the widow's son") he is identified with the biblical character Hiram of Tyre. He is mentioned in 1 Kings: 13-14: "And King Solomon sent and fetched Hiram out of Tyre. He was a widow's son out of the tribe of Naph-ta-li and his father was a man of Tyre, a worker in brass. And he came to King Solomon and wrought his works."

In Masonic lore, which is enacted in the rituals of the lower degrees of Freemasonry, it is believed that Hiram Abiff was murdered while working on the construction of King Solomon's Temple by three men – called Jubela, Jubelo and Jubelum – for refusing to reveal his secrets, including the Masonic word. Upon becoming a Freemason and on upon receiving further degrees in Freemasonry, initiates are given substitute words to help them identify fellow Freemasons and what degree in "the Craft" they hold. To save you spending time on the Internet trying to discover the secret word of the Master Mason, I can reveal that it is "Mah-Hah-Bone". Of course, what it actually means is a secret.

left The skull has a central place in the strange symbolism of the occult rituals practised by many of the higher degrees in Freemasonry.

THE SECRETS OF *OPUS DEI* AND ITS FOUNDER JOSEMARIA ESCRIVA

The ultra-secretive Catholic cult Opus Dei may not be the brutal searchers for the Holy Grail of the novel *The Da Vinci Code*, but they are linked with General Franco's fascist rule in Spain and dominate the lives of hundreds of prominent Catholic politicians. British Cabinet member Ruth Kelly regularly attends meetings and other Opus Dei events, but has not revealed whether she is a member.

The priest Josemaria Escriva de Balaguer formed Opus Dei in 1928. Its name means "the work of God". Teaching Catholic fundamentalism, it encourages members to lead holy lives. The vast majority of the members of Opus Dei live very normal and highly spiritual lives. At the extreme end of the scale, however, some members of the organization have allowed it to dominate their lives, right down to which books they should read and to supporting those who indulge in flagellation and self-harm. However, the organization strongly denies it is a cult.

When Escriva was made a Saint in 2002, the Catholic Church and Opus Dei itself worked hard to try and suppress information about the man. However, according to Carmen Tapia, a former secretary to Escriva, his attitude to women was misogynistic and with strong undercurrents of sexual degradation. He would often call women by names such as "sow", "bitch", and "whore". Expressing his anger in a meeting of senior Opus Dei members over a woman who had offended him, he said: "She has to be spanked throughout. Draw up her skirts, tear down her panties and give it to her in the ass! In the ass! Until she talks! Make her talk!"

Despite preaching a doctrine of self-denial and humility, he insisted upon gourmet dining and exorbitantly expensive wine always being served in his luxurious, palatial HQ in Rome. Given that Opus Dei was not only linked to Franco's fascist regime but to more recent far-right groups, it is no surprise they also try to keep secret Escriva's positive views on Hitler. Escriva not only said: "Hitler has been unjustly accused of killing six million Jews," he also claimed the Nazi leader had been good for Catholicism because: "Hitler was against the Jews, Hitler was against the Slavs."

It is reassuring to discover that the Catholic Church is so broad-minded when it comes to defining sainthood isn't it?

left Recognized Catholic saint and founder of Opus Dei, Josemaria Escriva supported fascists and wanted to see a woman spanked and given it in the ass.

MOONIE PROPAGANDA PLANS INCLUDE TRYING TO MAKE MOVIES WITH ELVIS AND SETTING UP *THE WASHINGTON TIMES* NEWSPAPER

In the early 1970s, it was common to read reports about the worrying activities of a cult nicknamed "the Moonies". There were proven cases of brainwashing and the extreme control exerted on the lives of the young followers, including providing them with previously unknown partners whom they would marry in mass-wedding ceremonies involving thousands of people.

Even as a child, I found the sight of the Reverend Sun Myung Moon, who proclaimed himself "the Messiah and mankind's perfect parent", marrying crowds of transfixed people in football stadiums, troubling and scary. Others felt the same way, because after years of bad press and Moon's imprisonment for tax evasion and conspiracy, the Korean billionaire and his Unification Movement decided to change tack.

Using the millions of dollars provided to the church by its followers, Moon and the Unification movement set up *The Washington Times* newspaper to promote right-wing views and provide an apparently impartial source of good publicity for the church. They also purchased United Press

International – the respected global news agency. The church used profits generated by arms manufacturers and more than 500 other front businesses owned by the Unification Movement and himself to fund a network of powerful US conservative groups that would be pro-Moonie. Moon even started to fund the production of movies that would promote conservative views and act as secret Moonie propaganda.

His first idea was to retell the story of Christ with a Unification Movement slant and Elvis in the lead role. Right up until the King's death, Moon made overtures to persuade him to exchange his Vegas capes for the robes of Christ. Presley refused to take a role that suggested Jesus was not the genuine king (according to Moon, as he himself was the Messiah, Jesus must have failed in his mission). Despite being knocked back by Presley, Moon went on to plough $48 million into the Korean-based war movie *Inchon*. Starring Laurence Olivier and Jacqueline Bisset, it was the most expensive and largest box office flop of its time. It seems that even Messiahs can make bad movies.

below Mankind's alleged perfect parent and media mogul and arms manufacturer, the Reverend Sun Myung Moon marries 22,000 believers in New York.

PUBLIC FACES, SECRET LIVES

"The great enemy of the truth is very often not the lie – deliberate, contrived and dishonest – but the myth, persistent, persuasive and unrealistic."
John F Kennedy

The cult of personality breeds many dangers including the tendency to refuse to acknowledge the truth about an icon's flaws and failings. Individual people, and sometimes even whole countries, invest so much emotion and pride in their heroes that they develop an inability even to be open to the possibility that they lied and concealed elements of their lives.

Respected, global figures, many of them regarded as national heroes and cultural icons, are just like you and me – they have certain secrets they would rather stay hidden. One difference, however, is that they tend to have a lot more people who are more than happy to lie and cover up to protect their inflated reputations for them.

When the propaganda and cheerleading machinery kicks in, history has a tendency to be re-written and flesh-and-blood political leaders can easily become saints, while any quirky signs of individuality such as mystical beliefs are repressed. All evidence of drug use, sexual adventures and personal misjudgement are ignored.

Some lies told by an icon's supporters are deliberately intended to bolster their public image. If these go unchecked because of the esteem in which they are held, they can become inflated to the status of almost universally held belief. However, the most common lies told about public figures are those of omission. These mislead people into having a less than complete picture of a well-known figure – especially about any earlier political beliefs or elements in their personal lives that conflicts with their later status.

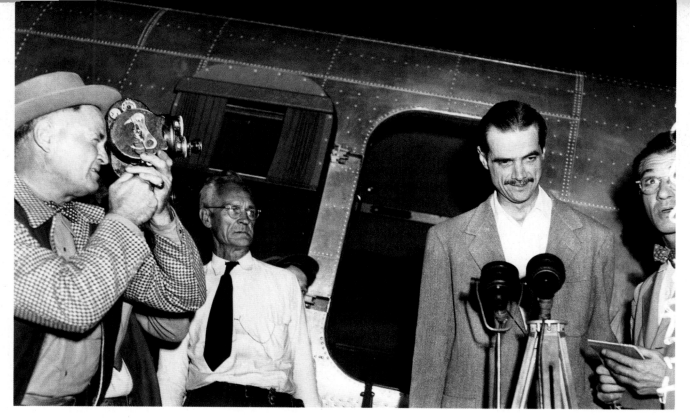

above The real thing? Hughes gives a rare interview, but after an air crash almost killed him he increasingly began to use doubles to avoid making public appearances.

MULTI-MILLIONAIRE HOWARD HUGHES EMPLOYED A DOUBLE SO CONVINCING THAT THE AMERICAN GOVERNMENT THOUGHT HE HAD DIED AND THE DOUBLE HAD TAKEN OVER

If you thought it was only paranoid world leaders who employed doubles to take the risk of being hit by the assassin's bullet while appearing for a photo opportunity, it is probably because you have not heard the secrets of the last years of Howard Hughes's life before.

Howard Hughes's early life saw him rise to prominence as an aviator, businessman and playboy (who bought a movie studio just to increase his chances of having sex with starlets ranging from Jane Russell to Ava Gardner). After the crash of the experimental XF-11 spyplane he was piloting in 1946, Hughes's mental state began to deteriorate.

Increasingly a recluse, he moved to Las Vegas. When the Desert Inn hotel threatened to evict him, he bought the hotel and lived in seclusion on the top two floors. With no one seeing him from year to year, wild rumours of his morbid obsession with germs and his strange behaviour spread. Hughes began to employ a series of doubles to impersonate him, including actor Brucks Randell. The aim

was to create false sightings and draw the attention of newsmen when the stretcher-bound Hughes occasionally left Vegas. The actors became so proficient at impersonating Hughes they could fool almost anyone.

In 1970, the American Internal Revenue Service (IRS) was convinced that Hughes was dead and "officials in charge of his empire are concealing it in order to prevent a catastrophic dissolution of his holdings". They believed they were doing this by using a double "schooled in his speech, mannerism and eccentricities". When Hughes moved to the Bahamas in the 1970s, a double was sent to meetings with the US ambassador and the Nicaraguan president, Anastasio Somoza. His double even fooled the CIA who employed Hughes in 1972 to try and secretly raise a Soviet submarine which had sunk near Hawaii four years before.

When the emaciated 90-pound body of Hughes was flown back to the States in April 1976, the IRS and the FBI both refused to believe it was Hughes and not his double until they could fingerprint the body.

HENRY KISSINGER ONCE BELIEVED NUCLEAR WAR WINNABLE AND IS BELIEVED BY MANY TO BE ONE OF THE INSPIRATIONS FOR DR STRANGELOVE

H enry Kissinger is regarded by many as the statesman supreme of the twentieth century and a regular and well-respected TV news talking head. Amongst the many areas of his career that Kissinger likes to keep quiet about are his former views on nuclear war. In the 1950s, Dr Kissinger wrote *Nuclear Weapons and Foreign Policy*. The book makes for frightening reading as Dr. K advocates just how the US should aim to use it nuclear weapons to win a war. His favoured option is an agreement with the Soviet Union to use only limited range nuclear weapons and only in European and other none homeland territories. If you read the book it is clear that Kissinger believes a nuclear war is winnable and at times the favoured option to achieve US dominance. Obviously, Kissinger no longer believes this to be the case.

It was such views that have convinced many experts and academics that Kissinger was one of the inspirations of the character of Dr Strangelove in Stanley Kubrick and Peter Sellers's hilariously scary movie *Dr. Strangelove or: How I Learned to Stop Worrying and Love the Bomb* .

In 1973, Kissinger was US Secretary of State and, with Nixon embroiled in the Watergate scandal, effectively the most powerful man in the world. On October 24, 1973, Nixon was too concerned with trying to save his presidency to make a meeting of military chiefs discussing fighting between Israeli and Egyptian forces. Kissinger attended and ordered the US move to DEFCON 3 because he thought the Soviets might intervene. During this high state of alert a false alarm led B-52 crews to rush to their planes. Thankfully the planes did not get airborne because with Dr. Strangelove in charge...

Henry Kissinger is a man who has played a pivotal role in world affairs. Even though no longer in government, he and his views on world affairs are still given a lot of airtime. Amongst the many areas of his career that Kissinger does not seem to talk about much in broadcast interviews are his former views on nuclear war. I do not share this view. I once declined appearing on a live television news programme, because I knew Kissinger was also going to be a guest. I could not trust myself not to turn to the presenter and say: "Why have you just given that man airtime"?

above and **right** The power behind the throne – Dr Kissinger in discussion with President Ford whilst Peter Sellers plays crazed nuclear madman Dr Strangelove.

PUBLIC FACES, SECRET LIVES

<above> Ladies man – Mahatma Gandhi claimed that his regular practice of sleeping naked with young girls was purely a spiritual exercise.

MAHATMA GANDHI REGULARLY SLEPT NAKED WITH YOUNG VIRGINS

There is a statue of Mohandas Karamchand Gandhi at Westminster Abbey. For many this does not seem incongruous as the Indian leader is seen by many as saint. Albert Einstein said: "Generations to come will scarcely believe that such a one as this, ever in flesh and blood, walked upon this earth." Voted "Man of the Millenium" and called Mahatma by his followers (often mistaken for his first name, it is a title meaning "Great Soul"), it is often difficult to tell if people believe he was a man or an incarnation of some higher force.

From Richard Attenborough's overblown movie *Gandhi*, to countless hagiographies, the truth about the more secretive aspects of Gandhi's life is usually – and consciously – omitted. While his role in fighting for civil liberties in South Africa and for Indian independence are repeated *ad infinitum*, you'll have to search hard for details of the Great Soul's habit of sleeping naked with young virgins.

Details of Gandhi's odd practice of sleeping naked with young women first emerged when it became known he was sleeping with a 19-year-old. When challenged to explain what was going on, Gandhi claimed it was his way of testing his vow of chastity, known as brahmacharya. His reasoning was that if he could spend the night in bed with an attractive young woman without any sexual thoughts, it showed he was keeping his vow in thought as well as deed. Gentleman readers are advised never to use this as an excuse for any of their indiscretions. The 19-year-old was not the only woman his tested brahmacharya with; a number of women as young as 18 shared the mattress of the Mahatma.

Gandhi's wife was not around to offer her views on the Great Soul's sleeping arrangements. She had died in a British prison from a lung infection. Gandhi had refused to allow her to be treated with antibiotics, claiming that drug treatment would go against his faith. However, when he contracted malaria a few weeks later, he seemed to find no problem in taking quinine tablets to aid his recovery.

PRINCE PHILIP CHEATED ON THE QUEEN AND BELIEVES THE WORLD NEEDS DEPOPULATING

The power behind the British throne is His Royal Highness Prince Philip (AKA the Duke of Edinburgh, Earl of Merioneth and Baron Greenwich, because for some people prince is just not enough of a title).

Although Buckingham Palace has been fighting a losing battle during the last 30 years trying to keep quiet some of the Philip's inexcusable verbal gaffs (including telling British students in China, "If you stay here much longer, you'll all be slitty-eyed"), they have done a better job at hiding his sexual shenanigans as well as his controversial political beliefs.

The extramarital affairs and sex scandals of the Prince's children and their spouses make it easy to forget that when Philip married Elizabeth, royal reporting was conducted in a totally different manner. In the 1950s and early 1960s, the Palace was able to control which stories ended up in the papers. This was good thing for Philip, as while many journalists knew he was cheating on the queen there was no chance that they would be able to report it.

Philip was a member of the exclusive Soho dining group, the Thursday Club, alongside David Niven and *Daily Express* editor Arthur Christiansen. It was notorious for its drunkenness and skirt chasing – an activity that the Prince and his equerry Mike Parker would often slip out of Buckingham Palace to engage in together. Alongside conducting a longstanding relationship with a French singer and actress, the Prince also had an affair with the Queen's cousin, Princess Alexandra. This affair was the last straw for the Queen and the resulting strain on the marriage seems to have brought Philip to heel.

Despite being meant to keep out of politics, the Prince has repeatedly made clear his extremist view that the world needs depopulating. Speaking to the German press in 1988, he said: "In the event that I am reincarnated, I would like to return as a particularly deadly virus, in order to contribute something to solve overpopulation." Quite what the Queen thinks Philip should be reincarnated as after his behaviour has not been publicly recorded.

above Deadly virus in waiting – Prince Philip has decided what he wants to be reincarnated as.

WINSTON CHURCHILL WAS A DRUID

Whatever image goes through your mind when you hear the name Winston Churchill, I sincerely doubt it is of the man voted "Greatest Briton" dressed in druids' robes, celebrating the solstice at an ancient megalithic site.

It is well known that Churchill was a Freemason for a few short years, leaving the Brotherhood in 1912. His membership of druidic orders and participation in various druidic rites and festivals is a fact that is banished from almost all of the hundreds of biographies on Britain's wartime leader.

Even the one or two biographies that make mention of his membership are always at pains to suggest it was either a brief flirtation or that his involvement was entirely honorific. While that might be the version the hagiographers of Churchill would like to have us believe, it is not the truth, as he remained a druid throughout his life.

Occult and mystical orders, especially those that are secret or semi-secret, do not tend to produce much in the way of written evidence such as membership lists. When Churchill was initiated into the Ancient & Archaeological Order of Druids in 1908, it was not a story covered in the national papers, even though the prospect of the then government cabinet member and President of the Board of Trade enrolling in an organization which carried out neo-pagan rituals was certainly newsworthy. In fact, it was not until the publication of Stuart Piggott's book *The Druids* that even many druids themselves knew that Churchill had been one of their number.

Churchill was not just an armchair druid. Although no firm evidence shows him joining other druids in celebrating the Midsummer Solstice at Stonehenge, Churchill did join the Albion lodge in Midwinter Solstice rituals held at the Rollright Stones (a stone circle in Oxfordshire). Whether his willingness to consider the occult during the Second World War stemmed from his occasional donning of white robes is a matter that historians have failed to look at – because they continue to pretend that he was too busy being a politician to do anything as interesting as being a druid.

HENRY FORD WAS ANTI-SEMITIC AND USED HIS CAR COMPANY TO DISTRIBUTE ANTI-JEWISH PROPAGANDA

Despite once saying "History is more or less bunk", Henry Ford has emerged as one of the most significant figures of the twentieth century. His application of assembly-line manufacturing techniques to automobiles led to a revolution in mass production. It also meant that cars became affordable enough to change the whole transportation culture of the world.

In most history books – bunk or not – you rarely find mention of Ford's rabid anti-Semitism, promotion of anti-Jewish conspiracy theories or financial support of Adolf Hitler. In school textbooks, a sanitized and sometimes even saintly version of Ford is put across. You certainly don't find his 1920 comment: "The international financiers are behind all war. They are what is called the International Jew – German Jews, French Jews, English Jews, American Jews. I believe that in all these countries except our own the Jewish financier is supreme. Here, the Jew is a threat."

Ford's anti-Semitism was so ardent that he set up his own newspaper, *The Dearborn Independent*, in 1919 that carried virulent anti-Jewish articles under his own name. The paper was distributed free via Ford dealerships across the USA and had a circulation of 700,000. Ford's articles were then collected into a four-volume book called *The International Jew, the World's Foremost Problem*, which was sent free of charge to major libraries.

Under pressure, Ford closed the paper in 1927 and apologized to the Anti-Defamation League while still continuing to praise Hitler. In fact, Ford had even helped finance Hitler's early rise to power in Germany in the 1920s, giving up to $75,000 to cover Nazi election expenses. Ford's company and the regime enjoyed a close relationship until the start of the Second World War. In 1938, on his 75th birthday, Ford was given Germany's highest award for a foreigner – the Order of the German Eagle – accompanied by a personal note of congratulations from Adolf (who had a portrait of Ford on a wall in his office). Ford refused to return the medal during the war and even hung on to it after details of the Holocaust emerged.

CARL SAGAN, ONE OF THE MOST FAMOUS SCIENTISTS IN THE WORLD, DID HIS BEST WORK WHILE TAKING DRUGS

Starman – Cosmic Carl Sagan was no stranger to the concept of out of this world trips to other planets, which might explain his secretly advocating marijuana

Aside from Einstein, there are not many poster boys when it comes to science. In fact, the scientists that members of the public can name are few and far between. Carl Sagan was a notable modern example. Through his pioneering work to popularize science through broadcasting with his worldwide hit TV show *Cosmos*, and with his host of best-selling science books, he reached out to the public in an unprecedented way. With the turning of his novel about extraterrestrial contact into the hit movie *Contact*, he reinforced his position as the most publicly recognized scientist around (a position assumed on his death by Stephen Hawking).

Outside of books and TV, Sagan racked up a number of significant accomplishments, including designing the plaque giving humanity's message to the stars on the Voyager space probes and developing the theory of a subsurface ocean on Jupiter's moon Europa (which was eventually confirmed by the Galileo spacecraft). Something that Sagan kept secret throughout his life was his regular use of marijuana and his belief that it helped him do some of his best work.

After his death, biographer Keay Davidson revealed his drug use and also exposed Sagan as "Mr. X" – the infamous contributor of an essay to Dr Lester Grinspoon's pro-pot book *Marihuana Reconsidered*. In 1999, Grinspoon confirmed that Sagan was Mr. X and that the scientist had even written his Pulitzer-Prize-winning book *Dragons of Eden* while under the influence of pot.

In the essay "Mr. X"/Carl Sagan comments: "The cannabis experience has greatly improved my appreciation for art, a subject which I had never much appreciated before." It also enhanced other things for Sagan: "Cannabis enhances the enjoyment of sex – on the one hand it gives an exquisite sensitivity, but on the other hand it postpones orgasm, in part by distracting me with the profusion of images passing before my eyes." Rather poetically, Sagan goes on to say: "Looking at fires when high, by the way, especially through one of those prism kaleidoscopes which image their surroundings, is an extraordinarily moving and beautiful experience."

SIGMUND FREUD USED AND PROMOTED THE USE OF COCAINE AFTER BEING PAID BY A DRUG COMPANY PRODUCING IT

Sigmund Freud, the founder of psychoanalysis, is lauded as one of the most important minds of the nineteenth century. The mention of any criticism or suggestion of impropriety can lead to a screaming assault on your ignorance by a rabid psychoanalyst. The great man's defenders have tried to suppress some of the more embarassing facts about his life and career, including his use and promotion of cocaine.

In 1884, Freud wrote a paper called *On Coca* that helped popularize the use of cocaine (the drug was entirely legal at this point in history). In it he writes: "I have tested this effect of coca, which wards off hunger, sleep and fatigue, and steels one to intellectual effort, some dozen times on myself." He became a public advocate for the regular use of cocaine claiming "lasting improvement" in users' mental ability.

Freud treated a friend's morphine addiction with cocaine, resulting in the man's slow, painful death as a cocaine addict. But even this did not stop his own use or prevent him from writing to his fiancée "In my last serious depression I took cocaine again and a small dose lifted me to the heights in a wonderful fashion. I am just now collecting the literature for a song of praise to this magical substance."

Documents from pharmaceutical company E Merck show that while Freud was promoting their brand of cocaine over others on the market he was also taking large sums of money from them and another American company for performing clinical trials on the drug. This shows a conflict of interest and a deliberate attempt to mislead by not revealing the drug company's financial backing.

If the pun can be forgiven, a close analysis of Freud's reputation shows it was built on a tissue of lies. He only wrote up six cases in his career, claiming to have cured all of them despite the fact that one patient was "totally shattered" and placed in an asylum, one committed suicide and two others claimed the treatment did not help them.

THE MASTERMIND OF THE BATTLE OF BRITAIN VICTORY – AIR CHIEF MARSHAL LORD DOWDING – SPOKE TO THE DEAD AND USED DOWSING AS TOOLS OF WAR

There is a good reason why governments keep secret the more eccentric beliefs of its military leaders from the public. Knowledge that commanders of the war believe they are reincarnations of historical characters (as was the case with General George Patton) or that they can contact the dead is not seen as good for morale on the battlefield or home front.

The fight for air supremacy over the skies of England between the Royal Air Force and the German Luftwaffe in 1940 saved Britain from Nazi invasion and has gone down in history as the Battle of Britain. It is acknowledged that victory was largely due to the work of the Commander-in-Chief of Fighter Command, Air Chief Marshal Hugh Dowding.

His appointment as head of Fighter Command in 1936 put him in charge of developing the Spitfire and Hurricane and the embryonic use of radar. During the Battle of Britain his understanding and careful use of fighter aircraft, combined with his expert knowledge of the air defence network, were crucial to victory. It was therefore a subject of much controversy that he was not promoted after 1940 and sidelined into economic planning. Dowding himself was so frustrated with the situation that he resigned from the RAF in 1942.

Although attributed in 1940 to political intrigue, one of the secret factors in his downfall was his advocacy of spiritualism and application of unorthodox techniques in warfare. A member of the Ghost Club of London, Dowding would recommend that widows of his fighter pilots lost in action visit mediums to contact their dead husbands. He himself believed he had the ability to talk to the dead and more than once took advice on strategic matters from the other sides believing that the spirits of dead aircrew might be able to provide information not obtainable by British spies. Dowding also used dowsing when trying to work out the best location to place air defence installations. Although not a patch on Nazi use of magic during the war, his colleagues much preferred to believe in Spitfires over spirits.

MARTIN LUTHER KING WAS A WOMANIZER AND PLAGIARIST

Martin Luther King is the only American to be honoured by an annual US national holiday held in his name every year. His status as a national hero and icon of freedom and justice has only grown in the years since his death. Given how elements of the FBI tried to destroy and discredit King while he was alive, there is a natural assumption that any negative accusations about him must be false. However, behind the national hero there are at least two dark secrets in King's life that many still deny today.

Due to the FBI's fear that King was a communist, a series of wiretaps were made by the Bureau. While to J Edgar Hoover's dismay hundreds of hours of surveillance could not prove King was a red, they did provide ample evidence that he was a serial womanizer and regularly used the money coming into his civil rights organization to hire prostitutes. Journalist Carl Rowan detailed how Hoover played a tape they had of King and his close friend Ralph Abernathy holding a sex party in a hotel to a congressional committee. On the tape King could be heard having sex with two women and making comments such as "I'm fucking for God!"

In 1990, researcher Theodore Pappas discovered that King had plagiarized more than a third of his doctoral thesis from the work of an earlier student. King had even duplicated the previous student's errors. The plagiarism continued after he had been falsely awarded his doctorate. Many of his famous civil rights speeches and papers were heavily plagiarized and the rousing end of his "I have a dream" speech was stolen directly from a 1950s speech made by black preacher named Archibald Carey.

The deepest truth about King is that he preached racial equality, love for all mankind, tolerance and peace in a time of massive injustice, extreme hatred and violence. No plagiarism or predilection for prostitutes can deny the reality that his voice and resistance to prejudice helped bring about the landmark civil rights legislation that America still benefits from today.

`right` Beautiful dreamer – the FBI could not prove that the civil rights hero Martin Luther King was a red, but they could prove whom he was having in his bed.

LIES, DAMNED LIES AND STATISTICS

17

"There are three kinds of lies: lies, damned lies and statistics."
Benjamin Disraeli

We have been culturally conditioned to find arguments more believable if accompanied by statistical evidence. We tend to take on trust that when someone quotes a percentage or a cost figure that it is accurate and there's a widespread belief that statistics equate to facts.

It was not until I started to have my first battles with Downing Street's spin doctors and the British government's political advisers, such as the infamous Jo Moore (who sent an email around on 9/11 advising government press officers that it was "a good day to bury bad news"), that I realized how statistics could be used to lie and cover up inconvenient political truths.

When you have a chance to see up close how the figures bandied around to support various arguments and claims made by governments have been manipulated to mislead the media and the public, you quickly loose your faith in the idea that any number quoted by a politician can be trusted.

We know governments rarely play fair when it comes to manipulating the information at their disposal. Surveys can be constructed to give you any answer you want, targets can always be met with a little bit of massaging and you can avoid discussions on controversial issues by simply not collecting any figures.

The same statistics those in power use to make their lies seem believable can also be used to explode long-established myths and expose information that those in government and big business definitely don't want you to know.

above Don't believe your eyes – an Egyptian family watch Princess Diana's funeral on television, but the majority no longer trust the media to tell us the truth.

STATISTICS THAT SHOW THAT ONLY 21 PER CENT OF US TRUST THE MEDIA

Of all the under-reported stories in the media, the one that should surprise us least about its suppression/convenient omission from news diaries (delete according to your level of cynicism) is that only just over one fifth of us trust the media to report fairly and accurately any more.

In 1974, more than 33 per cent of Americans and 36 per cent of Europeans expressed a "great deal of confidence" in the media, according to National Opinion Research Centre measures and academic studies. Twenty years later the figure has fallen to just over 10 per cent and in 2004 it was just under 10 per cent who expressed the same confidence.

A regular Gallop survey showed belief in the accuracy of the media falling from 54 per cent in 1989 to 36 per cent in 2004. *The Wall Street Journal* and NBC polls showed a similar decline to a figure of just 21 per cent of Americans believing that their newspapers and broadcasters got the facts right. When Gallop also asked people to rate the honesty and ethical standards of different professions, journalists only scored higher than lawyers, politicians and car salesmen.

A recent *E-Times* survey showed 41 per cent of people in America and 59 per cent of those surveyed in the UK attributed their recent decline in trust in the media to coverage of the lead-up to and invasion of Iraq, while more than 80 per cent of Americans said that they did not believe coverage of the presidential elections was fair and accurate. In total, only 20.5 per cent trusted the media to tell them the truth.

The former president of the American Society of Newspaper Editors, Robert H Giles, admitted: "To many the mass media has become the massive media – intrusive, sensational, uncaring and flawed by bias and inaccuracy. To many, we lack introspection, discipline, restraint and a capacity for self-scrutiny."

Maybe the media could start to get our trust back by beginning reports with, "We know most of you won't believe this, but…" or by quoting the secret "level of trust" surveys that most newspapers and broadcasters regularly conduct to find out what we think of them – but only publish if they like the results.

SECRET CAR COMPANY STATISTICS THAT COULD MEAN THE DIFFERENCE BETWEEN YOUR LIFE AND DEATH IN ONE OF THEIR VEHICLES

In the hands of big business, secret safety statistics can kill the customer. In the movie *Fight Club*, Edward Norton's character explains his job to a fellow aircraft passenger. To her horror he details how his job as a "recall co-ordinator" for a major car company involves him using statistics to work out whether to recall a car that he knows is dangerous will cost more than the resulting law suits. While it seems on the surface like a piece of dark satire with no basis in reality, it is in fact an accurate account of how some automobile manufacturers used statistics in their safety policies.

In 1977, investigative journalist Mark Dowie obtained a secret memo and other documents from the Ford Motor Company that clearly detailed how it knew that hundreds of its customers could potentially suffer needless and horrifically painful death in the company's Pinto models. The problem occurred when Ford produced the Pinto in the early 1970s. Engineers at the company discovered towards the end of the safety checking process a flaw in the car's fuel tank that meant in the event of a rear end collision it would rupture

easily. However, as the assembly-line machinery was already set up for production and making the necessary changes would add a cost of $11 per car produced, Ford went ahead and made the car without first making the necessary changes.

Statistics suggested 180 deaths by burning and 180 serious injuries were likely to be caused by 2,100 serious accidents relating to the faulty fuel tank. Managers at the car giant made a cost-benefit analysis. Working out that each death would cost them $200,000 in out-of-court settlements, and each serious accident $67,000 over the lifetime of the car production, they compared this to the cost of making the $11 change per car. Ford ultimately decided to proceed with the manufacture of the car without making any changes to the fuel tank.

Aside from this incident, Ford has an exemplary commitment to safety and no one could doubt that its products, since Pinto, have prioritized driver and passenger safety. While some other car manufacturers still continue to employ similar statistics methods today, Ford do not.

MANKIND IS THREE MILLION YEARS OVERDUE TO BE WIPED OUT BY A MAJOR CATASTROPHE

With more than six billion people living today, it's hard to contemplate a time in our past when the population of the planet was reduced to just 10,000 individuals.

However, *Homo sapiens* has come close to outright extinction, with the population falling to that genetic bottleneck figure twice in the last 100,000 years. Our ancestors were nearly wiped out in 100,000 BCE by climate change and again in 74,000 BCE when a volcanic super-eruption struck Sumatra and plunged the Earth into an instant ice age. Worryingly, statistically speaking we are now overdue an extinction level event.

The work by statisticians looking at the likelihood of an extinction level event reducing mankind to similar numbers again does not make for comfortable reading. According to Professor Richard Muller and Professor Robert Rohde from the University of California, there is a cycle of massive extinction every 62 million years. A detailed and extensive analysis of the fossil records has backed up their theory and even though they and colleagues across the globe have tried to

knock it down, they have all failed. According to the statistics, we are now three million years overdue for the next extinction.

If extinction does not come through the 62-million-year cycle of death, it could come from a shorter geological pattern, as we are 2,500 years overdue a massive super-volcano eruption. According to Professor Stephen Sparks of Bristol University, its fallout would "cause a 'volcanic winter' devastating global agriculture and causing mass starvation that would threaten the fabric of civilisation". America, the country with the most potential super-volcanoes, has not got any contingency plans.

Even ignoring these threats, one of the greatest minds on the planet, Stephen Hawking, Lucasian Professor of Mathematics at the University of Cambridge, believes that statistics show humanity is likely to be wiped out by a deadly virus. In an interview with the *Daily Telegraph*, he said: "I don't think the human race will survive the next thousand years, unless we spread into space. There are too many accidents that can befall life on a single planet."

CRACK COCAINE IS THE BIGGEST DRUG THREAT, BUT 85 PER CENT OF THE BUDGET IN THE WAR AGAINST DRUGS IS TARGETED AT MARIJUANA

When politicians talk about the war on drugs, they are really talking about the war on *some* drugs. The reasons for spending billions of dollars campaigning against illegal drugs are given as preventing death and reducing crime. The secret they don't want you to know is that following this logic, the war on drugs should be extended to cigarettes and alcohol as statistically they cause more deaths and crime than any illicit drug.

In the US – the first country to declare a "war on drugs", thanks to President Richard Nixon – the leading causes of death in 2000 – according to the American Medical Association – were tobacco (435,000 deaths; 18.1 per cent of total US deaths), poor diet and physical inactivity (400,000 deaths; 16.6 per cent), and alcohol (85,000 deaths; 3.5 per cent). All illicit drug use only accounted for 17,000 deaths. Perhaps aspirin should also have war declared on it because it killed 7,600 Americans in the same period.

According to the US Department of Justice, alcohol use was a factor in four out of ten convicted murderers' crimes and two out of three US prison inmates have previously been in a treatment programme for alcohol dependency. By comparison, the drug cited as the most dangerous to society, crack cocaine, featured only in one in ten murder convictions. There is no way of ignoring the statistical evidence that shows the $20 billion the US spent in the war on drugs in 2004 would have done a lot more to reduce deaths and crimes if spent on tackling cigarette and alcohol addiction.

An even bigger statistical shock comes from discovering that although politicians quote crack cocaine as the biggest problem illicit drug, the majority of the drug-busting budget is spent tackling marijuana. Judge Robert Sweet, the first Federal judge in America to reveal openly his opposition to the drug war, revealed that using the Department of Justice's own figures, 85 per cent of the cost of combating drugs was taken up with marijuana, which according to him is further evidence that: "The use of the criminal law to deal with the drug problem is expensive, ineffective and harmful."

`right` High times - Marijuana takes the lion share of the anti-drug funding in most western countries, but some countries such as the Netherlands have actually legalized it.

THE FUEL CONSUMPTION STATISTICS THAT SHOW CARS MADE TWENTY YEARS AGO WERE BETTER THAN THE ONES MADE TODAY

It's a sign of learning an unusually shocking truth, when it not only challenges your world view, but after discovering it you end up finding yourself supporting those you consider dangerous cranks. The scandalous and surprising truth that has placed me in the same camp as Greenpeace comes from statistics that prove cars made in the past were more fuel efficient than those being built today. It's a secret car makers don't boast about in their glossy commercials.

In 1975, in the aftermath of the OPEC oil export embargo in response to western support of Israel, the US government introduced a fuel efficiency programme. However, in 2001, the US Transportation Department released a report showing the average fuel economy of cars and light trucks sold in America was 24.5 miles (39.4 km) per gallon (3.8 litres). This was the lowest figure recorded since 1980. According to the Transportation Department, fuel efficiency has been in reverse since 1987, when the average fuel economy was 26.2 miles (42.2 km) per gallon. The real situation is worse, but is hidden because manufacturers get extra credits for making vehicles that can run on other fuel sources.

In response to this situation, the US Environmental Protection Agency said: "If this backslide continues, problems with fuel consumption will increase and global warming trends will worsen at a pace faster than is being assumed by analysts."

It would be easy to believe that this was purely an American problem due to the still low level of fuel prices paid by American drivers compared to most other countries in the western world. However, figures show that even in territories where petrol is double the cost of that in the US, a similar pattern emerges. In Japan and South Korea fuel efficiency has also dropped by 6 per cent.

While many may disagree with Greenpeace over the best methods for achieving a reduction in CO2 emissions, it is hard to argue with their assertion that: "So far, no country or manufacturer has taken concrete action to implement meaningful fuel efficiency." Until fuel efficiency beats 1980 levels, it is a claim that will continue to stand.

below Autogeddon – car trouble looms for the entire planet as the automobile has a dominant role in the economy and transport policy of western countries.

HOW THE UK GOVERNMENT DELIBERATELY MANIPULATES STATISTICS TO MAKE IT APPEAR THAT THE UK HAS LESS UNEMPLOYMENT AND HOMELESSNESS THAN IT ACTUALLY HAS

The British government is obsessed with statistics. Of course, Britain is not the only country where those in power rely heavily on bombarding the media and the public with statistical information to prove how good a job there are doing. However, in their last election campaigns, for every one statistic George W Bush mentioned, Tony Blair mentioned four.

With little ideological difference between the two major political parties, statistics are used more heavily to try and differentiate how effective they have been in government. Given the importance statistics have assumed in UK politics, it is even more disturbing that they are being deliberately manipulated either by presenting them as showing something they actually do not show or taking measures to falsify the collection of data behind them.

An example of presentational manipulation is the Labour government's claims that unemployment figures in the UK are better than those of its main competitors in Europe, thereby proving that their handling of the economy is better than its rivals. However, the lower unemployment figures in the UK are only achieved through the fact that 7 per cent of the British workforce is now registered as long-term sick and therefore not counted in the jobless figures. Germany only has 2 per cent of its workforce registered long-term sick and France only 0.3 per cent, which makes the comparisons the British government make a total sham.

Even worse is the use of techniques to falsify the data collected about the levels of homelessness in the UK. Knowing the date of the night on which the "headcount" survey of levels of homelessness in London was to be carried out, the government's Rough Sleeper Unit (RSU) moved sleepers off the streets for just that single night by threatening many of the homeless with arrest and also putting them in hostels that would not be able to provide a place for them again. The RSU also leaned on those who had taken the headcount to "reconsider" their figures so they appeared lower. Thanks to this approach, the government could lie better through statistics and claim that levels of homelessness had radically declined.

left Walk on by – the UK government fixes the homeless figures by ensuring there are less rough sleepers on the streets of London when it makes its official survey.

Blessed are the poor – if a rich man has trouble getting into heaven Bill Gates can afford to buy all of our prayers due to his $28 billion fortune.

HOW MUCH WEALTH IS ACTUALLY OWNED BY THE RICHEST 400 PEOPLE IN THE WORLD

According to *Forbes* magazine, the collective net worth of the world's wealthiest 400 people stood at $1.9 trillion in 2004. The publication of the *Forbes* list of the 400 richest Americans, and the *Sunday Times Rich List* in the UK, always leads to new statistics interpretations of what this concentration of money actually means.

The statistics will be seized upon by political groups and campaigners to illustrate the inequality between the world's rich and poor. Statistically speaking, the horrendous gap is self-evident and deplorable, which makes it all the more puzzling why some people have to lie about it.

In just one afternoon, I found 118 political parties and movements quoting: "Only 4% of the wealth of the world's richest 225 people – $40 billion – would be enough to end poverty and provide basic healthcare, food, safe water, sanitation and education for all of the world's people." Quoting a United Nation's report, it seems like a believable statistic until it is checked. Doing this reveals that on a conservative estimate, the UN believes at least $500 billion is required to halve world poverty.

As a spin-doctor, one thing I learnt was that you had to be scrupulous about telling the truth and the facts you use. Nothing undermines your credibility faster than providing false information to people. Quoting a fact without checking it suggests that one person somewhere got it wrong and a lot of people are too lazy to check what they are copying or that some of the politically motivated are not going to let a little thing like accuracy come between them and beating on the rich.

It is not hard to play with the real figures and come up with shocking but accurate statistics about the disparity between the world's wealthy and the world's poor. My favourite is that Bill Gates – the richest person on the planet with $28.95 billion, which increases by $4.12 million per day – could give every one of the 6.43 billion people on earth $4.50 and still have almost $18 million left in the bank. Now that is scary.

STATISTICS THAT REVEAL WHICH IS THE MOST AGGRESSIVE NATION

Although statistics are often abused and perverted to back up the official position, stripped-down numerical facts also possess a wonderful ability to cut through a miasma of lies, half-truths and conflicting claims to reveal unpleasant truths. When that happens, it becomes very clear why governments prefer to make policy on the basis of opinion rather than evidence. After all, surely it makes sense to adopt a defence strategy based on tackling the most aggressive country in the world?

It is not easy to develop a fair statistical formula for showing which nation holds the record for aggression since 1945, but two undeniable measures of aggression – bombing of another country and unprovoked military invasion of a sovereign nation – allow for a good objective assessment.

Although Africa remains the bloodiest continent, with the highest number of aggressive acts occurring on it, using the above objective criteria, no single African nation emerges as a challenger for the title of "The World's Most Aggressive Country". Even given its record for invasion of satellite states such as Hungary in 1956, Czechoslovakia in 1968 and Afghanistan in 1979, the former Soviet Union only manages to come in a distant second to the eventual winner.

The most aggressive nation is the United States of America. With 17 invasions of other countries and the bombing of 22 states since 1945, including the bombings of Korea, Cuba, Libya, Afghanistan, Vietnam and Iraq, as well as the less well-remembered bombings of Peru, Indonesia and Guatemala. It is also worth nothing that the USA spends more money on its military ($276.7 billion) than the next 12 nations combined.

It is a terrible irony that a country that has stood as a beacon of justice, democracy and freedom for so many in the world is revealed by statistics as the number one gangster. I do not know how a country so full of generous, open-hearted and principled people has allowed itself to earn the dubious title of the most aggressive nation in the world today, but I am certain it is a record that most Americans will be appalled by.

`below` Combat rock – US armed forces during the "Urgent Fury" invasion of Grenada, where they crushed the "New Jewel" revolutionary movement.

HOW THE US ARMY HIDES THE NUMBER OF CIVILIAN DEATHS IN IRAQ AND OTHER CONFLICTS BY NOT COLLECTING STATISTICS

By the time you read this, the figure of 1,587 US deaths, 87 UK deaths and 90 other "coalition of the willing" deaths will be out-of-date when it comes to recording the military deaths suffered since the invasion of Iraq in 2003. However, if you are curious to find the current toll, it will be easy to look up the latest official statistics about how many coalition soldiers have given their lives.

You will not be able to go online and discover an official Iraqi civilian death toll resulting from the invasion and subsequent occupation of Iraq. The simple reason for this is, as General Tommy Franks, who led the US forces into Iraq, has said: "We don't do body counts."

It has to be said, this is an unprecedented stroke of genius by the US military. It also shows that despite what many of its critics claim, it has learnt at least one lesson since the Vietnam War – that the reporting of civilian deaths at the hands of US forces increases public opposition to a conflict. Going one step further than

previous attempts to anaesthetize the folks back home to the horrors of war by relabelling civilian deaths "collateral damage" or getting the US media to under-report statistics (as they did in the US invasion of Afghanistan), doing away with collecting statistics means you don't have to lie or keep secrets as, officially, there are no civilian deaths.

Despite the fact that the Geneva Convention requires occupying forces to protect the civilian population and that this action, by definition, requires monitoring how many of them are dying and why, neither UK nor US governments have backed down over their policy of not keeping count of civilian deaths. In fact, when the Iraqi Health Ministry tried to collect data on deaths it was ordered to stop by American officials. No wonder that when Brigadier General Mark Kimmitt, Deputy Director of Coalition Operations, was asked what he would say to someone who saw the civilian deaths on TV and wondered why they were not reported, he commented: "Change the channel."

HOW MUCH AN END TO POVERTY AND FREE HEALTHCARE WOULD REALLY COST

For years, various peace campaigns and anti-world-poverty groups have used posters that claim: "The cost of ending world poverty is $450 billion – the same as is spent on arms in just one year." It's a neat lie to give the posters shock effect. Supporters of the idea that halting military spending could end poverty rarely check the statistical facts underpinning the claim. If they did, they would find that the truth is the sums do not add up.

Eight million people around the world die each year because they are too poor to stay alive and 1.1 billion people struggle to survive on less than $1 a day. Even using the most rigorously costed schemes to reduce world poverty provided by economists such as the UN's Jeffery Sachs, the cost of even halving poverty is in excess of $500 billion. The figure keeps rising as populations increase and the impact of global warming and environmental changes hit. Most figures quoted do not include health care as no one can agree on a definition of the minimum acceptable level.

Few doubt that simply diverting funds would solve the poverty problem. Reform of land rights, access to capital and an end to developed world protectionism would all also be needed. However, a realistic figure to end poverty is much closer to $1,250 billion than the figure campaigners usually quote.

The truth is that there is no single magic bullet that can end world poverty – not even scrapping all military spending. However, certain statistics remain. The cost of a single B-2 Stealth Bomber is $1 billion. If that money was spent elsewhere it could restore sight to 31,446,541 adults through cataract operations; remove more than one million landmines; create 1,150,510 clean water wells or provide three months' worth of medicine for 3,030,303 communities of up to a thousand people.

Somehow, I think the shock and awe provided by any of those is worth a lot more to world peace and the spread of democracy than turning downtown Baghdad into a deadly firework show for the 24-hour satellite news channels.

WHITEWASHES

18

"If there were twenty ways of telling the truth and only one way of telling a lie, the government would find it out. It's in the nature of governments to tell lies."
George Bernard Shaw

What happens when something people in power do not want you to know about threatens to become public? They set up an official inquiry or other form of investigation to ensure a good, old-fashioned whitewash where lies are supported by a phalanx of selective facts and the truth is a secret buried in an unreported footnote.

This might sound cynical, but any examination of the public inquiries, commissions, panels, committees and a host of other bureaucratic devices governments resort to when a public outcry is building shows they are rarely designed to reveal the truth.

Those in power recognize an inquiry can not only calm public fears of a cover-up and draw the political sting out of an issue but can also become a powerful mechanism for spreading the official version. If it is believed an inquiry is independent, the whitewash it produces can act as an enforcer of conformity and the orthodox view that reverberates throughout history.

Although sold to the public as independent mechanisms for exposing secrets and lies, the nature of their composition, terms of reference and limited investigative power means that right from the word go they will never produce a final report that reveals anything damaging to those who set up the investigation. The public rarely gets to see the hidden web of political patronage, shared interests and clandestine alliances that ensure that a supposedly autonomous commission has an invisible bias towards those in power, or most at risk, should the full facts ever get out.

THE IRAN-CONTRA SCANDAL

On October 6, 1986, a cargo plane crashed into the Nicaraguan jungle. It had been brought down with a surface-to-air missile as it was dropping weapons to Contra rebels. The only survivor to emerge was American mercenary Eugene Hasenfus. His capture by the Sandinista government led to the unravelling of what became known as the Iran-Contra scandal.

It emerged that the Reagan-Bush government was secretly selling arms to Iran in exchange for the release of American hostages held by Islamic extremists in Lebanon. The profits from these arm sales were being channelled to illegally fund the Contra rebels in Nicaragua in direct contravention of the Congressional ban on the US providing any such support.

Faced with mounting Congressional pressure, President Reagan was forced to announce that former Senator John Tower would head a Presidential Commission to investigate the matter. One US Senator, John Kerry, pressed for the commission to investigate not only the arms deals but evidence that the CIA was also using drug smugglers and profits from drug deals to help fund the Contras. He was ignored.

During Colonel Oliver North's public testimony to the commission about his role in the affair and his shredding of vital documents, two men unfurled a banner stating, "Ask about the cocaine smuggling" while a third man leapt up and started to shout out: "Ask about the cocaine!" As he was dragged out of earshot, his colleagues kept shouting out questions such as: "What about the cocaine dealing that the US is paying for?" and "Why don't you ask questions about drug deliveries?" Eventually security pulled them from the room. All three were arrested and charged with contempt of Congress and sentenced to a year in jail.

The Senators did not ask North about cocaine and when the commission published its findings in 1987, the drug smuggling issue was totally whitewashed out of the report. However, a decade later CIA Inspector General Frederick Hitz published a report admitting: "The Reagan administration knew from the outset that Contra-connected drug traffickers worked directly for National Security Council staff and the CIA."

right American hero – The truth, the whole truth and nothing but the truth as Oliver North gives evidence at the Iran-Contra hearings. No one did ask about the cocaine

Who watches the watchmen? The members of the Warren Commission failed to examine much of the crucial evidence relating to JFK's assassination.

THE WARREN COMMISSION ON THE ASSASSINATION OF JFK

In 2002, more than 500 hours of secret tapes made by the disgraced former president Richard Nixon were released. The tapes reveal Nixon's attempt to blame supporters of Democratic presidential hopefuls George McGovern and Edward Kennedy for the attempted assassination of the Governor of Alabama.

Discussing how to make it appear the work of a left-winger, Nixon commented to an aide "Just say you have it on unmistakable evidence." When questioned whether it would be believed, Nixon reminded his staff of the Warren Commission looking into the assassination of JFK and said: "It was the greatest hoax that has ever been perpetuated."

Within six days of Kennedy's shooting, President Lyndon B Johnson set up the President's Commission on the Assassination of President Kennedy. It quickly became known as the Warren Commission after its head, Earl Warren. It was made up of Democratic and Republican politicians alongside CIA director Alan Dulles and former World Bank President John J McCloy. Its job was to tell the public the truth about the assassination.

Rushed to make its final report before the next US presidential elections, the commission relied entirely on material provided to them by the Secret Service and the FBI. It never even examined the actual autopsy evidence and classified its own files to 2039. Only by accepting the "magic bullet" theory – that one bullet was responsible for several injuries sustained by Kennedy and the Texas Governor – were they able to state that the assassination was the work of Lee Harvey Oswald, who acted entirely alone. The one dissenting voice on the commission was Congressman Hale Boggs. He had "strong doubts" over the magic bullet theory and complained "the FBI is using *Gestapo* tactics", when a package of pornographic material relating to critics of the commission was sent to him.

Whether or not it was a hoax, the failure to explore the evidence makes the Warren Commission a whitewash. Even the later House Select Committee on Assassinations criticized the commission for failing to "investigate the potential of conspiracy" and stating "conclusions in its report in a fashion that was too definitive".

THE ROBERTSON PANEL ON UFOS

On July 19, 1952, radar operators at Washington National airport tracked an armada of blips on their screens while through the glass in the control tower their colleagues followed the fast-moving strange lights with their own eyes. The nearby Andrews Air Force Base, which also had the invaders of the US capital's airspace on their radar, scrambled attack jets. This set the pattern for the next three weeks – mass sightings of UFOs confirmed by civilian and military radar contact and fighters chasing UFOs over the White House itself.

Not surprisingly, these events knocked the Korean War and approaching US presidential elections off of the front pages. Occurring at the height of the Cold War, it is not surprising the UFO flap meant the public in Washington DC were on the edge of hysteria. At the risk of losing all credibility for being unable to control the capital's airspace and unable to provide an explanation, the intelligence services formed the Advisory Panel on UFOs, Office of Scientific Intelligence.

Headed up by physicist and CIA employee H P Robertson, the group of experts quickly became known as the Robertson Panel. However, instead of conducting a scientific and impartial investigation into what was happening in the skies above them, they quickly turned their considerable minds to conducting a whitewash that would calm top politicians' growing worries.

Although unable to derive a conventional explanation that fitted the facts, the Robertson Panel reported that most UFO sightings were the misidentification of clouds, planets and stars and the remaining cases could also be explained away if given enough study (even those that turned up on radar). The panel also suggested the government should begin a programme of serious "debunking" and run a secret public relations campaign using psychiatrists, astronomers and celebrities to reduce the public perception of UFOs as serious or threatening. They even suggested getting Walt Disney to help.

Given this, it's not surprising that the US military got away with giving an official version that the events of 1952 were caused by a "temperature inversion".

THE BLOODY SUNDAY INQUIRY

Since 1969 more than 3,300 people have been killed in Northern Ireland's "troubles". Although, disgracefully, many victims have quickly been forgotten by the public and politicians alike, no one has forgotten the 14 unarmed civil rights protesters and civilians shot dead by British paratroopers during a civil rights protest in the Bogside district of Derry on January 30, 1972, a date forever known as "Bloody Sunday".

Within days of Bloody Sunday, Prime Minister Edward Heath had appointed Lord Widgery to conduct an official inquiry into the events. Reporting 11 weeks later, Lord Widgery claimed that the soldiers had been fired on first and that the deceased had been in close contact with firearms. To come up with his conclusions Widgery had taken the soldiers at their word, failed to call key witnesses and had wilfully disregarded all forensic evidence that did not fit his version of events.

Recently declassified documents show UK politicians wanted the matter "buried as quickly as possible" and they knew Widgery's report was wrong in several key areas.

Despite knowing the report was full of flaws, Edward Heath said: "All shades of opinion concerned with the truth must feel indebted to him for his objective and painstaking analysis of events." The anger of the families of the dead at Widgery's whitewash led them to campaign for a fresh inquiry. Twenty-five years later, after new medical, ballistic and eyewitness evidence surfaced, further disproving Widgery's account, the British government set up the Saville Inquiry to reinvestigate Bloody Sunday.

When people are given a whitewash instead of the truth, they often get angry. In the years following the Bloody Sunday Inquiry, resentment over the killings and the lack of credible truth over the event fuelled a bitterness that propelled many people to join the Republican terrorist movement. Former Republican MP Bernadette Devlin was addressing the civil rights protesters when paratroopers opened fire. In 2001 she claimed that Bloody Sunday had worsened the violence in Northern Ireland, saying: "Three thousand and more coffins followed." If the public had been given the truth instead of whitewash, that number may have been reduced.

left Alternative Ulster — the killing of 13 civilians on Bloody Sunday strengthened the view of many that British soldiers were an occupying force suppressing Irish freedom.

THE 9/11 COMMISSION AND BUSH AND CHENEY'S SECRET EVIDENCE

For people to be able to judge truth from lies on an objective basis, they need to have access to the facts. If you get anything less than that during an official investigation of a subject any findings it makes will never amount to more than a whitewash that robs the public of their chance to determine what really happened.

When the issues that people want to know the truth about are the events that occurred in the months leading up to the 9/11 attacks, you would think that the White House would bend over backwards to ensure the American public was given a chance to make their own judgement by co-operating fully with the inquiry conducted by Congress. They didn't.

After months of pressure, President Bush finally allowed the establishment of the 9/11 Commission with Dr Henry Kissinger at its head. When Kissinger refused to provide details of his business clients, he was replaced as chairman by Thomas Kean. Naturally the commission was keen to interview the president to establish exactly what he and the White House staff knew about the al-Qaeda threat in advance of the attacks. Both President Bush and Vice President Dick Cheney refused to appear in public before the commission.

It took several months of behind-the-scene negotiations before Bush and Cheney would agree to meet the commissioners, and even then it was only under the following extraordinary conditions: they would not be under oath; they could appear together, and the session would not be recorded, transcribed or made public. Bush even refused to allow the families of those who had died access to the evidence that he and his vice president gave.

After a three-hour visit by the commissioners, George W Bush gave a short press conference in the White House Rose Garden. He said: "If we had something to hide we wouldn't have met with them in the first place." If there was nothing to hide, why was what was said kept secret? It's an important question to which the American people have yet to receive an answer.

`top` 9/11 - the day the world changed forever. The victims and their families deserve the truth, but secrets are still being kept.

`above` Condoleezza Rice's evidence may have seen her commit an act of perjury.

More tank top than tank commander - Former British Prime Minister John Major's government failed to release the report.

THE UK NATIONAL AUDIT OFFICE REPORT INTO THE AL YAMAMAH ARMS DEAL

When Margaret Thatcher signed the £20 billion Al Yamamah arms deal with Saudi Arabia in 1985, the *Financial Times* called it "the biggest sale of anything to anyone by anyone". In this remarkable arms-for-oil deal, the British sold Tornado and Hawk jets, a fleet of minesweepers and an array of other equipment to the Saudi military.

For once, the largest concerns over the deal centred not on providing arms to a repressive regime, but the corruption involved in the massive deal. There have been persistent claims – reinforced by evidence – showing British arms companies involved in the deal operated multi-million pound slush funds to pay Saudi officials, but the most vexing issue for various MPs was Margaret Thatcher's son Mark.

Given her central role in helping secure the massive Al Yamamah deal, any claims that Mark Thatcher benefited from being an intermediary by receiving illegal "commissions" was political dynamite. The persistent allegations of corruption over the Al Yamamah deal led to an investigation by the National Audit Office (NAO).

The NAO investigation took three years, but when it was completed the House of Commons Public Accounts Committee decided not to publish its findings. The chairman of the committee, Robert Sheldon MP, even refused to disclose the report to his fellow committee members, assuring them that there was "No evidence of fraud or corruption". Many of his fellow MPs regarded this as a monstrous whitewash. When in opposition, the Labour Party promised it would publish the report. This has been proven to be a lie as it has consistently refused to do so since it came to power in 1997.

Corruption can only thrive in conditions of secrecy or indifference and is always defeated by transparency. If the NAO report exonerates those concerned from all the accusations made, why do successive governments refuse to publish it? Given that it still remains secret, it is understandable why so many MPs and campaigners suspect that it may contain both the proof needed to proceed with prosecutions and the evidence that would destroy the reputations of politicians, businessmen and companies in both the UK and Saudi Arabia.

INVESTIGATIONS INTO SEXUAL ABUSE IN THE CATHOLIC CHURCH

The sexual abuse of a child by an adult is one of the most obscene breaches of trust and heinous crimes one human being can perpetrate on another. When a priest conducts the abuse, the evil seems compounded by extra layers of hypocrisy and the exploitation of faith.

The Roman Catholic Church is not alone in terms of religious organizations providing a cover for vile sexual predators, but its long-established official policy of secrecy and deception clearly single it out for justified exposure within the pages of this book. When investigative reporting by *The Boston Globe* helped expose the massive scale of systematic child abuse by Catholic priests in the Boston Archdiocese, and led to a series of lawsuits by former victims and prosecutions by the authorities in 2002, it lifted the lid not only on predatory perverts across the US but also on the Roman Catholic Church's despicable policies aimed at whitewashing over the problem.

Documents uncovered during legal actions show that the Church was well aware of not only the massive scale of abuse in churches in countries across the globe, but had a secrecy strategy endorsed by the pope himself. From 1962, when Pope John XXIII signed a document entitled *Instruction on the Manner of Proceeding in Cases of Solicitation*, it was official policy that when a priest was accused of abusing a child (or committing an act of bestiality) he would be tried in secret by his local church and that the police and other secular authorities were not to be told of the abuse.

Updated approaches to the issue still allow for the Holy See to decide how to handle suspected cases of abuse and whether to proceed with a secret tribunal to judge accusations or whether to place the case in the hands of the relevant secular authorities. In many countries, such as Ireland, Poland and Argentina, abuse scandals have cost bishops and archbishops their jobs, but the whitewash over the issue and public downplaying of the problem continues to put many children at risk in the future.

THE INVESTIGATION INTO THE DEATH OF PRINCESS DIANA

Few disagree with the maxim that for justice to be done, it must be seen to be done. However, it also requires that any legal process involved be open to scrutiny and impartial. On these grounds alone justice was taking a holiday when it came to the investigation of the death of Princess Diana. The official inquiries that have been undertaken are without doubt whitewashes.

Disregarding the conspiracy theories that proliferate about what happened on August 31, 1997, when the Mercedes driven by chauffeur Henri Paul carrying Diana and her lover Dodi Al Fayed crashed into a pillar in Pont e l'Alma tunnel in Paris, it is clear that the truth has not emerged – due to failings in the official French inquiry into her death.

Taking two years to report, the full 6,000 pages of the French Public Prosecutor's investigation is still kept secret, with only employees of the police and the Department of Justice allowed access. Even in its public executive summary form it is obvious that the report is a whitewash due to its failure to address several serious issues, which if they had

been investigated could have at a stroke eliminated much of the wild speculation about what happened.

Despite a series of legal challenges by Dodi's father in the United States, which exposed the fact that the US National Security Agency (NSA) was monitoring Diana in Paris and holding more than a thousand still-classified documents on her death, the French Public Prosecutor made no attempt to discover what the NSA knew. Nowhere in the 6,000 pages is there any investigation of how Henri Paul, whose salary was £20,000 per year, managed to maintain 13 different bank accounts containing in total more than 1.2 million francs or from where large sums paid into those accounts had come. The Public Prosecutor also failed to question a number of witnesses.

The impartiality of the British inquiry must be called into question by the fact it was carried out by Royal Coroner Michael Burgess. In fact, the Surrey Coroner called the inquests into the death of Diana and Dodi "a waste of time and public money".

THE WHITEWATER INVESTIGATION INTO BILL AND HILARY CLINTON

In 1994, President Clinton faced a crisis when it emerged that the White House chief counsel Bernard Nussbaum had taken documents concerning the Whitewater Development Corporation from the office of Deputy White House Counsel Vince Foster when his dead body was found in Fort Macy Park. Bill and Hilary Clinton had invested in the property company and had been accused of fraud when the Securities and Exchange Commission investigated its bankruptcy.

Facing a barrage of press speculation, Clinton did what most politicians in similar situations do: he called for an independent inquiry. Attorney General Janet Reno appointed a special prosecutor to investigate. When Kenneth Starr replaced original prosecutor Robert Fiske, the Clintons' allies claimed that the investigation was a "witch hunt", while Hilary Clinton talked of a "vast right-wing conspiracy".

Using the classic tactics of refusing to co-operate and encouraging others to do the same (key witness Susan McDougal spent 18 months in jail for contempt after refusing Starr's questions), the inquiry dragged on until the public

and press were bored. It was only when Starr discovered evidence of Bill Clinton's sexual activities with Monica Lewinsky that the story was brought to life again.

During this period Clinton famously said: "I want to say one thing to the American people. I want you to listen to me. I did not have sexual relations with that woman, Miss Lewinsky." Starr sent his report showing Clinton's perjury, obstruction of justice, witness tampering and abuse of authority to Congress, but in a total whitewash ignoring all of the evidence the Democratic Party-dominated Senate acquitted Clinton of all charges.

In March 2002, Robert Ray, the third prosecutor appointed to the case, finally delivered his report. It showed that, after eight years of investigation costing more than $52 million, Bill Clinton could have been charged and might have been convicted in a Federal Court for lying under oath and other offences. However, Mr Clinton's lawyers struck a deal with Mr Ray to spare the president from criminal charges the day before he left office in January 2001, ensuring a Whitewater whitewash to the end.

THE HUTTON INQUIRY INTO THE DEATH OF DR DAVID KELLY

When BBC journalist Andrew Gilligan reported in May 2003 that Tony Blair's government had "sexed up" its dossier of intelligence information about Saddam Hussein's weapons of mass destruction and "probably knew" that the claim the weapons could be launched in 45 minutes was wrong, everything changed.

Within weeks, Gilligan's source for the report – government scientist Dr David Kelly – was exposed in the press by the government and later found dead (apparently from suicide), and the BBC was under attack from Number 10. Gilligan was suspended and Tony Blair established an inquiry under Lord Hutton to investigate the claims. After six weeks and £2.54 million in taxpayers' money, Hutton produced a report clearing the government of any responsibility for Dr Kelly's death and suggesting that the accusations about the dossier were false. Even the normally loyal pro-Labour papers thought it was a whitewash. However, Blair demanded an apology. Gilligan left the BBC, as did its chairman and director general.

A later inquiry by Lord Butler into the intelligence used to justify the war against Iraq showed just how much of a whitewash the Hutton inquiry had been. It proved that Tony Blair had lied when he twice claimed that Lord Hutton had seen all the intelligence on the case for war. It also showed that MI6 and the Joint Intelligence Committee knew intelligence had been withdrawn, but had not told this to Lord Hutton. Most importantly it proved without a doubt that pressure had been brought by Number 10 to strengthen the report and that important caveats about the 45-minute claim had been removed. Sorry, Tony, that is "sexing up".

When the Butler report was published, Blair said he took "full responsibility" for any mistakes made, but claimed that they were "made in good faith". According to Blair: "No one lied. No one inserted things into the dossier against the advice of the intelligence services." Given that this is the same man who lied about the number of bodies found in mass graves in Iraq and non-existent atrocities occurring in Kosovo to justify war, it will be hard for many to believe him.

right Bliar Bliar – Credibility under fire Protestors made their feelings clear when Tony Blair turned up to give evidence to the Hutton inquiry.

DON'T PANIC

19

We all try to hide from certain truths. The comfort zone an illusion built around a framework of lies can give us is often more appealing than facing up to the harsh realities about ourselves and the society in which we live.

It can be very hard to get through the day if we don't ignore certain troubling facts and buy into a series of falsehoods. The money spent purchasing this book could have saved someone's life, and your freedom to read it was bought at the expense of a series of war crimes and atrocities. However, if you begin to think like that too much, not only will I be out of a job, but you are probably going to have a very grim lifestyle.

Possibly one of the biggest illusions we have bought into is the belief that we live in a relatively safe world. When we think of dangers, they tend to be the ones that our governments – supported by media reporting that fails to challenge underlying assumptions – want us to be worried about.

We are all aware of the threat of terrorism, but few people are aware of the potential to kill millions that a failed shuttle launch containing a nuclear cargo could mean. Which is the bigger threat to the public? Secrets have been kept and lies continue to be told over the real dangers we face because the one thing that governments fear more than a disaster is an informed public challenging their dangerous policies.

HOW A FAULTY COMPUTER ALMOST CAUSED THE THIRD WORLD WAR

The fact that you are reading this book instead of scrabbling around in radioactive rubble is something of miracle (or the result of dumb luck depending on your religious perspective). In his groundbreaking book *The Limits of Safety*, Professor Scott D Sagan at Stanford University revealed just how many times and how close to the edge of nuclear war we have been due to mishaps since 1945.

From a series of coincidences during the Suez Crisis to the time during the Cuban Missile Crisis when faulty wiring on a klaxon led to US nuclear bombers moving down the runway ready for take-off, false alarms have almost triggered nuclear war more times than your sanity will allow you to dwell on. While safety measures such as the famous hotline between leaders of the US and the USSR are well known, there has been a persistent culture of keeping the near misses as secret as possible.

Some of the more worrying close calls have involved computers. At 8:50 am on November 9, 1978, the US went from DEFCON 5 (the lowest level of perceived threat and military readiness) to DEFCON 1 (the highest level) when the computer displays at NORAD and the Pentagon showed a full-scale nuclear attack. President Carter could not be found and without their Commander-in-Chief around, the military prepared to retaliate. Six minutes into the situation and with the clock ticking toward apocalypse, it emerged that military training exercise computer programmes were running without anyone knowing, so causing the false displays and information.

At 2:25 am on June 3, 1980, the computer displays in NORAD that usually showed "0000 enemy intercontinental and surface launched missiles detected" started registering "0002" then "0003". Preparations for retaliation were made – missiles were primed in their silos and the US Pacific Command's nuclear-equipped planes took to the air – only for it to be discovered that the readings were down to a single faulty computer chip.

If you want a comfortable night's sleep, then just remember that some missile bases in the former Soviet Union are still using technology introduced in 1980.

THERE HAVE BEEN MORE THAN TWENTY ACCIDENTS INVOLVING NUCLEAR WEAPONS IN THE UK

On July 27, 1956, the county of Suffolk in England almost became a nuclear wasteland. An American B-47 bomber coming in to land at RAF Lakenheath crashed and careered into a nuclear weapons storage bunker. The plane exploded and showered the three Mark VI US bombs in the bunker with burning jet fuel. Fire fighting teams managed to dowse the blaze before the conventional explosive in the bombs could trigger a nuclear detonation.

The commanding officer of the US 7th Air Division sent a memo to General Curtis LeMay, commander of US Strategic Air Command, stating: "Preliminary exam by bomb disposal says a miracle that one Mark Six with exposed detonators didn't go."

Setting a policy of secrecy and deceit that continues until this day, the American Government and the British Ministry of Defence (MoD) decided to deny that an accident had happened. Even in 1985, the MoD still claimed that the B-47 had hit a stationary plane and no fire had occurred.

Declassified documents from the 1960s show that in the event of a major accident involving American nukes, the British government would have stopped the US from ordering evacuations and releasing details in an attempt to avoid panic.

Until 2003, the MoD continued to refuse to admit that any accident involving British nuclear weapons had occurred at all. After a sustained campaign by *The Guardian* newspaper, they admitted to seven incidents. Among these was the dropping of a torpedo on top of a store of nuclear warheads on the submarine *HMS Tiger* while it was anchored off Malta in 1974. They also acknowledged three road accidents that had involved convoys carrying British nukes.

However, they refused to provide details of any other mishaps involving nuclear weapons because they claimed they did not "involve any threat to public safety". Given that an investigation by the MoD's chief scientific adviser Ronald Oxburgh hints at more than 20 mishaps, and that the MoD had decided not to tell the public of any accidental nuclear detonation in the UK, not many people will find that reassuring.

THE USAF ACCIDENTALLY DROPPED ATOMIC BOMBS ON NORTH CAROLINA

The fear of Mutually Assured Destruction (MAD – surely the most apt acronym of all time) may have kept a fragile peace, but the policy of constantly flying B-52 bombers carrying thermonuclear devices across your own territory must rank as an insane risk in anyone's book.

It is a risk that on more than one occasion almost had disastrous consequences. The US military admits to 32 accidents involving nuclear weapons since 1945, but looking at the evidence it is clearly under-reporting. One notable event actually saw two atomic bombs dropped on North Carolina.

When a B-52 broke up in mid-air due to structural failure, its payload of two 24-megaton hydrogen bombs fell to earth near Goldsboro. The parachute of one bomb opened and was easily recovered; however, the other bomb plummeted into a swamp. Try as they might, the military could not retrieve it and in 1992 they admitted that: "A portion of one weapon, containing uranium, could not be recovered despite excavation to a depth of 50 feet." The land has been bought by the military and they continue to monitor it.

Many documents relating to the accident remain classified, but it is known five of the six fail-safe triggers on the bomb failed. Dr Ralph Lapp of the Office of Naval Research said: "Only a single switch prevented detonation and nuclear fire over a wide area."

It would be tempting and reassuring to think that the Goldsboro incident was a one-of-a-kind event. However, the truth is that less than two months after the crash in North Carolina, on March 14, a B-52 carrying two nuclear weapons crashed in California. Luckily, the high explosive did not detonate. Nor was 1961 the only bad year for the B-52s. They continued to crash regularly throughout the 1960s and 1970s – one almost crashed on top of the Big Rock nuclear power plant in Michigan. If the plane had hit Big Rock, no amount of luck would have stopped the mother of all nuclear explosions devastating the Great Lakes area for years to come.

above Bombs away - USAF B-52s and their atomic cargoes have often posed more of a threat to American soil than to that of foreign nations.

THE DANGER OF A 300-FOOT-HIGH TSUNAMI IN THE NORTH ATLANTIC IF THE CUMBRE VIEJA VOLCANO ERUPTS

The unquestionably dire blockbuster movie *The Day After Tomorrow* (it is no secret that all films directed by Roland Emmerich are dire) contains one memorable scene – a 200-foot-high wave crashing into Manhattan and giving the armpits of the Statue of Liberty a good wash with saltwater. While there is debate over whether the science depicted in the film is likely, one scenario that could generate such a New York-bashing tsunami is the collapse of the Cumbre Vieja volcano.

Situated on La Palma, (one of the Canary Islands situated in the Atlantic Ocean off the northwestern coast of Africa), Cumbre Vieja has a long history of seismic activity. Eruptions have been recorded since 1585, with the last eruption occurring in 1971. During an eruption in 1949, the western half of Cumbre Vieja slipped several metres into the ocean, resulting in a mile-long fracture. This fracture weakened the structure of the island and has led some scientists to warn that a further eruption could send a piece of Cumbre Vieja weighing more than 500 billion tons crashing into the ocean.

If this happens, it could create a mega-tsunami reaching a height of 300 feet and travelling at the speeds of a jet plane. It would hit the coast of North Africa in three hours, hit Britain in five hours and reach North America in less than 12 hours. With the wave travelling up to a mile inland, the effects would result in the largest devastation in recorded history. Professor Bill McGuire of the Benfield Research Centre reassuringly said: "There's no if about it. It will happen, it's just a question of when."

You would think that our governments are secretly planning how to cope and ensure they have adequate early warning systems in place. The sad truth is that they are doing next to nothing. The amount of money spent on seismological monitoring of Cumbre Vieja since 1971 would not buy a single armoured tank. It seems that defending the population has a narrow definition in government circles, amounting to little more than keeping them in the dark about the dangers they face and spending the money elsewhere.

SPACECRAFT MISHAPS THAT HAVE RELEASED PLUTONIUM INTO THE ATMOSPHERE

As a child born in the 1970s when man was still going to the Moon, the exploration of space has always seemed to me one of humanity's greatest accomplishments. One of the few benefits of the Cold War was that it provided the fuel of political pride for the space race. Unfortunately, the fuel used to power many satellites was nuclear.

While the rockets used to power space missions are non-nuclear, missions often contain nuclear payloads and many satellites used plutonium-238 as fuel in the form of a long-lasting battery known as a radioisotope thermal generator. Although plutonium-238 does explode, during its half-life of 87.8 years it is 270 times more radioactive than the plutonium-239 used in nuclear weapons. It's not a substance conducive to human health.

This makes the several spacecraft mishaps that have resulted in plutonium-238 being released into the atmosphere extremely worrying. There is not the space to detail even a fraction of the accidents that have occurred, but a typical example is that of a 1964 US navigational satellite which failed to attain orbit after take-off. The nuclear-powered satellite broke up as it fell back to Earth, releasing 2.1 pounds of plutonium-238 into the atmosphere. According to Dr John Gofman, Professor of Medical Physics at the University of California at Berkeley, this accident alone led to an increase in global lung cancer rates. Of course, the US authorities didn't exactly promote this information, and details of many satellite mishaps remain secret.

In 1985, author Karl Grossman got NASA to admit that there was "a very small risk" of releasing plutonium-238 in its missions, but that the odds were "100,000-1 against due to the high reliability inherent in the design of the space shuttle". Within weeks of saying this, the *Challenger* shuttle exploded. The next Space Shuttle mission was due to carry a payload of 24.2 pounds of plutonium-238. Scientists estimate that 24 pounds of plutonium-238 released into the atmosphere could have resulted in several million deaths. Plutonium-238 may feature in many of NASA's future planned missions.

THE LUCKY ESCAPE AND LATER LIES ABOUT THE WINDSCALE FIRE

In the 1950s the British people were sold a lie by their government. They were informed nuclear power was being introduced to provide cheap and clean power. The real reason was that a nuclear power programme was needed if the British were to build their own nuclear bomb. However, the biggest nuclear lie the public was told was that nuclear power was safe.

On October 8, 1957, at the Windscale nuclear plant on the Cumbrian coast of England, a heat sensor failure led to a fire in the Windscale Pile No. 1 reactor. Two days later, air samplers picked up high levels of radioactivity which led staff to realize one of their reactors had been blazing for two days, carrying plumes of radioactive material out of a chimney. With temperatures rising at 20 degrees a minute, staff had a stark choice: risk meltdown or risk an explosion by dowsing the pile with water. They used water and their gamble paid off.

Even with this close scrape, the Windscale fire was the world's worst nuclear power disaster of its time. Windscale Pile No. 1 was not just generating electricity, it was producing plutonium for use in British bombs. The fire released radioactive material, including tellurium-132, caesium-137, strontium-90, polonium-210 and iodine-131 in a nuclear cloud that drifted over England and as far across Europe as Denmark. As iodine-131 easily enters the food chain, millions of litres of milk from an area of 250 square miles surrounding Windscale had to be poured away during the following four months.

Prime Minister Harold Macmillan classified almost all details of the fire for 30 years to try and quell public fears. He ordered a massive pro-nuclear power publicity campaign and that the medical impact of the disaster should be downplayed. Later expert investigation suggests that the accident claimed more than 1,000 lives (mainly through cancer). Between 1950 and 1977 there were 194 accidents at Windscale, 11 involving fires and 45 that led to plutonium releases. Details of many of these incidents remain classified. It seems that, like radioactive isotopes, lies have half-lives and can take a very long time to decay.

above Up in smoke – It took two days for anyone at Windscale (AKA Sellafield) to realize a nuclear fire was burning and sending radioactive material up one its chimneys.

ATOMIC BOMBS HAVE BEEN ACCIDENTALLY DROPPED ON GREENLAND AND SPAIN

To drop atomic bombs on your own country by accident is one thing, but to nuke your allies inadvertently seems not only careless, but also rather impolite. However, given that it was America doing the nuking, the Danish and Spanish governments should at least be grateful that they tried to clean up the resulting mess given the US military's woeful track record of tackling the nuclear pollution it has caused on its home soil.

When a B-52 bomber collided with a refuelling plane above the tiny Spanish village of Palomares on January 17, 1966, the resulting explosion sent both planes crashing to the ground – along with the bomber's payload of four MK28FI nuclear bombs. Each bomb had a potential yield of 1.5 megatons - more than 75 times the raw destructive power that had flattened Hiroshima in 1945. Under a virtual media blackout helpfully provided by the regime of fascist dictator General Franco, the US military searched the area using more than a thousand troops.

One bomb was lost at sea and took four months to find, while another bomb landed harmlessly. The conventional explosive material in the other two bombs detonated when they hit the ground, leading to the release of radioactive material. It cost the Department of Defense $50 million to remove more than 1,400 tons of contaminated soil, but recent tests have shown that the land and the sea still show traces of radiation to this day.

Even more secrecy surrounds another American nuking of foreign soil which occurred in January 1968, when a B-52 bomber crashed while attempting an emergency landing at US Thule Air Force Base in Greenland. The high explosive components of three nuclear weapons the craft was carrying exploded, contaminating 880,000 square feet of rock, snow, ice and water with plutonium. The American military and the Danish government (which controls Greenland) claimed that all four bombs on the plane had exploded. In 2000, however, the Danish newspaper *Jyllands Posten* printed evidence that only three of the four nuclear bombs were retrieved. Leaked classified documents suggest that a bomb with the serial number 78252 may still lie in the sea off Greenland.

`below` Catch of the day – It took the US Navy 81 days to recover one of the nuclear bombs it had lost from the sea around the Spanish village of Palomares.

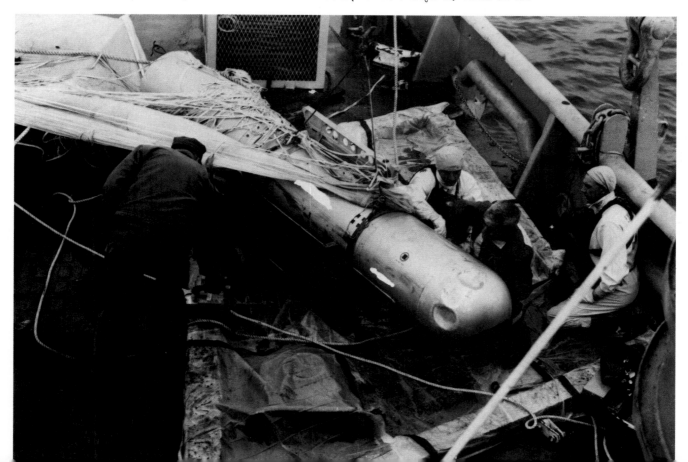

FALLOUT FROM NUCLEAR BOMB TESTS DRIFTED IN CIVILIAN AREAS AND POLLUTED THE ATMOSPHERE IN THE US WITH THE RADIOACTIVE ELEMENT IODINE-131

On December 28, 1966, the People's Republic of China made what could be considered a nuclear assault on the USA. Chinese scientists conducted a 300-kiloton open-air nuclear test. Within four days, US scientists were tracking the resulting cloud of fallout as it travelled across America.

In secret maps not revealed until 30 years later, Oak Ridge National Laboratory not only monitored where the fallout went, but the amount of radioactive iodine-131 the explosion had produced. They estimated that the American people were exposed to more than 15 million curries (radioactive units) of iodine-131 – a similar level was thrown up by the Chernobyl nuclear disaster – with high levels of the radioactive element entering the food chain through milk produced by cows which had fed on contaminated grass.

Iodine-131 is one of the primary radioactive airborne isotopes that result from nuclear tests and is known for being directly linked to thyroid cancer. If you are feeling outraged by the fact that the Chinese test was kept secret from the American people, prepare to have your anger go up another notch, because higher levels of iodine-131 were released into civilian areas by the Americans's own nuclear weapon tests.

On top of weapon tests, scientists even purposefully released clouds of radiation. During its Green Run tests, the Hanford Nuclear Facility in Richland, Washington, regularly released iodine-131 to see how far downwind it went. In doing so, it subjected unknowing citizens to radiation levels hundreds of times higher than that produced by the nuclear power plant accident at Three Mile Island.

Even though the American people never experienced the horror of being attacked by an enemy nation armed with nuclear weapons, the tests by their own military have resulted, and continue to result, in a horrendous civilian death toll. In the 1990s, the US National Cancer Institute produced a 10,000-page report which estimated that between 75,000-100,000 cases of thyroid cancer in the US are the direct result of the fallout from the 443 American weapon tests that released iodine-131 into the atmosphere. Every year, as more evidence becomes available, those figures are revised upward.

THE TICKING TIME BOMB AT THE BOTTOM OF THE THAMES

Living by the Thames Estuary, I've always identified with the lyrics of The Clash's "London Calling" (which I won't repeat for copyright reasons and because you should already know them) and known I was close to a ticking time bomb left over from World War Two.

The SS Richard Montgomery was an American Liberty ship used to move ammunition across the Atlantic during the war. Having survived U-boats, the ship ran aground in 1944 in the Thames Estuary, two miles from Sheerness in Kent and five miles from Southend in Essex. It contained a cargo of 13,064 250lb bombs; 9,022 cases of fragmenting bombs; 7,739 armour-piercing bombs; 1,522 cases of fuses; 1,429 cases of phosphorous bombs; and 1,427 cases of 100lb demolition bombs. Oh, and lots of boxes of bullets.

The SS Richard Montgomery and its deadly cargo is still there today as it was deemed too risky to attempt a salvage operation at the time of its sinking. For years the UK Ministry of Defence claimed the risk of explosion was minimal and if one occurred would present little risk to those in the surrounding areas. As a boy, I can remember seeing the mast of the wreck at low tide. I don't know why, but I did not believe it when I was told it was safe. Years later it turns out I was right to have had that unshakeable cynicism inherent in a young child.

In 2005, the government admitted: "Our understanding of risk has changed and some of the assumptions used are no longer valid." Translated into practical terms, it means if the ship explodes it would be one of the biggest non-nuclear blasts ever and would devastate the surrounding area. It also means that they lied about the level of threat for nearly 60 years. At risk from terrorism and seabed tremors, the biggest problem is the deterioration of the fuses in the bombs. Many experts believe that this factor makes it a case of not if the SS Richard Montgomery explodes, but when. And I can still see the mast from where I live.

MURUROA ATOLL COULD COLLAPSE AND RELEASE RADIOACTIVE DEBRIS INTO THE PACIFIC

At the present time, the thing France is most famous for sinking in the Pacific is the Greenpeace ship *Rainbow Warrior*. The boat was planning to breach the exclusion zone around Mururoa Atoll to protest against French nuclear testing on the island when, on July 10, 1985, agents from the French intelligence service DGSE planted two bombs aboard the ship that sank it and killed one of its crew.

Soon, the French could be responsible for sinking a whole island as a result of their nuclear tests rather than a single ship, as it has emerged that there is an increasing risk that the whole of Mururoa Atoll could collapse into the ocean.

The French government continues to keep secret the nature and long-term impact of the 178 nuclear bombs it exploded on Mururoa and Fangataufa Atolls between 1966 and 1996. However, the French Atomic Energy Commission admitted in 2001 that: "We are observing an acceleration of the natural, seaward progression of certain perimeter areas in the north-eastern zone. There has definitely been a weakening of the

atoll rock that has been amplified by the nuclear tests." Putting this into plain English, the former test site is crumbling and there is a strong chance the atoll could collapse.

This is in complete contrast to the French position before 1996 when they ridiculed suggestions by environmentalists saying the same things and accusing them of being liars. Even in the face of photographic evidence of fissures, subsidences and slides gathered by campaigners, the French government continued to lie. In 1995 it even threatened to sue *Le Monde* when it printed a leaked map showing various cracks and fissures on Mururoa.

A collapse could cause a catastrophic tsunami wiping out thousands of lives across the Pacific area. Huge amounts of radioactive material would be released into the ocean. An expert on the atoll, Nic Maclellan, believes that much of the plutonium would be dispersed, but gaining accurate information is difficult due to continuing French secrecy and its classification of the island as a National Defence Protected Zone.

left Hollywood actor Martin Sheen is just one of the countless individuals and organizations who have protested over French nuclear testing at Moruroa Atoll.

INSTITUTIONS

"Ye shall know the truth, and the truth shall make you mad."
Aldous Huxley

The reason why some secrets can remain hidden in plain sight and certain blatant lies can be told and believed freely is that the institutions concerned are so trusted that they are rarely given any real scrutiny. The institutions that control so much of our lives and dominate global culture are treated with respect and rarely have their motives doubted – lucky for them as when you start digging it becomes clear they are already working overtime to keep their cloak-and-dagger activities hidden.

As children we receive by osmosis widespread beliefs such as the paper money in our pockets is "real money", that the police always enforce the law and that museums are places dedicated to spreading knowledge. We have all been shaped by society to believe in a handful of organizations that have a huge impact on our financial, spiritual and cultural lives. The underlying reasons for their existence or basic questions about whether they serve the public interest are rarely asked.

Those who do question them often end up perpetuating their own lies. The belief that every institution is part of a conspiracy is a lie many have bought into. The resulting level of paranoia blinds them from the truth that most cover-ups often conceal cock-ups rather than grand evil plans.

Ultimately, our most important institutions only lie and repress information out of fear of us. They don't want us to know the truth because their biggest secret is that they only have power over us because we allow them to have it.

above Going underground - Churchill described the Admiralty Citadel that links up to Q-Whitehall as "The vast monstrosity which weighs on the Horse Guards Parade".

TUNNELS AND ESCAPE PLANS FOR THE BRITISH MONARCHY IF THERE IS EVER A REVOLUTION OR WAR IN THE UK

In the event of an invasion of Britain or a mass uprising of the English people, the royal family has no plans to show bravery or face the music; they intend to make a quick getaway and escape to exile in Canada.

If the brutal honesty of the above shocks anyone who clings to images of the royal family defying the *Luftwaffe* by staying at Buckingham Palace during the Blitz, maybe you will feel less shocked if I also tell that this cosy myth was simply wartime propaganda and the Windsor family regularly took refuge in a secret government bunker in Curzon Street in Mayfair.

If the evacuation of the queen and any other members of the royal family by road is impossible, or a speedier exit is required, the plan is to airlift them using helicopters. If the helicopters might be vulnerable to surface-to-air missiles, then any fleeing royals will use the secret tunnels that link Buckingham Palace to various points under the streets of central London in a vast government network of bunkers and buildings.

Once in the tunnel, the queen could travel to the Wellington Barracks, continue on to Horseferry Road Rotunda or emerge at St James Park tube station. It is more likely that she would enter the tunnel that runs under the Mall to a massive underground citadel known as Q-Whitehall. Investigative journalist Duncan Campbell, who discovered that it lies 100 feet under Westminster and Whitehall and extends as far north as Holborn, explored this vast complex of linked buildings. In 1992, a £100 million nuclear bunker and computer centre was added to the complex, with tunnels linking it directly to Downing Street and indirectly to the Buckingham Palace rat routes.

The one secret I cannot tell you about the queen's escape plans is which picture she intends to take off the Buckingham Palace walls and into exile with her. My acquaintance, who was once told by the queen which one she intended to grab in case of emergency, cannot remember if it was one of her Rubens or Van Dycks.

THE VATICAN HELPED NAZI WAR CRIMINALS ESCAPE TO NEW LIVES

In May 2000, Pope John Paul II prayed at the shrine of the Virgin Mary in Fatima, Portugal. Although the town is known for its once secret prophecy, it still has more tangible things to cover up. In 1942 the Catholic shrine there received 110 pounds (49.9 kg) of gold ingots from Nazi Germany that were secretly held on to until, as the Church admitted, "they disappeared in 1970 to an unknown destination."

The exact nature of the Vatican's relationship with the Nazi regime during the Second World War is one of its most closely guarded secrets. However, it is proven that the Nazi regime had close ties with the Vatican through its use of the Vatican bank to assist in transferring illegally obtained SS gold to non-European accounts during the war. It is also known that the Vatican played a significant role in helping Nazi war criminals escape justice.

Klaus Barbie, Adolf Eichmann, Heinrich Mueller, Franz Stangl and a raft of other Nazis were able to leave Europe for Latin America through what has become known as the Vatican "rat-line". Operated largely by a bishop named Alois Hudal, it is a matter of debate how much Pope Pius XII knew of the activities that helped members of the SS leave Italy with false identities and large amounts of cash. Given that the pope gave Hudal a mission to visit German POW camps to find occupants worthy of special assistance from the Vatican, innocence is difficult to presume.

It was not just German Nazi officials the Vatican helped. It sheltered Croatian Nazi collaborators – known as the Utashe – within Vatican properties after the war and helped them escape to Argentina, including their leader Ante Pavelic. The Vatican bank also helped launder $200 million which Utashe leaders had stolen. While being hid, members of the Utashe met Pope Pius XII's acting secretary of state, Giovani Montini.

The Vatican continues to refuse to reveal its papers relating to the "rat-line" and the Nazi gold. Maybe some secrets are just too shocking for the faithful?

left Papal infallibility? Pope Pius XII head of the Catholic Church when it operated its infamous "rat-run" that allowed Nazi butchers to escape justice.

THE TRUTH BEHIND THE UNITED NATION'S ROLE IN THE RWANDAN MASSACRES

In the aftermath of the Second World War and the genocidal horrors of the Holocaust unleashed upon the Jews and gypsies by the Nazis, the United Nations was created with the words "never again" ringing loudly in its ears. Charged with preventing genocide, it seems unimaginable that the UN not only failed the people of Rwanda, but also lied about its role in the terror.

In 1994, about one million of the minority Tutsis population of Rwanda were killed as government-backed militias made up from the majority Hutu population carried out a pre-planned programme of ethnic cleansing. Men, pregnant women, children and babies – none were spared by the machete-wielding militias who not only murdered with ferocity, but tortured, raped and laughed at their victims.

The UN could have prevented the genocide. The UN already had a peacekeeping force in the country, UNAMIR – the United Nations Assistance Mission for Rwanda. Its commander, Lt. Gen. Romeo Dallaire, sent a fax to Undersecretary-General of the UN, Kofi Annan, Chief of the Department of Peacekeeping, warning him of the risk of genocide. He asked for permission to take preventative action. It was refused by Annan. To make matters worse, Annan and Secretary General Boutros Boutros-Ghali decided not to give the information to the UN's Security Council to act on. Boutros-Ghali later lied and claimed he did pass on the information, whilst Annan refused to apologize for his actions and backed his spokesman's slanderous attacks on journalists trying to uncover the story.

When the genocide started on April 6, General Dallaire pleaded for reinforcements to prevent it. Instead of this, the UN supressed information coming out of Rawanda and reduced the UNAMIR force to 260 men. Officially, the reduction of the UNAMIR force was made for the safety of its members. However, the advice given to the UN by Dallaire was that the reduction was more likely to endanger the UNAMIR men and potentially lead to a higher number of fatalities among them. More than a decade on, the reasons for the UN's actions in its response to the situation in Rwanda remain disputed by many of the individuals involved.

It was not until May 17, that the UN conceded "acts of genocide may have been committed", by which time 500,000 Rwandans were dead. The UN belatedly agreed to send troops, but deployment was delayed over arguments about the costs involved. On June 22, the French sent its own forces in to stop the killing and end the UN's mendacity and inaction.

above One life saved – amongst the personal horrors, the greatest tragedy of Rwanda was hundreds of thousands of lives could have been saved if the UN had acted properly.

THE PAPER MONEY ISSUED BY THE US FEDERAL RESERVE BANK IS ILLEGAL UNDER THE AMERICAN CONSTITUTION

Despite the fact that the seventh President of the United States, Andrew Jackson, abolished the Bank of the United States in 1833 and the US showed it could do very well without any other privately owned institution issuing currency, in 1913 Congress passed the Owen-Glass Act and created the Federal Reserve (known as the Fed).

Acting as the central bank of the United States, unlike many other central banks across the world, the Federal Reserve is a quasi-privately-owned bank which has assumed a monopoly position in terms of issuing the money that the people of America carry in their wallets. It is the Fed and not the US government that issues bank notes.

According to Article One, Section 10, of the United States Constitution it is forbidden to: "coin money; emit bills of credit; make any thing but gold and silver coin a tender in payment of debts." In 1982 the Ninth Circuit Federal Court of Appeals ruled that Federal Reserve Banks are "independent, privately owned and locally controlled corporations". If they put out bank notes that cannot be redeemed for silver or gold, those notes are illegal under the Constitution.

This wasn't a problem in 1914 when the Fed issued its first notes, as they stated on them: "This Note is Redeemable in Gold on Demand." It was not a problem in 1950 when the text on bank notes was revised to: "This Note is Redeemable in Lawful Money", because as defined in the US Constitution itself, "lawful money" must only be made of gold or silver.

In 1963, President Kennedy signed executive order No. 11210 which issued $5 billion of currency directly from the US mint and bypassed the Fed. These notes could be redeemed for silver and gold. However, after Kennedy's assassination, President Johnson recalled these notes and the Fed changed the text on its notes yet again to: "This note is Legal Tender for all Debts, Public and Private." The shocking truth is all notes issued since 1964 are no longer exchangeable for gold, silver or lawful money; they are all illegal under the Constitution.

above The strong arm of the law – UK police have often broken the law and ignored basic civil liberties when trying to prevent legitimate political protest.

THE UK POLICE OFTEN BREAK THE LAW WHEN POLICING DEMONSTRATIONS

I t's no secret that UK policing has a long and dishonourable history of bent coppers, and it would be no challenge to catalogue the thousands of lies told by corrupt police officers.

The fact UK police regularly break the law when policing demonstrations is so woefully under-reported that it can be considered a secret. Any regular demonstrator will be able to recount stories of police illegally obscuring their identity numbers, casual use of unnecessary violence, blocking access to public footpaths and other infringements of the law. These breaches have been commonplace for decades, but in recent years the UK police have begun to break the law regularly by illegally detaining protestors to prevent demonstrations taking place. Two good examples of this are cases in which the police have been successfully prosecuted.

In 2002, 23 protestors from the Movement Against Monarchy were arrested for attempting to stage a mock execution at Tower Hill. At the time of arrest, they were having a quiet drink in a pub. The protestors subsequently took legal action against the police and won £3,500 damages each for unlawful arrest and false imprisonment.

It was not an isolated example. The next year Gloucester police stopped three coaches of protestors on their way to a demonstration against the war in Iraq. Having stopped and searched the 120 protestors, the police forced them back into their coaches, barred the doors and made them drive back non-stop for three hours under police escort with the passengers forcibly detained on board. When the case came to court, Lord Justice May found that the police actions could not be justified under either common law or the European Convention on Human Rights.

Justified or not, despite denials the police continue to use illegal detention as a protest prevention technique, so reducing to a blatant lie the claims that UK citizens are free to protest and have their human rights protected.

THE MASONIC LODGES IN THE HOUSE OF COMMONS

In his 1995 autobiography, *Who Goes Home?*, former Member of Parliament and Deputy Leader of the Labour Party Roy Hattersley unwittingly gave confirmation of one of the oldest and strongest rumours that does the rounds in the Houses of Parliament – that there is a hidden Masonic temple in the Palace of Westminster.

The now Baron Hattersley recalled being mistaken for a Freemason by fellow Labour MP George Brown. Thinking Hattersley was about to leave the Houses of Parliament to attend a lodge meeting, George Brown told him: "You don't have to go outside. There is a special parliamentary lodge. Shall I get you transferred?"

With two lodges of MPs and peers and the Gallery Lodge (the Masonic lodge made up of journalists working in the Houses of Parliament), it is not surprising there is a temple for their use within the building. The fact that it is real has been confirmed to me both by non-MP masons who have been shown it while visiting the Palace of Westminster and by current MPs who have testified to its existence.

The use of Masonic symbolism in the Palace of Westminster has long been established, from the chessboard floor of the debating chamber of the House of Commons (which has given us the famous phrase "the floor of the house") to the precise symbolic measurements and gothic design elements incorporated into the building when it was rebuilt by Charles

below House of mystery, house of secrets – the British Parliament contains a Masonic temple.

Barry and Augustus Pugin (both noted Freemasons) after a fire in 1870. It now appears they also built a Masonic temple into the Palace as well.

The exact location of the temple within the Palace of Westminster is difficult to determine (there is a security presence which makes exploring difficult). However, with almost a thousand rooms, a hundred staircases and more than two miles of passageways there is more than enough space to accommodate it. As recently as the 1990s, several rooms which had been "lost" and unused for more than 70 years were rediscovered. It seems, however, that the temple continues to stay purposefully "lost".

THE INTERNATIONAL ATOMIC ENERGY AGENCY FAIL TO TACKLE THE MASSIVE PROBLEM OF MISSING URANIUM AND OTHER NUCLEAR MATERIAL

The UN's International Atomic Energy Agency (IAEA) is upfront on the problems of nuclear materials going missing in the former Soviet Union. It has made constant calls for increased funds to combat the problem. According to the IAEA, there have been 175 nuclear smuggling attempts related to the former Soviet republics. In the worst instance, three men were arrested trying to sell 3.75 pounds (1.7 kgs) of weapon-grade uranium.

The reports from the IAEA send shivers down the spines of those trying to combat terrorism and prevent the creation of a "dirty bomb" (a conventional bomb packed with radioactive material that could make a city uninhabitable for years). However, even though the IAEA is charged with preventing nuclear proliferation by monitoring the use of nuclear material and investigating any losses, it is strangely complacent about losses that occur in some countries.

In 2004 it was revealed that 65 pounds (29.48 kgs) of plutonium – enough to make seven conventional nuclear bombs – was "unaccounted for in auditing records" (in non-spin speak, that means missing) from the UK's Sellafield nuclear plant. The UK Atomic Energy Authority downplayed this as their accounting standards allow for this type of discrepancy. The year before Sellafield had reported of 42 pounds (19.05 kgs) of "unaccounted" plutonium.

The IAEA took no steps to conduct an in-depth investigation to verify whether the plutonium was really an accounting error or actually missing. Some feel they should have. The British Nuclear Fuels reprocessing plant at Sellafield has a record for lying and falsifying documents. In 2000 Japanese officials exposed them as having lied and deliberately falsified quality control records on batches of uranium and plutonium they sent back to Japan. BNF responded by improving management systems after criticism from the UK Nuclear Installations Inspectorate. The BNF did not contest the facts, it admitted liability and took appropriate action with the staff responsible for falsification of the control records. The IAEA said that an in-depth investigation was not necessary, claiming the discrepancy was within acceptable tolerances and that they were confident that it was an administrative error.

Just as worrying, in 2002, ex-Labour MP Tony Benn told how he had been lied to when he was Energy Minister and only later discovered that plutonium created by the UK nuclear power stations secretly went to America for their military programme. He also told how accounting errors were used to hide the fact that the plutonium, which allowed Israel to develop its nuclear bombs, had also come from Britain.

THE SMITHSONIAN INSTITUTE'S DISRESPECT FOR AMERICAN SCIENTIFIC HEROES

The Smithsonian Institution in Washington DC is one of the most famous museums in the world. Broken down into 16 separate museums and seven research centres with more than 142 million items in its collections, it plays a definitive role in preserving and celebrating the history of American achievement. However, it has a secret history of disrespecting some of the most important American scientific heroes.

The most famous exhibit in the Smithsonian's National Air and Space Museum is the most important aircraft of all time – the original Wright Flyer which made the first controlled, powered flight in 1903. However, the aircraft first went on display at the Science Musuem in London in 1928 because of the appalling treatment of the Wright brothers by the Smithsonian.

Due to claims that its Secretary Samuel P Langley had built an earlier aircraft in 1896, the Smithsonian refused to believe the Wright brothers had achieved powered flight despite public demonstrations and even photographs of them flying. It was not until President Theodore Roosevelt ordered trials of the aircraft at Fort Myers in 1908 that the Smithsonian accepted their claim. The Smithsonian compounded this insult by assisting a rival aircraft developer in a prolonged legal fight over patents. It's not surprising Orville Wright sent the plane to England. It did not return to America and the Smithsonian's possession until after his death in 1948.

Other American science heroes still suffer appalling disrespect at the hands of the Smithsonian. The electrical pioneer Nikola Tesla is one of the worst sufferers. His invention of the radio is incorrectly credited to Marconi, one of his inventions on display is incorrectly credited to Thomas Edison, his name is omitted from several Smithsonian-produced books, including their *The Beginning of the Electrical Age*, despite the fact he was the inventor of the alternating current power system and built the world's first hydro-electric dam at Niagara Falls.

There is something very wrong when you can't even rely on an institution created to "increase the diffusion of knowledge" to tell the truth about its own heroes.

above Pride of place - The Wright Flyer on display at the Smithsonian. The Smithsonian's treatment of the Wright brothers almost led to it being given to an English museum.

THE METROPOLITAN MUSEUM OF ART IN NEW YORK AND OTHER TOP MUSEUMS CONTAIN NUMEROUS FAKE PAINTINGS AND ARTEFACTS

Pablo Picasso once said: "We all know that art is not truth." If he had been talking about certain paintings and artefacts displayed in top museums around the globe, he may have had a point.

In 1961, the Metropolitan Museum of Art in New York had to withdraw three terracotta statues of "Etruscan" warriors which for more than 40 years had been displayed as having come from the sixth century BCE. Many doubted their authenticity, especially after tests undertaken in 1960 proved the glaze on the statues contained substances Etruscans never used. Even then the museum still claimed them as genuine. It took the confession of one of the statues' fakers before the museum admitted its mistake.

The same museum continues to claim its disputed self-portrait of Van Gogh, three of its Goyas, their 1997 acquisition "Riverbank" – which the Metropolitan maintains is an exceptionally rare 1,000-year-old Chinese silk scroll – and more than 40 other artworks and artefacts are the genuine articles. The Met also used to make the same claim for many of its pre-Columbian artefacts, which later turned out to be forgeries.

Former Director of the Metropolitan Museum, Thomas Hoving, has admitted the museum contains many unacknowledged fakes, but has also pointed out: "There is not a major museum or gallery in the world that doesn't have at least one fake." Dr Jane Walsh, who established in 2005 that the crystal skull in the British museum previously thought to be pre-Columbian was a nineteenth-century German fake, has also revealed that even items in the Holocaust Museum, such as prison uniforms and Star of David badges, are forgeries. However, museums refuse to allow testing of many artworks and objects to reveal the truth.

As the career of Elmyr de Hory (who forged Picasso paintings that sold to galleries for millions of pounds) showed, the line between what is real and fake relies on the opinion of experts. As the institutions that own the suspected works of art employ the majority of these experts, the likelihood of us knowing the full truth seems remote.

THE INTERNAL PAPER FROM THE INTERNATIONAL MONETARY FUND THAT ADMITS THEIR POLICIES DO NOT WORK

Right now, somewhere in the developing word, there is a protest involving thousands of people against the International Monetary Fund. In 2004, there were 471 significant anti-IMF protests. As none of them involved major riots in a western capital or major city, they weren't covered on the television news.

Even when the reaction against the IMF causes major riots in the developed world, such as those in Seattle in 1999, it is often difficult to tell from the reporting what the protestors' beef is. The IMF claims it is: "An organisation of 184 countries, working to foster global monetary cooperation, secure financial stability, facilitate international trade, promote high employment and sustainable economic growth, and reduce poverty." This sounds as sinister as a tea dance and unworthy of so many protests.

With North Korea and Cuba the only major states not participating in the IMF, it has a global reach and a mandate to "provide assistance to countries that experience serious economic difficulties". In return for helping countries in crisis, the IMF demands that those they bail out introduce a range of ecomonic reforms (known as "Conditionalities"). These reforms usually include privatization of state-owned assets and massive reductions in welfare payments to the poor of the country. Few countries on the edge of financial collapse can afford to reject the IMF's offer of conditional help. Over the years IMF has rejected ciriticism of the social problems its Conditionalities have been shown to cause on the basis that the economic stability they create is worth it in the long run.

However, in a series of leaked reports in 2003 it emerged that internally the IMF acknowledges that there is little evidence that its policies work. The reports show that those countries adopting the Conditionalities often suffer "a collapse in growth rates and significant financial crises". The reports also showed 47 of the world's poorest countries had become poorer after IMF intervention and that the IMF distorted it claims of success by including countries it had not helped, such as China. Maybe the hidden truth explains why there are so many protests.

EPILOGUE –
THE BIGGEST LIE,
THE GREATEST SECRET

"In a time of universal deceit, telling the truth is a revolutionary act."
George Orwell

If you are an impatient sort of person who cannot wait to find out what the biggest secret and greatest lie are, skip the next few paragraphs and look at the last couple of lines. For those with a modicum of patience, the reward will be to learn a little about some of the secrets and lies that did not make it into this book and why.

Let us not be hypocritical. We all keep secrets. We all lie. On November 30, 2003, I woke up to find some of my secrets on the front page of *The Sunday Times*. For months, the lobby organization I worked for (the British Retail Consortium) had been in secret discussions with MI5 and Scotland Yard's Special Branch about potential al-Qaeda attacks in the United Kingdom. I had been asked to ensure these meetings were not disclosed because "unnecessarily

alarming the public is a terrorist victory". As there was nothing to suggest the public were at any immediate risk, I kept quiet.

MI5 did not. Whether it wanted to increase the level of fear in order to gather support for unpopular restrictions on civil liberties, such as ID cards (as I was later told by my MI5 contacts), or because it had access to new information that it was not sharing with us (therefore acting in a way likely to increase the chance of a terrorist attack), it decided to leak some of the details that it had discussed with us to the press.

To wake on a Sunday morning to find your name on the front page and realize that you are better at keeping secrets than MI5 – but nowhere near as good at lying – is an odd experience, even to a world-weary former journalist such as myself. It led people I knew to wonder what else I was keeping secret and why. As I said, we all keep secrets and even in this book I have held some things back.

I chose not to reveal the names of two CIA agents I know are currently working within the media in the UK. If I printed their names, their covers would be blown – and given their line of work, their lives would be at risk. I am sure that both they and the CIA would not to be happy with me either. I've already generated enough potential problems for myself by writing this book. Two pissed-off CIA agents on my doorstep is one situation I have decided to try to avoid by leaving their names out of the entry on the CIA's penetration of major news networks and newspapers.

Two names I desperately wanted to include were those of senior politicians who had achieved high positions of power. One of them likes to flaunt his family in photo-ops, presenting himself as a loving husband and father while having had a secret fling with a 16-year-old. I have no interest in anyone's sex life except my own, but when the happy family card is played to win votes, my revulsion at such hypocrisy rises. The other politician was someone whose own ex-police protection officer was so revolted by his behaviour he told me: "I'd like to have shot the bastard myself."

To have named either of these men and disclosed details of their activities would have risked putting my sources of information at great risk. Therefore, because of the journalistic code of ethics I adhere to, I cannot expose their sordid secrets. The fact that other journalists also know the facts in both cases, yet have been prevented from getting their stories published, also suggests that even if my ethics had not got in the way, there would have been other good reasons for keeping quiet.

I could have published the names of two well-known comedians, a major English singer and two football players who have embraced Haitian Vodon and regularly use its magical practices. The reason I haven't done so is because I believe they have the right to keep their religious beliefs a secret if they so desire. If any of them had the hypocrisy to proclaim themselves fundamentalist Christians in a television interview, I might be tempted to sell the story of their cigar-smoking, rum-drinking rituals and possession by ancestral spirits to the tabloids.

I also don't consider such things as particularly important secrets, and certainly not the type of lie that the public ought to be concerned about. I am much more concerned by the lies we are told about the issues that really matter, and which affect the lives of millions, and I am appalled by the cultural mendacity and media manipulation that occurs on a daily basis and which we allow to go unchallenged.

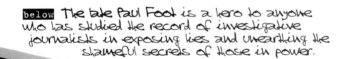

`below` The late Paul Foot is a hero to anyone who has studied the record of investigative journalists in exposing lies and unearthing the shameful secrets of those in power.

Having worked both as a journalist and as a spin-doctor, I can tell you with some authority that you are being lied to constantly, and subtly presented with a version of reality very different from the facts every time you switch on the television, open a paper or click on an Internet news feed.

Aside from the outright whopping lies (Saddam Hussein has weapons of mass destruction, no mistreatment of Iraqi prisoners is occurring, there will be no long-term occupation of Iraq), there is a constant and pernicious process of omission of facts, under-reporting of alternative views and an Orwellian manipulation of language that would not be out of place in the "Ministry of Truth" from the novel 1984.

Known in the spin-doctoring trade as relabelling, parents concerned over additives in vaccines become "fear mongers"; pensioners peacefully protesting against the cost of the British monarchy become "a small anarchist element" and, one of the best, anyone with an alternative view becomes a "conspiracy theorist". If you think relabelling is not a conscious process, consider this example. Up until September 28, 2001, the Chechen groups fighting against Russian control of Chechnya were described as "freedom fighters" by CNN. On September 29, 2001, the Russian government pledged to back America in the war against terror. From that point onwards, CNN relabelled the Chechen rebels as "terrorists".

It would be easy to read a book like this and become pessimistic. It is only natural after realizing that so much of what you have been told is wrong – after realizing just how routinely you are lied to and just how much information is kept from you – to adopt a cynical attitude. Please don't. Cynicism is the worst type of cop out.

The truth genuinely is out there. You can find it in lots of places. The fact that this book has slipped through the radar is a small victory, but it is nothing compared to the tireless work in exposing secrets and lies that certain journalists do on a daily basis. The late radical investigative journalist Paul Foot was always one of my personal heroes because, like the best of his colleagues, he was dedicated to the truth. His work helped send corrupt businessmen to jail (John Poulson), bring down double-dealing politicians (Reginald Maudling) and free the innocent that were rotting in jail (the Birmingham Six).

Type the name of other pioneering investigative journalists such as Duncan Campbell or Greg Palast into a search engine and you will get more truth than can be comfortably handled. However, don't just passively believe in something even if it is coming from a trustworthy source. Wake up your inner sheep, check things out for yourself and become your own investigator of secrets and lies.

Humour is one of the only ways left to slip unwelcome truths and secrets into the public arena, to share with others the horrors that we know about. The work of comedian Mark Thomas is a perfect example of this. His pioneering use of comedy as a tool of investigative journalism, and the combination of jokes, stunts and relentless research, has led to positive changes in UK law. More importantly, it has helped awaken many people to the fact that they themselves possess the power to confront and expose secrets and lies. When comedian Bill Hicks was asked for his motivation, he said: "I want to expose the lies and deflate the hypocrisy."

It's a job he did well, but one we can all do. It is also a necessary job, because as Bill frequently reminded his audiences: "The truth will set you free."

Just off Pall Mall in London, near the Duke of York steps, there is a door that leads down to the covert Q-Whitehall underground complex. There is also a nearby manhole cover that is reasonably easy to lift. It would be irresponsible of me to suggest you could investigate secrets and lies by slipping beneath the city streets, but there are thousands of other ways in which you can discover the things that you are not supposed to know.

The biggest lie you have been told is that you have no power to change the world, but the biggest secret is why, when you realize this, you don't get up off your backside and do something about it.

`below` King of comedy – Bill Hicks like many of the best comedians used his act to expose people to truths that those in power did not want them to hear.

INDEX

Mau Mau 74
Medical scans 115
Mental health 117, 119
Menwith Hill 105
Metal Storm 122
Meyer, Mary Pinchot 81
MI5 14, 46, 49, 60, 186
MI6 10, 11, 14, 57, 167
Microwave weapons 123
Ministry of Defence 61, 106, 108, 110, 169, 174
MK-ULTRA 14, 114, 123
Monkeys 20
Moon, Reverend Sun Myung 139
Mossad 8, 10, 12
Mount Weather 110
Mururoa Atoll 175
Museums 17, 176, 185

Nation of Islam 134
National Security Agency (NSA) 13, 75, 105, 121, 166
Nazis 25, 31, 32, 37, 39, 52, 60, 77, 92, 97, 107, 114, 178
Nestlé 37
New Zealand 42, 121, 126
Newton, Sir Isaac 24
Nicaragua 10, 43, 141, 161
Nixon, Richard 47, 48, 84, 102, 142, 153, 162
Northern Ireland 14, 32, 163
Nuclear fallout 171, 172, 174, 175
Nuclear weapons 109, 142, 169, 170, 172, 173, 175
Number stations 10
Nuremberg 31, 113, 123

Opus Dei 138
Orwell, George 56, 98, 188

Pan Am Flight 103 82
Papacy 107, 165, 178, 115
Parsons, Jack 25
Pearl Harbour 76
Pentagon 59, 61, 129, 169
Piccadilly Circus 109, 182–183
Plutonium 171, 172, 173, 183
Police breaking law 181
Police corruption 62, 69
Powell, Colin 28, 35

Presidential debates 50
Presidential election 45
Presley, Elvis 102, 139
Prince Philip 145
Princess Diana 166
Princess Margaret 101
The Prisoner 9
Project Blue Book 81
Pulsed Energy Projectiles 124

Q-Whitehall 177, 189

Raëlians 136
RAF Boscombe 108
Reich, Wilhelm 86, 92
Relativity 22, 86, 91
RFID 129
Robertson Panel 162
Room 801 106
Roswell 72
Royal Air Force 106, 108, 110 148
Royal family 101, 110, 177, 145, 166
Rudloe Manor 106, 110
Rwanda 42, 53, 179

Sagan, Carl 22, 147
Scientific establishment 16, 86
Scientology 25, 132
Scotland Yard 62, 69, 186
Skull & Bones Society 135
Sellers, Peter 101, 142
Shannon Airport 77
Sheldrake, Rupert 86, 90
Sony 40
Smithsonian Institution 184
South Africa 11, 134, 144
Soviet Union 13, 49, 51, 70, 72, 88, 142, 158, 169, 183
Space Command 111, 105
Space Shuttle 168, 171
Spears, Britney 103
Special Air Squadron (SAS) 15, 108
Special Boat Squadron (SBS) 108, 110
Spin doctors 46, 150, 70

Task Force 121 15
Terrorism 8, 15, 58, 62, 168, 186
Thames 13, 174
Thatcher, Margaret 49, 165

Thomas, Mark 189
Tobacco 41, 153
Transient Lunar Phenomena 87
Tsunami bombs 126, 171, 175

UFOs 72, 75, 81, 106, 110, 111, 134, 136, 162
Underground complexes 104, 110, 189
United Nations 11, 35, 76, 157, 179
United States Air Force 29, 81, 125, 169, 170
United States Army 27, 33, 58, 61, 76, 159
United States Congress 10, 30, 164, 180
United States Constitution 48, 180

Vaccines 118
VALIS 88, 114
Vatican Bank 67, 178
Vatican Library 107
Vietnam 26, 28, 30, 49, 59, 158, 159
Voodoo 43, 188

Warren Commission 84, 162
Wayne, John 61, 96
Weapons of Mass Destruction 35, 44, 76, 186
Weather control 128
White House 58, 61, 83, 84, 162, 166
Whitewater 166
Wilson, Harold 49
Windscale 172
World War Two 9, 12, 31, 32, 77, 110, 126, 128, 146, 148

DEDICATIONS

For my Aunt Barbara, who taught me that reading and writing were subversive and always believed that I'd write a book that would upset people in authority.

And for Sean, B.B.A.M., who should have written this with me but was probably too busy watching wrestling and *Doctor Who*.

ACKNOWLEDGEMENTS

Professional thanks to: Amie McKee for giving me such fun work and being a brilliant editor and Steve Behan for finding great pictures of all the mad gear I asked of him.

Personal thanks to: Mum for everything; Andrew Collins for being the most brilliant friend and mentor; Stephen Grasso for doctoring, being there and CHC chats; Ian Lawton, the type of friend I need and the type of researcher I aspire to be; Richard Ward for his knowledge of all things magical and drug-related; Brendon Hunt for DavidSouthwell.com; Sue Collins; Liz Swanson; Cheryl Twist; Brendan and Lesley Wilson; Hugh and Gaetane Phillips; David Smith; Danny and Kiyomi; Brendan Bannon; Louise, Claire, Julie, Miriam and Dr Martin Forker; extra special love and thanks to Annie and to my grandparents.

Research Assistance thanks: Dickon Springate – master of detection, I'm sorry about the MI5 file; James "What you got for me, dog-tits?" Harborne; my "obviously anonymous" friends at SIS; Piggy; MANDI – cryptic messages received; Harry of the Yard; Inspector "X"; Peter from the Palace; the London Tunnel Rats; THC; April Cole; Joscelyne Hynard; Jessica Faleiro; Kate Ison; Jeremy Marsh; James Muslic; Nuong Trieu; James Tyrrell and Sarah Winterton.

Inspirational thanks to: Luke Haines, T V Smith and John Barry for providing the soundtrack; the spirits of Bill Hicks and Paul Foot; Mark Thomas; Duncan Campbell; *Private Eye*; Billy Bragg; Captain Fred Holroyd; Dr Jack Sarfatti; Mark Steel; Hunter S Thompson; Robert Anton Wilson; Paul Weston; Charles Anglin, who I expect to at least lie with more style when he becomes an MP; Paul Crosbie, Sarah Ryle, Philip Thornton and George MacDonald; Mark Ryan for helping me find the gun of the "Mad Major"; Robin Ramsey and *Lobster* Magazine; Warren Ellis, Gary Russell, Julian Barratt, Noel Fielding and Russell T Davis for providing the only things I stopped to read, listen and watch during writing this; Ken MacLeod, whose secret is that he writes the most inspiring books you can find.

If you have a secret to share or know an interesting lie: **inside.knowledge@gmail.com**

PICTURE CREDITS

The publishers would like to thank the following sources for their kind permission to reproduce the pictures in the book.

Photograph location indicator: t-top, b-bottom, l-left, m-middle, r-right, c-centre.

Aquarius Collection: 9, 56; /Corbis: 28r, 52, 79; /Bettmann: 12, 24-25, 30, 43, 52-53, 65, 66, 72, 75, 81, 84, 95, 119, 133, 139, 141, 142-143, 162, 172, 173, 178; /Patrick Chauvel: 23; /CinemaPhoto: 99; /Urraca Claude: 158; /Ric Ergenbright; 41; /Owen Franken: 153; /Michael Freeman: 113; /George Hall: 29; /Thomas Hartwell: 151; /Rob Howard: 164t; /Hulton-Deutsch Collection: 74, 146; /James A. Finley/Reuters: 50; /Brooks Kraft: 135; /Daniel Laine: 114; /James Leynse: 17; /Massimo Listri: 107; /Wally McNamee: 51; /Oliver Coret/In Visu: 34-35; /Reuters: 40, 59, 122, 157, 165, 170; /Derek Trask: 154-155; /Getty Images: 42; /AFP/Choo Youn-Kong: 126-127; /Slim Aarons: 101; /Frank Barratt/Keystone: 48-49; /Central Press: 37; /Express Newspapers: 132; /Fox Photos: 145; /Ronald S. Haeberle/Time Life Pictures: 28Eugene Hoshiko: 15; /Hulton Archive: 38; /Alexander Joe/AFP: 179; /Keystone: 60; /David Levenson: 73; /Peter Muhly/AFP: 77; /National Archive/Newsmakers: 102; /Mike Nelson/AFP: 175; /Opus Dei Rome: 138; /Paul Schutzer/Time Life Pictures: 47; /Hugo Philpott: 167; /Tony Prime/The Observer: 180-181; /Santi Visalii Inc. 147; /Howard Sochurek: 149; /Terrence Spencer/Time Life: 11t; /Thopson/AFP: 163; /Chris Wilkins/AFP: 161; /Photo12.com: Collection Cinema: 68, 143, 171; /Coll-Dite-Usis: 80r; /Interfoto: 98; /Keystone Pressedienst: 39, 80l; /Musee de la Franc-Maconnerie: 136-137; /U.S. Air Force/Snark Archives: 71; /Ullstein Bild: 144; /Picture-Desk/The Kobal Collection: Colombia/Revolution Studios/Sidney Bald: 61; /Paramount: 28; /Rex Features: 121, 188; /Action Press: 103; /Nicholas Bailey: 177; /Roger Bamber: 97; /Peter Brooker: 57; /David Buchan: 13; /Everett Collection: 96, 189; /James Fraser: 63; /James Kidd: 82; /Lapi: 32; Patsy Lynch: 164b; / James D. Morgan: 182-183; /NBC/Everett: 58; /Heathcliff O'Malley: 124; /Photo News Service: 69; /Alex Segre: 11b; /Sipa Press: 55, 83, 131; /Frank Siteman: 116; /Ken Straiton: 105; /Jeremy Sutton Hibbert: 46; /Voisin/Phanie: 118; /Edward Webb: 156; /Bill Samuel: 128; /Science Photo Library: Julian Baum: 125; /Novosti: 20-21; /James Stevenson: 7; /Topfoto.co.uk: 67, 11; /Ian Yeomans: 18-19; /U.S. Air Force: 108

Every effort has been made to acknowledge correctly and contact the source and/or copyright holder of each picture, and Carlton Books apologises for any unintentional errors or omissions, which will be corrected in future editions of this book.